Year 2

Chemistry

Exam Board: OCR A

Ah, Chemistry. That moment when your eyes meet meaningfully with a beautiful stranger's across the ballroom and a fuzzy haze descends, enveloping you in happiness...

OK, enough daydreaming — you've got A-Levels to look forward to. And while this CGP book isn't the most romantic dance partner, it will help you waltz through the exams.

It's packed with crystal-clear study notes explaining every OCR A Year 2 topic, plus plenty of realistic exam questions (with answers at the back). To make your joy complete, there's even a free Online Edition you can read on your computer or tablet! Bliss.

How to access your free Online Edition

This book includes a free Online Edition to read on your PC, Mac or tablet.
You'll just need to go to **cgpbooks.co.uk/extras** and enter this code:

0683 9484 8757 0738

By the way, this code only works for one person. If somebody else has used this book before you, they might have already claimed the Online Edition.

A-Level revision? It has to be CGP!

Published by CGP

Editors:
Mary Falkner, Charles Kitts, Andy Park and Sarah Pattison.

Contributors:
Mike Bossart, Robert Clarke, Ian H. Davis, John Duffy, Lucy Muncaster, David Paterson and Paul Warren.

ISBN: 978 1 78908 037 7

With thanks to Paul Jordin, Glenn Rogers and Jamie Sinclair for the proofreading.
With thanks to Jan Greenway for the copyright research.

Cover Photo **Laguna Design**/Science Photo Library

Clipart from Corel®
Printed by Elanders Ltd, Newcastle upon Tyne.

Based on the classic CGP style created by Richard Parsons.

Contents

The Scientific Process

'How Science Works' is all about the scientific process — how we develop and test scientific ideas.
It's what scientists do all day, every day (well except at coffee time — never come between scientists and their coffee).

Scientists Come Up with **Theories** — Then **Test Them...**

Science tries to explain **how** and **why** things happen. It's all about seeking and gaining **knowledge** about the world
around us. Scientists do this by **asking** questions and **suggesting** answers and then **testing** them, to see
if they're correct — this is the **scientific process**.

1) **Ask** a question — make an **observation** and ask **why or how** whatever you've observed happens.
   E.g. Why does bromine water react easily with cyclohexene but not with benzene?

2) **Suggest** an answer, or part of an answer, by forming a **theory** or a **model** (a possible **explanation** of the
   observations or a description of what you think is happening actually happening).
   E.g. Benzene has a ring of carbon atoms with delocalised electrons, so the negative
   charge is spread over the whole molecule. This makes it more stable than if it
   contained three double bonds, with a region of high electron density at each double bond.

   A theory is only scientific if it can be tested.

3) Make a **prediction** or **hypothesis** — a **specific testable statement**,
   based on the theory, about what will happen in a test situation.
   E.g. The enthalpy change for the hydrogenation of benzene (an exothermic reaction — see p.65) will be less
   than three times the enthalpy change of the hydrogenation of cyclohexene, which contains one double bond.

4) Carry out **tests** — to provide **evidence** that will support the prediction or refute it.
   E.g. Use a calorimeter to measure the enthalpies of hydrogenation of benzene and cyclohexene. If the value
   for benzene is less than three times the value for cyclohexene, then the evidence supports the hypothesis.

...Then They **Tell** Everyone About Their **Results...**

The results are **published** — scientists need to let others know about their work. Scientists publish their results
in **scientific journals**. These are just like normal magazines, only they contain **scientific reports** (called papers)
instead of the latest celebrity gossip.

1) Scientific reports are similar to the **lab write-ups** you do in school. And just as a lab write-up is **reviewed**
   (marked) by your teacher, reports in scientific journals undergo **peer review** before they're published.

   Scientists use standard terminology when writing their reports. This way they know that other scientists will
   understand them. For instance, there are internationally agreed rules for naming organic compounds, so that
   scientists across the world will know exactly what substance is being referred to. See page 87.

2) The report is sent out to **peers** — other scientists who are experts in the **same area**. They go through it
   bit by bit, examining the methods and data, and checking it's all clear and logical. When the report is
   approved, it's **published**. This makes sure that work published in scientific journals is of a **good standard**.

3) But peer review **can't guarantee** the science is **correct** — other scientists still need to **reproduce** it.

4) Sometimes **mistakes** are made and bad work is published. Peer review **isn't perfect** but it's
   probably the best way for scientists to self-regulate their work and to publish **quality reports**.

...Then **Other Scientists** Will **Test** the Theory Too

1) Other scientists read the published theories and results, and try to **test the theory** themselves. This involves:
   - Repeating the **exact same experiments**.
   - Using the theory to make **new predictions** and then testing them with **new experiments**.
2) If all the experiments in the world provide evidence to back it up, the theory is thought of as **scientific 'fact'**.
3) If **new evidence** comes to light that **conflicts** with the current evidence the theory is questioned all over again.
   More rounds of **testing** will be carried out to try to find out where the theory **falls down**.

> This is how the scientific process works — evidence supports a theory, loads of other scientists read it and test
> it for themselves, eventually all the scientists in the world agree with it and then bingo, you get to learn it.

This is how scientists developed the theory that acids are proton acceptors and bases are proton donors (see p.23). As is often
the case, it took years and years for the model to be developed and accepted, and there are still problems with it even today.

The Scientific Process

If the **Evidence** Supports a Theory, It's **Accepted** — **for Now**

Our currently accepted theories have survived this '**trial by evidence**'. They've been tested **over and over again** and each time the results have backed them up. **BUT**, and this is a big but (teehee), they never become totally indisputable fact. Scientific **breakthroughs** or **advances** could provide new ways to question and test the theory, which could lead to **changes and challenges** to it. Then the testing starts all over again...

And this, my friend, is the **tentative nature of scientific knowledge** — it's always **changing** and **evolving**.

For example, when CFCs were first used in fridges in the 1930s, scientists thought they were problem-free — there was no evidence to say otherwise. It was decades before anyone found out that CFCs were actually making a massive hole in the ozone layer.

Evidence Comes From **Lab Experiments**...

1) Results from **controlled experiments** in **laboratories** are **great**.
2) A lab is the easiest place to **control variables** so that they're all **kept constant** (except for the one you're investigating).
3) This means you can draw meaningful **conclusions**.

> For example, if you're investigating how temperature affects the rate of a reaction, you need to keep everything but the temperature constant, e.g. the pH of the solution, the concentration of the solution, etc.

...But You **Can't** Always do a Lab Experiment

There are things you **can't** study in a lab. And outside the lab controlling the variables is tricky, if not impossible.

- *Are increasing CO_2 emissions causing climate change?*
  There are other variables which may have an effect, such as changes in solar activity. You can't easily rule out every possibility. Also, climate change is a very **gradual process**. Scientists won't be able to tell if their predictions are correct for donkey's years.

- *Does drinking chlorinated tap water increase the risk of developing certain cancers?*
  There are always differences between groups of people. The best you can do is to have a **well-designed study** using **matched groups** — **choose two groups** of people (those who drink tap water and those who don't) which are **as similar as possible** (same mix of ages, same mix of diets etc). But you still can't rule out every possibility. Taking new-born identical twins and treating them identically, except for making one drink gallons of tap water and the other only pure water, might be a fairer test, but it would present huge **ethical problems**.

Samantha thought her study was very well designed — especially the fitted bookshelf.

Science Helps to Inform **Decision-Making**

Lots of scientific work eventually leads to **important discoveries** that **could** benefit humankind — but there are often **risks** attached (and almost always **financial costs**). **Society** (that's you, me and everyone else) must weigh up the information in order to **make decisions** — about the way we live, what we eat, what we drive, and so on. Information can also be used by **politicians** to devise policies and laws.

- **Chlorine** is added to water in **small quantities** to disinfect it. Some studies link drinking chlorinated water with certain types of cancer (see page 67). But the risks from drinking water contaminated by nasty bacteria are far, far greater. There are other ways to get rid of bacteria in water, but they're heaps **more expensive**.

- Scientific advances mean that **non-polluting hydrogen-fuelled cars** can be made. They're better for the environment, but are really expensive. And it'd cost a lot to adapt filling stations to store hydrogen.

- Pharmaceutical drugs are really expensive to develop, and drug companies want to make money. So they put most of their efforts into developing drugs that they can sell for a good price. Society has to consider the **cost** of buying new drugs — the NHS can't afford the most expensive drugs without **sacrificing** something else.

So there you have it — how science works...

Hopefully these pages have given you a nice intro to how science works. You need to understand it for the exam, and for life. Once you've got it sussed it's time to move on to the really good stuff — the chemistry. Bet you can't wait...

Rates of Reaction

This section's a whole lot of fun. Well, it is if you like learning about speed of reactions anyway, and who doesn't...

The **Reaction Rate** tells you How Fast **Reactants** are Converted to **Products**

The **reaction rate** is the **change in the amount** of reactants or products **per unit time** (normally per second).

The units depend on **what** you're measuring. For example, if the reactants are in **solution**, the rate'll be **change in concentration per unit of time** and the units will be, e.g. **mol dm^{-3} s^{-1}**.

There are **Loads** of Ways to **Follow the Rate of a Reaction**

Although there are quite a few ways to follow reactions, not every method works for every reaction. You've got to **pick a property** that **changes** as the reaction goes on. Here are some methods you can use:

- Measure the **volume** of gas evolved.   *These are covered*
- Measure the **loss in mass** as a gas is evolved.   *in Year 1.*
- Use **colorimetry** to measure the colour change of a reaction — see below.
- Measure the **pH change** of a reaction.

Colorimeters Measure **Absorbance** of **Light**

Colorimeters measure the absorbance of a **particular wavelength** of light by a **solution**. If they're set to measure the absorbance of a wavelength that is absorbed by one of the **reactants** but **not** by the products (or vice versa), then the **change in absorbance** over the course of the reaction can be used to measure the **rate**. Here's how you use a colorimeter:

1) First, set the colorimeter to measure the wavelength of light that you're interested in measuring.

2) Next, calibrate the colorimeter. Place a sample of distilled water in a sample tube, known as a cuvette, and place it in the colorimeter. Set the absorbance to zero.

3) Carry out your reaction. You should take samples from the reaction mixture at regular intervals, and measure the absorbance of each one using the colorimeter.

To convert from absorbance to concentration you can use a **calibration curve**. A calibration curve is made by measuring the absorbances of a set of **standard solutions** (solutions of known concentrations) of the reactant or product you're interested in, then plotting a **graph** of absorbance against concentration and drawing a **line of best fit**.

To find the concentration of an unknown sample, **read across** from its **absorbance** to the line of best fit then **down to the concentration** on the *x*-axis.

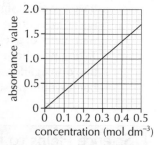

Work Out **Reaction Rate** from a **Concentration-Time Graph**

A tangent is a line that just touches a curve and has the same gradient as the curve does at that point.

1) By repeatedly taking **measurements** during a reaction (continuous monitoring) you can plot a **concentration-time** graph.

2) The rate at any point in the reaction is given by the **gradient** (slope) at that point on the graph.

3) If the graph is a curve, you'll have to draw a **tangent** to the curve and find the gradient of that.

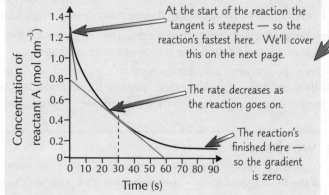

At the start of the reaction the tangent is steepest — so the reaction's fastest here. We'll cover this on the next page.

The rate decreases as the reaction goes on.

The reaction's finished here — so the gradient is zero.

E.g. here, the gradient of the blue tangent is the rate of the reaction after **30 seconds**.

$$\text{Gradient} = \frac{\text{change in } y}{\text{change in } x}$$

$$= \frac{-0.8}{60} = -0.013 \text{ mol dm}^{-3}\text{ s}^{-1}$$

So, the rate after 30 seconds is **0.013 mol dm^{-3} s^{-1}**.

4) The **sign** of the gradient doesn't really matter — it's a **negative** gradient when you're measuring **reactant concentration** because the reactant decreases. If you measured the **product concentration**, it'd be a **positive** gradient.

Rates of Reaction

Initial Rates Tell You How Rates Depend on the Reactant Concentration

The **initial rate of a reaction** is the rate right at the **start** of the reaction.
You can find this from a **concentration-time** graph by calculating the **gradient**
of the **tangent** at **time = 0**. Here's how it works:

1) Carry out the reaction, continuously monitoring **one reactant**.
   Use this to draw a **concentration-time graph**.

2) Repeat the experiment using a **different initial concentration** of the reactant.
   Keep the concentrations of other reactants the same. Draw another **concentration-time graph**.

3) Use your graphs to calculate the **initial rate** for each experiment using the method on p.4.

4) Repeat the process for **each reactant** (different reactants may affect the rate differently).

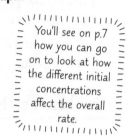

Initial rate = $\frac{y}{x}$

You'll see on p.7 how you can go on to look at how the different initial concentrations affect the overall rate.

Clock Reactions can be used to Simplify the Initial Rate Method

The method described above involves lots of measuring and drawing graphs.
In clock reactions, the initial rate can be **easily estimated**.

1) In a clock reaction, you measure how the **time taken** for a **set amount** of **product**
   to form **changes** as you vary the concentration of **one** of the **reactants**.

2) There is usually an **easily observable endpoint**, such as a colour change,
   to tell you when the desired amount of product has formed.

3) The **quicker** the clock reaction finishes, the **faster** the initial rate of the reaction.

4) You need to make the following assumptions:
   - The **concentration** of each **reactant** doesn't change significantly over the time period of your clock reaction.
   - The **temperature** stays constant.
   - When the endpoint is seen, the reaction has not proceeded **too far**.

   As long as these assumptions are reasonable for your experiment, you can assume that the rate of reaction stays constant during the time period of your measurement. So the rate of your clock reaction will be a good estimate for the initial rate of your reaction.

The most famous clock reaction is the **iodine clock reaction**. The reaction you're monitoring is:

$$H_2O_{2\,(aq)} + 2I^-_{(aq)} + 2H^+_{(aq)} \rightarrow 2H_2O_{(l)} + I_{2\,(aq)}$$

- A small amount of sodium thiosulfate solution and starch are added to **an excess** of hydrogen peroxide and iodide ions in acid solution. (Starch is used as an **indicator** — it turns blue-black in the presence of iodine.)

- The **sodium thiosulfate** that is added to the reaction mixture reacts **instantaneously** with any iodine that forms:

$$2S_2O_3^{2-}_{(aq)} + I_{2\,(aq)} \rightarrow 2I^-_{(aq)} + S_4O_6^{2-}_{(aq)}$$

- To begin with, all the iodine that forms in the **first reaction** is used up **straight away** in the second reaction. But once all the sodium thiosulfate is used up, any more iodine that forms will stay in solution, so the starch indicator will suddenly turn the solution blue-black. This is the **end** of the clock reaction.

- Varying iodide or hydrogen peroxide concentration while keeping the others constant will give **different times** for the colour change.

Colorimetry is a great way of monitoring this reaction due to the change in colour of the starch indicator when iodine is present.

Warm-Up Questions

Q1 Give two ways of monitoring the rate of reaction in which a gas is evolved.

Q2 How would you work out the rate of a reaction from a concentration-time graph?

Exam Question

Q1 A student investigates the rate of the following reaction by monitoring the concentration of HCl over time:

$$CH_3(CH_2)_2CHCH_{2\,(l)} + HCl_{(aq)} \rightarrow CH_3(CH_2)_2CHClCH_{3\,(l)}$$

Suggest a way of monitoring the concentration of HCl.

[1 mark]

I hate mornings — I just have a really bad alarm clock reaction...

If you're working out the rate of a reaction from a graph, make sure you show all your steps. Draw the tangent on the graph and write down the values you're using in your calculation. It shows the examiners you know what you're doing.

Reaction Orders

A reaction order is not just a reaction being really demanding. Nope, instead it tells you how the rate of the reaction depends on the concentrations of the reactants. You can work them out with the help of a few experiments.

Orders Tell You How a Reactant's Concentration Affects the Rate

1) The **order of reaction** with respect to a particular reactant tells you how the **reactant's concentration** affects the **rate**.

If you double the reactant's concentration and the rate stays the same, the order with respect to that reactant is **0**.

If you double the reactant's concentration and the rate also doubles, the order with respect to that reactant is **1**.

If you double the reactant's concentration and the rate quadruples, the order with respect to that reactant is **2**.

2) A reaction will also have an **overall order**. This is the **sum** of the orders of all the different reactants.

3) You can only find **orders of reaction** from **experiments**. You **can't** work them out from chemical equations.

You Need to Monitor How Each Reactant Affects the Rate One by One

Think about the generic reaction: $A + B \rightarrow C$

Imagine you want to find out the **order** of the reaction with respect to the **concentration of A**.
You have to use **experimental data** to work out the order, and you've got two options:

- Continuously monitor the change in concentration of A against time to construct a rate-concentration graph.
- Use an initial rates method to find out how the initial rate changes as you vary the concentration of A.

Whichever way you choose, you have to make sure that the concentrations of any reactants you're **not investigating**, here it's just B, are in **excess** — there's loads more B than there is A. This means the concentration of B won't change much during the reaction (it will be pretty much constant, and the reaction is effectively zero order with respect to B). This means any change in the **rate** can **only** be due to the change in concentration of A (the reactant you're investigating).

The Shape of a Rate-Concentration Graph Tells You the Order

You can use your concentration-time graph to construct a **rate-concentration graph**, which you can then use to work out the order of the reaction. Here's how:

1) Find the **gradient** (which is the rate, remember) at various points along the concentration-time graph. This gives you a **set of points** for the rate-concentration graph.

2) Just **plot the points** and then **join them up** with a line or smooth curve, and you're done. The **shape** of the new graph tells you the **order**...

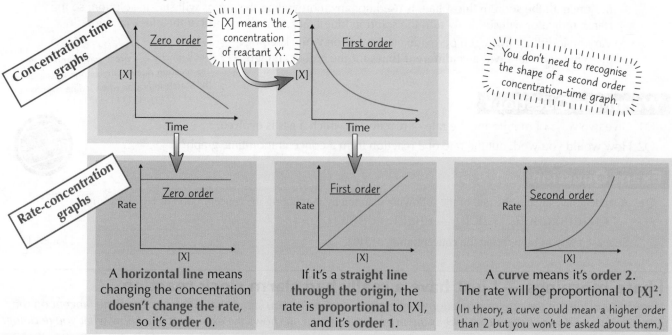

Reaction Orders

The **Initial Rates Method** Can Be Used to Work Out **Orders** Too

You saw how to work out the initial rate of a reaction on page 5 — you often do this to see how the rate right at the **start** of a reaction changes if you change the concentration of one of the reactants.

The initial rates method is a great way of working out the **orders** of different reactants in a reaction.

Example: The table below shows the results of a series of initial rate experiments for the reaction:

$$NO_{(g)} + CO_{(g)} + O_{2(g)} \rightarrow NO_{2(g)} + CO_{2(g)}$$

Write down the order with respect to each reactant.

Experiment number	$[NO_{(g)}]$ (mol dm^{-3})	$[CO_{(g)}]$ (mol dm^{-3})	$[O_{2(g)}]$ (mol dm^{-3})	Initial rate (mol dm^{-3} s^{-1})
1	2.0×10^{-2}	1.0×10^{-2}	1.0×10^{-2}	0.176
2	4.0×10^{-2}	1.0×10^{-2}	1.0×10^{-2}	0.704
3	2.0×10^{-2}	2.0×10^{-2}	1.0×10^{-2}	0.176
4	1.0×10^{-2}	1.0×10^{-2}	2.0×10^{-2}	0.0440

1) Look at experiments 1 and 2 — when $[NO_{(g)}]$ doubles (but all the other concentrations stay constant), the rate **quadruples**. So the reaction is **second order** with respect to NO.

2) Look at experiments 1 and 3 — when $[CO_{(g)}]$ doubles (but all the other concentrations stay constant), the rate **stays the same**. So the reaction is **zero order** with respect to CO.

3) All that's left is to calculate the order for O_2. The only experiment where $[O_2]$ changes is experiment 4. Between experiments 1 and 4, $[NO_{(g)}]$ has **halved** and $[O_{2(g)}]$ has **doubled**. You've already worked out that the rate is second order with respect to NO so halving its concentration will cause the rate to be four times less than in experiment 1: **$0.176 \div 4 = 0.0440$**. This is the same as the reported rate of the reaction. So doubling the concentration of O_2 must have **no effect** on the rate. This means the reaction is **zero order** with respect to O_2.

Warm-Up Questions

Q1 What does the order of a reaction with respect to a particular reactant tell you?
Q2 If you double the concentration of reactant X, the rate doubles.
What is the order of reaction with respect to reactant X?
Q3 How do you work out the overall order of a reaction?
Q4 Sketch a typical rate-concentration graph for a second order reaction.

Exam Questions

Q1 It takes 200 seconds to completely dissolve a 0.4 g piece of magnesium in 25 cm^3 of dilute hydrochloric acid.
It takes 100 seconds if the concentration of the acid is doubled.

a) What is the order of the reaction with respect to the concentration of the acid? [1 mark]

b) Sketch a graph to show the relationship between the concentration of the acid and the overall rate of the reaction. [2 marks]

c) What physical parameter could be measured to follow the rate of this reaction in more detail? [1 marks]

Q2 A reaction between two compounds has an overall order of 2.
Which of the following could represent the order of reaction with respect to each of the reactants?
A Both reactants have an order of 2.
B One reactant has an order of 1, the other has an order of 2.
C Both reactants have an order of 1. [1 mark]

Look at those great curves...

...sorry, chemistry gets me a bit over-excited sometimes. I think I'm OK now. Remember that you can never (ever) tell the order of a reaction from its equation — you've got to do an experiment. And then you have to interpret your results, so make sure you know how the shapes of concentration-time graphs and rate-concentration graphs relate to the order.

The Rate Constant

*The rate constant links the concentration of your reactants, their orders and the rate of your reaction.
I'll warn you now — there's a little bit of maths involved. It's really not too bad though... promise...*

The **Rate Equation** Links **Reaction Rate** to **Reactant Concentrations**

Rate equations look mean, but all they're really telling you is how the **rate** is affected by the **concentrations of reactants**. For a general reaction: $A + B \rightarrow C + D$, the **rate equation** is:

The units of rate are mol dm^{-3} s^{-1}.

$$\text{Rate} = k[A]^m[B]^n$$

Remember — square brackets mean the concentration of whatever's inside them.

1) k is the **rate constant** — the bigger it is, the **faster** the reaction.

2) **m** and **n** are the **orders of the reaction** with respect to reactant A and reactant B.
   m tells you how the **concentration of reactant A** affects the **rate** and **n** tells you the same for **reactant B**.

Example: The chemical equation below shows the acid-catalysed reaction between propanone and iodine.

$$CH_3COCH_{3(aq)} + I_{2(aq)} \xrightarrow{H^+_{(aq)}} CH_3COCH_2I_{(aq)} + H^+_{(aq)} + I^-_{(aq)}$$

This reaction is first order with respect to propanone and $H^+_{(aq)}$ and zero order with respect to iodine. Write down the rate equation.

Even though $H^+_{(aq)}$ is a catalyst, rather than a reactant, it can still appear in the rate equation.

The rate equation is: rate $= k[CH_3COCH_{3(aq)}]^1[H^+_{(aq)}]^1[I_{2(aq)}]^0$

But $[X]^1$ is usually written as $[X]$, and $[X]^0$ equals **1** so is usually **left out** of the rate equation.

So you can **simplify** the rate equation to: rate $= k[CH_3COCH_{3(aq)}][H^+_{(aq)}]$

Think about the powers laws from maths.

You can Calculate the **Rate Constant** from the **Orders** and **Rate of Reaction**

Once the rate and the orders of the reaction have been found by experiment, you can work out the **rate constant**, k. The **units** of the rate constant vary, so you have to **work them out**.

Example: The reaction below was found to be second order with respect to NO and zero order with respect to CO and O_2. The rate is 1.76×10^{-3} mol dm^{-3} s^{-1} when $[NO_{(g)}] = [CO_{(g)}] = [O_{2(g)}] = 2.00 \times 10^{-3}$ mol dm^{-3}.

$$NO_{(g)} + CO_{(g)} + O_{2(g)} \rightarrow NO_{2(g)} + CO_{2(g)}$$

Find the value of the rate constant.

First write out the **rate equation**: Rate $= k[NO_{(g)}]^2[CO_{(g)}]^0[O_{2(g)}]^0 = k[NO_{(g)}]^2$

Next insert the **concentration** and the **rate**. **Rearrange** the equation and calculate the value of k:

Rate $= k[NO_{(g)}]^2$, so $1.76 \times 10^{-3} = k \times (2.00 \times 10^{-3})^2 \implies k = \dfrac{1.76 \times 10^{-3}}{(2.00 \times 10^{-3})^2} = 440$

Find the **units for k** by putting the other units in the rate equation:

Rate $= k[NO_{(g)}]^2$, so mol dm^{-3} s^{-1} $= k \times$ (mol dm^{-3})$^2 \implies k = \dfrac{\text{mol dm}^{-3}\,\text{s}^{-1}}{(\text{mol dm}^{-3})^2} = \dfrac{\text{s}^{-1}}{\text{mol dm}^{-3}} = \text{dm}^3\,\text{mol}^{-1}\,\text{s}^{-1}$

So the answer is: $k = 440$ **dm^3 mol^{-1} s^{-1}**

Rate-Concentration Graphs Give the Rate Constants of **First Order** Reactions

If the overall reaction is **first order**, then the **rate constant** is equal to the **gradient** of the **rate-concentration graph** of that reactant.

Rate

[X]

The rate equation of a first order reaction is: rate = k[X], so a graph of rate against [X] has a gradient equal to the rate constant, k.

The Rate Constant

Half-life is the Time for Half the Reactant to Disappear

1) The **half-life** of a reaction is the time it takes for **half of the reactant** to be used up.

2) The **half-life** of a **first order reaction** is **independent of the concentration**.
   So each half-life will be the **same length**.

3) This means the half-life of a first order reaction can be read off its **concentration-time graph** by seeing how long it takes to halve the reactant concentration.

4) If you know the **half-life** of a **first order reaction** you can work out the **rate constant** using the equation:

Chocolate cake has a very short half-life.

The units are: $\dfrac{\text{no units}}{\text{s}} = s^{-1}$ $\qquad k = \dfrac{\ln 2}{t_{1/2}}$

Example: This graph shows the decomposition of hydrogen peroxide, H_2O_2.
Use the graph to measure the half-life at various points
and work out the rate constant of the reaction.

$[H_2O_2]$ from **4** to **2** mol dm^{-3} = **200** s,
$[H_2O_2]$ from **2** to **1** mol dm^{-3} = **200** s,
$[H_2O_2]$ from **1** to **0.5** mol dm^{-3} = **200** s.

The half-life is always **200 s**, regardless of the concentration,
so it's a **first order reaction** with respect to $[H_2O_2]$.

The rate constant is: $k = \dfrac{\ln 2}{t_{1/2}} = \dfrac{\ln 2}{200\,\text{s}} = 3.47 \times 10^{-3}\,s^{-1}$

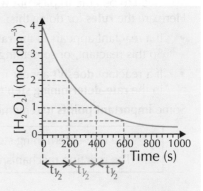

Warm-Up Questions

Q1 How can you use a rate-concentration graph to work out the value of k for a first order reaction?

Q2 What's a half-life?

PRACTICE QUESTIONS

Exam Questions

Q1 The following reaction is second order with respect to NO and first order with respect to H_2.

$$2NO_{(g)} + 2H_{2(g)} \rightarrow 2H_2O_{(g)} + N_{2(g)}$$

a) Write a rate equation for the reaction. [1 mark]

b) The rate of the reaction at 800 °C is 0.00267 mol dm^{-3} s^{-1} when $[H_{2(g)}]$ = 0.00200 mol dm^{-3}
   and $[NO_{(g)}]$ = 0.00400 mol dm^{-3}. Calculate the value for the rate constant at 800 °C, including units. [2 marks]

Q2 The table shows the results of an experiment on the decomposition of nitrogen(V) oxide at constant temperature. The reaction is first order.

$$2N_2O_5 \rightarrow 4NO_2 + O_2$$

Time (s)	0	50	100	150	200	250	300
$[N_2O_5]$ (mol dm^{-3})	2.50	1.66	1.14	0.76	0.50	0.32	0.22

a) Plot a graph of these results. [3 marks]

b) Calculate the rate constant for the reaction at this temperature. [2 marks]

Q3 The graph on the right shows how the rate of the following reaction changes with the concentration of ester at 298 K:
$CH_3COOCH_3 + H_2O \rightarrow CH_3COOH + CH_3OH$
The reaction is first order with respect to CH_3COOCH_3.
Calculate the rate constant of the reaction. [2 marks]

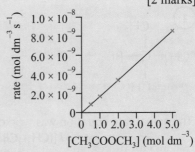

Spiffing page, that — really first rate...

What a lot of calculations and nasty-looking graphs. I'm sure you're thinking a cup of tea and a biscuit wouldn't go a miss after all that maths. I'm sorry to say we're only just getting started with rates though — there's much more to come...

The Rate-Determining Step

You know when you're trying to get out of a room to go to lunch, but it takes ages because not everyone can get through the door at the same time? Well getting through that door is the rate determining step. Talking about lunch...

The **Rate-Determining Step** is the **Slowest Step** in a Multi-Step Reaction

Reaction mechanisms can have **one step** or a **series of steps**.
In a series of steps, each step can have a **different rate**.
The **overall rate** is decided by the step with the **slowest** rate — the **rate-determining step**.

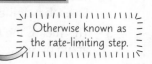
Otherwise known as the rate-limiting step.

Reactants in the **Rate Equation** Affect the **Rate**

The rate equation is handy for helping you work out the **mechanism** of a chemical reaction.
You need to be able to pick out which reactants from the chemical equation are involved in the **rate-determining step**.
Here are the **rules** for doing this:

- If a reactant appears in the **rate equation**, it must affect the **rate**.
  So this reactant, or something derived from it, must be in the **rate-determining step**.

- If a reactant **doesn't** appear in the **rate equation**, then it **isn't** involved
  in the **rate-determining step** (and neither is anything derived from it).

Catalysts can appear in rate equations, so they can be in rate-determining steps too.

Some **important points** to remember about rate-determining steps and mechanisms are:

1) The rate-determining step **doesn't** have to be the first step in a mechanism.

2) The reaction mechanism **can't** usually be predicted from **just** the chemical equation.

You Can Predict the **Rate Equation** from the **Rate-Determining Step**...

The **order of a reaction** with respect to a reactant shows the **number of molecules** of that reactant which are involved in the **rate-determining step**.

So, if a reaction's second order with respect to X, there'll be two molecules of X in the rate-determining step.

Example: The mechanism for the reaction between chlorine free radicals and ozone, O_3, consists of **two steps**:

$$Cl\bullet_{(g)} + O_{3(g)} \rightarrow ClO\bullet_{(g)} + O_{2(g)} \text{ — slow (rate-determining step)}$$
$$ClO\bullet_{(g)} + O_{(g)} \rightarrow Cl\bullet_{(g)} + O_{2(g)} \text{ — fast}$$

Predict the rate equation for this reaction.

$Cl\bullet$ and O_3 must both be in the rate equation, so the rate equation is of the form: rate $= k[Cl\bullet]^m[O_3]^n$.
There's only **one** $Cl\bullet$ radical and **one** O_3 molecule in the rate-determining step,
so the **orders**, m and n, are both **1**. So the rate equation is rate $= k[Cl\bullet][O_3]$.

...And You Can Predict the **Mechanism** from the **Rate Equation**

Knowing exactly which reactants are in the **rate-determining step** gives you an idea of the reaction **mechanism**.

For example, here are two possible mechanisms for the reaction $(CH_3)_3CBr + OH^- \rightarrow (CH_3)_3COH + Br^-$.

1

$$CH_3-\underset{\underset{CH_3}{|}}{\overset{\overset{CH_3}{|}}{C}}-Br + OH^- \rightarrow CH_3-\underset{\underset{CH_3}{|}}{\overset{\overset{CH_3}{|}}{C}}-OH + Br^-$$

The actual **rate equation** was worked out by rate experiments:
$$\text{rate} = k[(CH_3)_3CBr]$$

OH^- isn't in the **rate equation**, so it **can't** be involved in the
rate-determining step. So, **mechanism 2** is most likely to be correct
— there is **1 molecule** of $(CH_3)_3CBr$ (and **no molecules** of OH^-)
in the **rate determining step**. This agrees with the **rate equation**.

2

$$CH_3-\underset{\underset{CH_3}{|}}{\overset{\overset{CH_3}{|}}{C}}-Br \rightarrow CH_3-\underset{\underset{CH_3}{|}}{\overset{\overset{CH_3}{|}}{C^+}} + Br^-$$
— slow
(rate-determining step)

$$CH_3-\underset{\underset{CH_3}{|}}{\overset{\overset{CH_3}{|}}{C^+}} + OH^- \rightarrow CH_3-\underset{\underset{CH_3}{|}}{\overset{\overset{CH_3}{|}}{C}}-OH$$
— fast

The Rate-Determining Step

You have to Take Care when Suggesting a Mechanism

If you're suggesting a mechanism, **watch out** — things might not always be what they seem.
For example, when nitrogen(V) oxide, N_2O_5, decomposes, it forms nitrogen(IV) oxide and oxygen:

$$2N_2O_{5(g)} \rightarrow 4NO_{2(g)} + O_{2(g)}$$

From the chemical equation, it looks like **two** N_2O_5 molecules react with each other.
So you might predict that the reaction is **second order** with respect to N_2O_5... but you'd be wrong.

Experimentally, it's been found that the reaction is **first order** with respect to N_2O_5 — the rate equation is:

$$rate = k[N_2O_5]$$

This shows that there's only one molecule of N_2O_5 in the rate-determining step.
One **possible mechanism** that fits the rate equation is:

Only one molecule of N_2O_5 is
in the rate-determining step,
fitting in with the rate equation.

$N_2O_{5(g)} \rightarrow NO_{2(g)} + NO_{3(g)}$ — slow (rate-determining step)
$NO_{3(g)} + N_2O_{5(g)} \rightarrow 3NO_{2(g)} + O_{2(g)}$ — fast

The two steps add up to the overall
chemical equation. You can cancel the
$NO_{3(g)}$ as it appears on both sides.

Warm-Up Questions

Q1 What is meant by the rate-determining step?

Q2 Is the rate-determining step always the first step in the reaction?

Q3 What is the connection between the rate equation and the rate-determining step?

Q4 How can the rate-determining step help you to understand the mechanism?

PRACTICE QUESTIONS

Exam Questions

Q1 The following reaction is first order with respect to H_2 and first order with respect to ICl.
$$H_{2(g)} + 2ICl_{(g)} \rightarrow I_{2(g)} + 2HCl_{(g)}$$

a) Write the rate equation for this reaction. [1 mark]

b) The mechanism for this reaction consists of two steps.

i) Identify the molecules that are in the rate-determining step. Justify your answer. [2 marks]

ii) A chemist suggested the following mechanism for the reaction.

$$2ICl_{(g)} \rightarrow I_{2(g)} + Cl_{2(g)} \quad \text{slow}$$

$$H_{2(g)} + Cl_{2(g)} \rightarrow 2HCl_{(g)} \quad \text{fast}$$

Suggest, with reasons, whether this mechanism is likely to be correct. [2 marks]

Q2 The reaction between HBr and oxygen gas occurs rapidly at 700 K.
It can be represented by the equation $4HBr_{(g)} + O_{2(g)} \rightarrow 2H_2O_{(g)} + 2Br_{2(g)}$
The rate equation found by experiment is: $Rate = k[HBr][O_2]$.

a) Explain why the reaction cannot be a one-step reaction. [2 marks]

b) Each of the 4 steps of this reaction involves the reaction of 1 molecule of HBr. Two of the steps
are the same. The rate-determining step is the first one and results in the formation of $HBrO_2$.
HBrO is formed in step 2. Suggest equations for the full set of 4 reactions. [4 marks]

I found rate-determining step aerobics a bit on the slow side...

*These pages show you how rate equations, orders of reaction and reaction mechanisms all tie together and how each
actually means something in the grand scheme of Chemistry. It's all very profound. So get it all learnt and answer the
questions and then you'll have plenty of time to practise the quickstep for your Strictly Come Dancing routine.*

The Arrhenius Equation

The Arrhenius Equation. As the name suggests, it's a bit heinous to learn I'm afraid, but super useful. It links together reaction constants, activation energies and temperatures — all pretty important in the world of reaction rates.

Temperature Changes Affect the Rate Constant

You learnt in Year 1 that increasing the **temperature** of a reaction will increase its **rate**. Here's a quick recap of what goes on:

1) For a reaction to happen, the particles need to:

- **Collide** with each other.
- Have enough energy to react (i.e. have at least the **activation energy**).
- Have the **right orientation**.

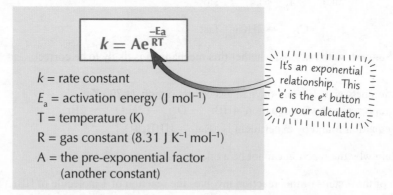

Rate constants are shape-shifters. Here's one in its true form.

2) Increasing the temperature gives the reactant particles more **kinetic energy**. This means the particles **speed up**, so they collide **more often**.

3) Increasing the temperature also means **more** reactant particles will have the required **activation energy** for the reaction, so a greater **proportion** of the collisions will result in the reaction **actually happening**.

4) In other words, **increasing temperature** increases the **reaction rate**.

5) According to the rate equation, reaction rate depends **only** on the rate constant and reactant concentrations.

$$\text{rate} = k[\text{A}]^m[\text{B}]^n$$

6) So changing the temperature must **change the rate constant**.

The **rate constant** applies to a **particular reaction** at a **certain temperature**. At a **higher** temperature, the reaction will have a **higher** rate constant.

Remember — the higher the rate constant, the faster the rate.

The Arrhenius Equation Links the Rate Constant and Activation Energy

The **Arrhenius equation** (nasty-looking thing in the green box) links the **rate constant** (k) with **activation energy** (E_a, the minimum amount of kinetic energy particles need to react) and **temperature** (T).

This is probably the **worst** equation you're going to meet. Luckily, it'll be on your **data sheet** in the exam, so you don't have to learn it off by heart. But you do need to know what all the different bits **mean**, and how it works. Here it is:

$$k = Ae^{\frac{-E_a}{RT}}$$

k = rate constant
E_a = activation energy ($J\,mol^{-1}$)
T = temperature (K)
R = gas constant ($8.31\ J\,K^{-1}\,mol^{-1}$)
A = the pre-exponential factor (another constant)

It's an exponential relationship. This 'e' is the e^x button on your calculator.

1) As the activation energy, E_a, gets **bigger**, k gets **smaller**. You can **test** this out by trying **different numbers** for E_a in the equation... ahh go on, be a devil.

2) So, a **large E_a** will mean a **slow rate**. This **makes sense** when you think about it... If a reaction has a **high activation energy**, then not many of the reactant particles will have enough energy to react. So only a **few** of the collisions will result in the reaction actually happening, and the rate will be **slow**.

3) The equation also shows that as the temperature **rises**, k **increases**.

The Arrhenius Equation

Use the Arrhenius Equation to Calculate the Activation Energy

Putting the **Arrhenius equation** into **logarithmic form** makes it a bit easier to use.

$$\ln k = -\frac{E_a}{RT} + \ln A$$

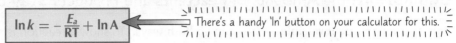 There's a handy 'ln' button on your calculator for this.

You can use this equation to create an **Arrhenius plot** by plotting **ln k** against $\frac{1}{T}$.

This will produce a graph with a **gradient** of $\frac{-E_a}{R}$ and a **y-intercept** of ln A.

So once you know the gradient, you can find both the **activation energy** and the **pre-exponential factor**.

Example: The graph below shows an Arrhenius plot for the decomposition of hydrogen iodide.
Calculate the activation energy and the pre-exponential factor for this reaction. R = 8.31 J K⁻¹ mol⁻¹.

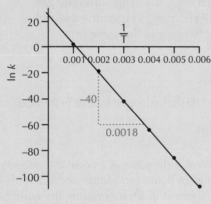

The gradient, $\frac{-E_a}{R} = \frac{-40}{0.0018} = -22\ 222$

So, $E_a = -(-22\ 222 \times 8.31) = 184\ 666$ J mol⁻¹
$= 185$ **kJ mol⁻¹** (3 s.f.)

The y-intercept, ln A, = **24.0**

So, A = e²⁴·⁰ = **3 × 10¹⁰**

Remember — 1 kJ = 1000 J

You can check your value of A by substituting it, along with your value of E_a, into the equation ln k = -E_a/RT + ln A. You can use any data point from your graph to give you a value for ln k and 1/T.

Warm-Up Questions

Q1 How does temperature affect the value of k?

Q2 In the Arrhenius equation, what do the terms k, T and R represent?

Q3 The Arrhenius equation is $k = Ae^{-E_a/RT}$. Which one of the following answers is true as E_a increases?

A k increases and rate of reaction increases.   **B** k increases and rate of reaction decreases.

C k decreases and rate of reaction increases.   **D** k decreases and rate of reaction decreases.

Q4 How would you find the activation energy from a graph of ln k against 1/T?

Exam Question

Q1 The table on the right gives values for the rate constant of the reaction between hydroxide ions and bromoethane at different temperatures.

a) Complete the table. [2 marks]

b) Use the table to plot a graph that would allow you to calculate the activation energy of the reaction. [3 marks]

c) Calculate the activation energy of the reaction. (R = 8.31 J K⁻¹ mol⁻¹) [2 marks]

d) Calculate the value of the pre-exponential factor, A. [1 mark]

T (K)	k	1/T (K⁻¹)	ln k
305	0.181	0.00328	−1.71
313	0.468		
323	1.34		
333	3.29	0.00300	1.19
344	10.1		
353	22.7	0.00283	3.13

Who knew rates of reaction could be such a pain in the ar...

...rhenius? That equation's fiddly to learn, but luckily you don't have to — it'll be on your data sheet in the exam. Hurrah. Be careful when you're plotting graphs to work out the activation energy though. There are lots of calculations to do before you get started, so check all your numbers before you draw anything so you don't make any silly mistakes.

The Equilibrium Constant

You met the equilibrium constant in Year 1 — charming fellow, I'm sure you'll agree.
I realise that was a while ago though, so there's a quick recap before any of the new stuff.

At **Equilibrium** the Amounts of Reactants and Products **Stay the Same**

1) Lots of reactions are **reversible** — they can go **both ways**. To show a reaction is reversible, you stick in a $\rightleftharpoons$.

2) A system is said to be in **dynamic equilibrium** if the rate of the **forward reaction** is the **same** as the rate of the **reverse reaction**.

3) At dynamic equilibrium, the forwards and backwards reactions **cancel** each other out and there's no **overall change** in the concentrations of the reactants and products.

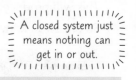
A closed system just means nothing can get in or out.

4) A **dynamic equilibrium** can only happen in a **closed system** at a **constant temperature**.

5) Equilibria can be set up in **physical systems**, e.g.:

> When **liquid bromine** is shaken in a closed flask, some of it changes to orange **bromine gas**. After a while, **equilibrium** is reached — bromine liquid is **still** changing to bromine gas and bromine gas is still changing to bromine liquid, but they are changing at the **same rate**.
>
> $Br_{2(l)} \rightleftharpoons Br_{2(g)}$

...and **chemical** systems, e.g.:

> If **hydrogen gas** and **iodine gas** are mixed together in a closed flask, **hydrogen iodide** is formed.
>
> $$H_{2(g)} + I_{2(g)} \rightleftharpoons 2HI_{(g)}$$
>
> Imagine that **1.0 mole** of hydrogen gas is mixed with **1.0 mole** of iodine gas at a constant temperature of **640 K**. When this mixture reaches equilibrium, there will be **1.6 moles** of hydrogen iodide and **0.2 moles** of both hydrogen gas and iodine gas. No matter how long you leave them at this temperature, the **equilibrium** amounts **never change**. As with the physical system, it's all a matter of the forward and backward rates **being equal**.

6) The **ratio** of products and reactants at dynamic equilibrium is shown by the **equilibrium constant**, K_c.

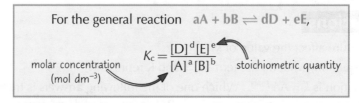

For the general reaction $aA + bB \rightleftharpoons dD + eE$,

$$K_c = \frac{[D]^d [E]^e}{[A]^a [B]^b}$$

molar concentration (mol dm^{-3})   stoichiometric quantity

The **Units** of K_c Depend on Your **Reaction**

1) You saw how to calculate K_c in Year 1 — you just have to stick the **equilibrium concentrations** of the components into the **expression** for K_c.

2) You calculate the **units** of K_c just like you calculated the units of the rate constant — you have to plug all your units into your expression and **cancel** them as much as possible.

Example: Calculate K_c, including units, for the reaction: $PCl_{5(g)} \rightleftharpoons PCl_{3(g)} + Cl_{2(g)}$
At 600 K, the equilibrium concentrations are:
$[PCl_5] = 0.024$ mol dm^{-3}, $[PCl_3] = 0.016$ mol dm^{-3}, $[Cl_2] = 0.016$ mol dm^{-3}

From the expression above, you can see that $K_c = \dfrac{[PCl_3][Cl_2]}{[PCl_5]}$

So if you put your equilibrium concentrations into the expression, you get: $K_c = \dfrac{0.016 \times 0.016}{0.024} = 0.011$

Now work out the units for the rate constant by substituting the units for each component into the

expression for K_c: $\dfrac{(\text{mol dm}^{-3})(\text{mol dm}^{-3})}{(\text{mol dm}^{-3})} = \dfrac{(\text{mol dm}^{-3})}{1} = \text{mol dm}^{-3}$

So $K_c = 0.011$ mol dm^{-3}

The Equilibrium Constant

Reactions Can be Homogeneous or Heterogeneous

If all the reactants and products in a reaction are in the same **state** (e.g. they're all gases, or all in solution) then the reaction is **homogeneous**. The dynamic equilibria you've met so far have all been homogeneous.

But if the reactants and products in a reaction are in **different states** the reaction is **heterogeneous**.
A **heterogeneous** reaction can change **what** you put in the **equilibrium constant expression**. The rule is:

- If the mixture is homogeneous, all the reactants and products are put into the expression for the equilibrium constant.

- If the mixture is heterogeneous only gases and aqueous substances go into the expression for the equilibrium constant (any solids or liquids get left out).

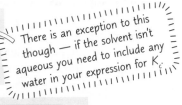
There is an exception to this though — if the solvent isn't aqueous you need to include any water in your expression for K_c.

Example:

a) Write an expression for the equilibrium constant of the following reaction:
$$Cu_{(s)} + 2Ag^+_{(aq)} \rightleftharpoons Cu^{2+}_{(aq)} + 2Ag_{(s)}$$

The reactants and products are a **mixture** of **aqueous** and **solid**. So the reaction is **heterogeneous**. Only the **aqueous** substances go into the equilibrium constant.

So $K_c = \dfrac{[Cu^{2+}]}{[Ag^+]^2}$

b) At a certain temperature, there are 0.431 mol dm^{-3} Ag$^+$ and 0.193 mol dm^{-3} Cu^{2+} at equilibrium. Calculate K_c and give its units.

$$K_c = \frac{[Cu^{2+}]}{[Ag^+]^2} = \frac{0.193}{(0.431)^2} = 1.04$$

The units are $\dfrac{(\text{mol dm}^{-3})}{(\text{mol dm}^{-3})^2} = \dfrac{1}{(\text{mol dm}^{-3})} = \text{mol}^{-1}\,\text{dm}^3$

So at 298 K, $K_c = 1.04\ \text{mol}^{-1}\,\text{dm}^3$

Warm-Up Questions

Q1 Write the expression for K_c for the following reaction: $N_{2(g)} + O_{2(g)} \rightleftharpoons 2NO_{(g)}$ *

Q2 What are the units for K_c in the reaction in question 1? *

Q3 What's a heterogeneous reaction?

PRACTICE QUESTIONS

*Answer on page 118.

Exam Questions

Q1 A sample of pure $N_2O_{4(g)}$ is placed in a sealed 6.00 dm^3 flask at 298 K and allowed to reach equilibrium with $NO_{2(g)}$.

$$N_2O_{4(g)} \rightleftharpoons 2NO_{2(g)}$$

At equilibrium there are 23.0 g $N_2O_{4(g)}$ and 0.389 g $NO_{2(g)}$.

Hint: You'll first need to convert the masses into concentrations. You'll need the equations
$$\text{moles} = \frac{\text{mass}}{M_r} \text{ and concentration} = \frac{\text{moles}}{\text{volume}}.$$

Calculate K_c for the equilibrium at 298 K and give its units. [4 marks]

Q2 Hexaaqua cobalt(II) ($[Co(H_2O)_6]^{2+}$) and ammonia (NH_3) react to form the following equilibrium:

$$[Co(H_2O)_6]^{2+}_{(aq)} + 6NH_{3(aq)} \rightleftharpoons [Co(NH_3)_6]^{2+}_{(aq)} + 6H_2O_{(l)}$$

At 30 °C, the equilibrium concentrations are:
$[Co(NH_3)_6]^{2+}_{(aq)} = 2.19$ mol dm^{-3}, $[Co(H_2O)_6]^{2+}_{(aq)} = 0.541$ mol dm^{-3} and $[NH_{3(aq)}] = 0.234$ mol dm^{-3}.

a) Write an expression for K_c for this reaction. [1 mark]

b) Calculate the value of K_c at 30 °C and give its units. [2 marks]

Understanding equilibria — it's a constant struggle...

Look carefully at the state symbols when you're writing out your expression for K_c. If the reaction is heterogeneous then liquids and solids never ever go in your expression for K_c. But in a homogeneous reaction you would put everything into your expression for K_c. Make sure you get that under your belt, so you don't end up in a pickle.

Equilibrium Concentrations

*A few more calculations using K_c coming up. You'll need to look carefully at the reaction equations in each case —
they can give you clues about the concentrations of different components at equilibrium.*

K_c can be used to Work Out **Concentrations** in an **Equilibrium Mixture**

You may be given K_c and **some** of the equilibrium concentrations, and asked to **work out** the concentrations of the
other components. You can do this by just **rearranging** your expression for K_c.

Example: When ethanoic acid was allowed to reach equilibrium with ethanol at 25 °C, it was found that
the equilibrium mixture contained 2.0 mol dm⁻³ ethanoic acid and 3.5 mol dm⁻³ ethanol.
The K_c of the equilibrium is 4.0 at 25 °C. What are the concentrations of the other components?

$$CH_3COOH_{(l)} + C_2H_5OH_{(l)} \rightleftharpoons CH_3COOC_2H_{5(l)} + H_2O_{(l)}$$

Write out the expression
for K_c and substitute in all
the values you know:

$$K_c = \frac{[CH_3COOC_2H_5][H_2O]}{[CH_3COOH][C_2H_5OH]} \longrightarrow 4.0 = \frac{[CH_3COOC_2H_5][H_2O]}{2.0 \times 3.5}$$

Rearranging this gives:

$$[CH_3COOC_2H_5][H_2O] = 4.0 \times 2.0 \times 3.5 = 28.0$$

But from the equation, $[CH_3COOC_2H_5] = [H_2O]$.

The equation tells you that for every mole of $CH_3COOC_2H_5$
produced, one mole of H_2O is also produced, so their
concentrations will always be equal. (The reactant concentrations
aren't the same since they were different at the start).

So: $[CH_3COOC_2H_5] = [H_2O] = \sqrt{28} = 5.3$ mol dm⁻³

The concentration of $CH_3COOC_2H_5$ and H_2O is **5.3 mol dm⁻³**.

The **Reaction Equation** Helps You Work Out **Equilibrium Concentrations**

If you know the initial concentrations of all of your reactants, and the equilibrium
concentration of one of them, you can use the reaction equation to work out the concentrations
of all the components at equilibrium. You can use this to calculate K_c.

Example: 500 cm³ 0.10 mol dm⁻³ iron(II) sulfate solution is added to 500 cm³ 0.10 mol dm⁻³ silver nitrate at
298 K to set up the following equilibrium reaction:

$$Fe^{2+}_{(aq)} + Ag^+_{(aq)} \rightleftharpoons Fe^{3+}_{(aq)} + Ag_{(s)}$$

Once the solution has reached equilibrium, a sample is taken and the concentration of Fe^{2+} ions is
found by colorimetry. Given that at equilibrium, $[Fe^{2+}_{(aq)}] = 0.0439$ mol dm⁻³, calculate K_c.

The starting concentrations of Ag^+ and Fe^{2+} are the same
and equal to $(0.10 \div 2) = 0.05$ mol dm⁻³.

500 cm³ of each solution is diluted to 1000 cm³,
so the concentration of each reactant is halved.

The colorimetry result gives you an equilibrium concentration for Fe^{2+} of 0.0439 mol dm⁻³.

The equation tells you 1 mole of Fe^{2+} reacts with 1 mole of Ag^+ to form 1 mole of Fe^{3+} and 1 mole of Ag.
In this particular reaction solid silver is formed, so you don't need to include it in the expression for K_c.

The equilibrium concentration of Ag^+ will be the same as Fe^{2+} i.e. 0.0439 mol dm⁻³.
The equilibrium concentration of Fe^{3+} will be $0.05 - 0.0439 = 0.00610$ mol dm⁻³.

So $K_c = \frac{[Fe^{3+}]}{[Fe^{2+}][Ag^+]} = \frac{0.00610}{0.0439 \times 0.0439} = 3.17$

The reaction is heterogeneous, so
solids and liquids are omitted from
the expression for K_c (see page 15).

The units of K_c are: $\frac{mol\,dm^{-3}}{(mol\,dm^{-3})(mol\,dm^{-3})} = mol^{-1}\,dm^3$

At 298 K, K_c for this reaction = 3.17 mol⁻¹ dm³

Equilibrium Concentrations

Use the Equilibrium Concentration of a **Product** to Find the Others

You might have to figure out some of the **equilibrium concentrations** before you can find K_c. You can do this if you know the **initial concentrations** of your **reactants** and the **equilibrium concentration** of your product.

Example: 0.100 mol dm^{-3} Cu^{2+} ions are mixed with 0.300 mol dm^{-3} HCl to form the following equilibrium:

$$Cu^{2+}_{(aq)} + 4Cl^-_{(aq)} \rightleftharpoons [CuCl_4]^{2-}_{(aq)}$$

a) At equilibrium, there are x moles of $[CuCl_4]^{2-}_{(aq)}$. Write an expression for K_c in terms of x.

From the equation, you can see that for every mole of $[CuCl_4]^{2-}_{(aq)}$ formed, you will lose
1 mole $Cu^{2+}_{(aq)}$ and **4 moles $Cl^-_{(aq)}$** from your initial reactant concentrations.
So if x moles of $[CuCl_4]^{2-}_{(aq)}$ have **formed**, you will have **lost** x moles $Cu^{2+}_{(aq)}$ and $4x$ moles $Cl^-_{(aq)}$.
So the equilibrium concentrations will be:
$Cu^{2+}_{(aq)}$ = (initial $Cu^{2+}_{(aq)}$ concentration) $- x$ and $Cl^-_{(aq)}$ = (initial $Cl^-_{(aq)}$ concentration) $- 4x$
You can use this information to construct a table:

Equilibrium component	$Cu^{2+}_{(aq)}$	$Cl^-_{(aq)}$	$[CuCl_4]^{2-}_{(aq)}$
Initial concentration (mol dm^{-3})	0.100	0.300	0
Equilibrium concentration (mol dm^{-3})	$0.100 - x$	$0.300 - 4x$	x

From your equilibrium concentrations, you can see that: $K_c = \dfrac{[[CuCl_4]^{2-}]}{[Cu^{2+}][Cl^-]^4} = \dfrac{x}{(0.100 - x)(0.300 - 4x)^4}$

b) At 291 K, the concentration of $[CuCl_4]^{2-}$ in solution is 0.0637 mol dm^{-3}. Calculate K_c.

You can work out K_c by substituting the concentration of $[CuCl_4]^{2-}$ at equilibrium for x:

$x = 0.0637$ mol dm^{-3}, so $K_c = \dfrac{0.0637}{(0.100 - 0.0637)(0.300 - 4 \times 0.0637)^4} = $ **4.20×10^5 mol^{-4} dm^{12}**

Warm-Up Questions

Q1 Write down an expression you could use to work out [C] for the reaction $A + B \rightleftharpoons C$.*

Q2 Calculate [C] given that at equilibrium [A] = 0.152 mol dm^{-3},
[B] = 0.586 mol dm^{-3} and K_c = 7.35 mol^{-1} dm^3.*

Exam Questions

*Answer on page 118.

Q1 When 42.5 g nitrogen dioxide was heated in a vessel of volume 22.8 dm^3 at 500 °C,
it dissociated to form x mol dm^{-3} of oxygen in the equilibrium mixture. $2NO_{2(g)} \rightleftharpoons 2NO_{(g)} + O_{2(g)}$.

a) Calculate the starting number of moles of nitrogen dioxide. [1 mark]

b) Write an expression for K_c in terms of x. [2 marks]

c) Calculate the value for K_c at 500 °C, and give its units,
given that there were 14.1 g oxygen in the equilibrium mixture. [3 marks]

Q2 0.100 moles of dichromate(VI) ions and 0.100 moles of water were mixed together in a non-aqueous solvent
and allowed to reach equilibrium at a fixed temperature: $Cr_2O_7^{2-}_{(aq)} + H_2O_{(l)} \rightarrow 2CrO_4^{2-}_{(aq)} + 2H^+_{(aq)}$

a) Write an expression for K_c for this reaction. [1 mark]

b) At equilibrium there were 0.0300 moles of $Cr_2O_7^{2-}$ ions.
If the total volume of the solution was 100 cm^3, calculate the equilibrium concentrations of:
i) H_2O ii) CrO_4^{2-} iii) H^+ [3 marks]

c) Calculate a value for K_c at this temperature. [2 marks]

Want to find K_c? It'll need your concentration...

Lots of maths on these pages, so make sure you've worked through all the examples and understand what's happening. Whatever question you're doing, always start by writing down an expression for K_c and all the concentrations you know.

Gas Equilibria

It's easier to talk about gases in terms of their pressures rather than their molar concentrations. If you want to do this, you need a slightly different equilibrium constant — it's called K_p (but I'm afraid it's got nothing to do with peanuts).

The **Total Pressure** is **Equal** to the **Sum** of the **Partial Pressures**

In a mixture of gases, each individual gas exerts its own pressure — this is called its **partial pressure**.

> The total pressure of a gas mixture is the sum of all the partial pressures of the individual gases.

You might have to put this fact to use in pressure calculations:

Example: When 3.0 moles of the gas PCl_5 is heated, it decomposes into PCl_3 and Cl_2: $PCl_{5(g)} \rightleftharpoons PCl_{3(g)} + Cl_{2(g)}$

In a sealed vessel at 500 K, the equilibrium mixture contains chlorine with a partial pressure of 263 kPa. If the total pressure of the mixture is 714 kPa, what is the partial pressure of PCl_5?

From the equation you know that PCl_3 and Cl_2 are produced in equal amounts, so the partial pressures of these two gases are the same at equilibrium — they're both 263 kPa.

Total pressure = $p(PCl_5) + p(PCl_3) + p(Cl_2)$ ← *p just means partial pressure.*

714 = $p(PCl_5)$ + 263 + 263

So the partial pressure of PCl_5 = 714 − 263 − 263 = **188 kPa**

Partial Pressures can be Worked Out from **Mole Fractions**

A '**mole fraction**' is just the **proportion** of a gas mixture that is a particular gas. So if you've got four moles of gas in total, and two of them are gas A, the mole fraction of gas A is ½. There are **two formulas** you've got to know:

> 1) Mole fraction of a gas in a mixture = $\dfrac{\text{number of moles of gas}}{\text{total number of moles of gas in the mixture}}$
>
> 2) Partial pressure of a gas = **mole fraction of gas × total pressure of the mixture**

Example: When 3.0 mol of PCl_5 is heated in a sealed vessel, the equilibrium mixture contains 1.75 mol of chlorine. If the total pressure of the mixture is 714 kPa, what is the partial pressure of PCl_5?

PCl_3 and Cl_2 are produced in equal amounts, so there'll be **1.75 moles** of PCl_3 too.
1.75 moles of PCl_5 must have decomposed so (3.0 − 1.75 =) **1.25 moles** of PCl_5 must be left at equilibrium.
This means that the total number of moles of gas at equilibrium = 1.75 + 1.75 + 1.25 = **4.75**
So the mole fraction of $PCl_5 = \dfrac{1.25}{4.75} = 0.263$
The partial pressure of PCl_5 = mole fraction × total pressure = 0.263 × 714 = **188 kPa**

The **Equilibrium Constant K_p** is Calculated from **Partial Pressures**

The expression for K_p is just like the one for K_c — except you use partial pressures instead of concentrations.

> For the equilibrium $aA_{(g)} + bB_{(g)} \rightleftharpoons dD_{(g)} + eE_{(g)}$: $K_p = \dfrac{p(D)^d p(E)^e}{p(A)^a p(B)^b}$

There are no square brackets because they're partial pressures, not molar concentrations.

To **calculate K_p**, you just have to put the partial pressures in the expression. You work out the **units** like you did for K_c.

Example: Calculate K_p for the decomposition of PCl_5 gas at 500 K (as shown above).
The partial pressures of each gas are: $p(PCl_5)$ = 188 kPa, $p(PCl_3)$ = 263 kPa, $p(Cl_2)$ = 263 kPa

$K_p = \dfrac{p(Cl_2)p(PCl_3)}{p(PCl_5)} = \dfrac{263\,\text{kPa} \times 263\,\text{kPa}}{188\,\text{kPa}} = 368$

The units for K_p are worked out by putting the units into the expression instead of the numbers, and cancelling (like for K_c): $K_p = \dfrac{\text{kPa} \times \text{kPa}}{\text{kPa}} = \text{kPa}$. So, K_p = **368 kPa**

Gas Equilibria

K_p can be Used to Find Partial Pressures

You might be given the K_p and have to use it to calculate **equilibrium partial pressures**.

> **Example:** An equilibrium exists between ethanoic acid monomers, CH_3COOH, and dimers, $(CH_3COOH)_2$.
> At 160 °C the K_p for the reaction $(CH_3COOH)_{2(g)} \rightleftharpoons 2CH_3COOH_{(g)}$ is 180 kPa.
> At this temperature the partial pressure of the dimer, $(CH_3COOH)_2$, is 28.5 kPa.
> Calculate the partial pressure of the monomer in this equilibrium and state the total pressure
> exerted by the equilibrium mixture.
>
> First, use the chemical equilibrium to write an expression for K_p: $\quad K_p = \dfrac{p(CH_3COOH)^2}{p((CH_3COOH)_2)}$
>
> This rearranges to give: $p(CH_3COOH)^2 = K_p \times p((CH_3COOH)_2) = 180 \times 28.5 = 5130$
>
> $\qquad\qquad p(CH_3COOH) = \sqrt{5130} = 71.6$ kPa
>
> So the total pressure of the equilibrium mixture = 28.5 + 71.6 = **100.1 kPa**

Add the two partial pressures together to get the total pressure.

K_p for Heterogeneous Equilibria Still Only Includes Gases

You met the idea of homogeneous and heterogeneous equilibria on page 15.
Up until now we've only thought about K_p expressions for **homogeneous equilibria**.
If you're writing an expression for K_p for a **heterogeneous equilibrium**, you don't include **solids** or **liquids**.

> **Example:** Write an expression for K_p for the following reaction: $NH_4HS_{(s)} \rightleftharpoons NH_{3(g)} + H_2S_{(g)}$.
>
> The equilibrium is heterogeneous — a solid decomposes to form two gases.
> Solids don't get included in K_p, so $K_p = p(NH_3)\,p(H_2S)$.

There's no bottom line as the reactant is a solid.

Warm-Up Questions

Q1 What is meant by partial pressure?
Q2 How do you work out the mole fraction of a gas?
Q3 Write the expression for K_p for the following equilibrium: $NH_4HS_{(g)} \rightleftharpoons NH_{3(g)} + H_2S_{(g)}$

PRACTICE QUESTIONS

Exam Questions

Q1 At high temperatures, SO_2Cl_2 dissociates according to the equation $SO_2Cl_{2(g)} \rightleftharpoons SO_{2(g)} + Cl_{2(g)}$.
When 1.50 moles of SO_2Cl_2 dissociates at 700 K, the equilibrium mixture contains SO_2
with a partial pressure of 60.2 kPa. The mixture has a total pressure of 141 kPa.

   a) Write an expression for K_p for this reaction.   [1 mark]

   b) Calculate the partial pressure of Cl_2 and the partial pressure of SO_2Cl_2 in the equilibrium mixture.   [2 marks]

   c) Calculate a value for K_p for this reaction and give its units.   [2 marks]

Q2 When nitric oxide and oxygen were mixed in a 2:1 mole ratio at a constant temperature
in a sealed flask, an equilibrium was set up according to the equation $2NO_{(g)} + O_{2(g)} \rightleftharpoons 2NO_{2(g)}$.
The partial pressure of the nitric oxide (NO) at equilibrium was 36 kPa and the total pressure in the flask was 99 kPa.

   a) Deduce the partial pressure of oxygen in the equilibrium mixture.   [1 mark]

   b) Calculate the partial pressure of nitrogen dioxide in the equilibrium mixture.   [1 mark]

   c) Write an expression for the equilibrium constant, K_p,
for this reaction and calculate its value at this temperature. State its units.   [2 marks]

Pressure pushing down on me, pressing down on you... Under pressure...

Partial pressures are like concentrations for gases. The more of a substance you've got in a solution, the higher the concentration, and the more of a gas you've got in a container, the higher the partial pressure. It's all to do with how many molecules are crashing into the sides. With gases though, you've got to keep the lid on tight or they'll escape.

More on Equilibrium Constants

In Year 1, you saw how changing conditions can change the position of the equilibrium. That's great, but you also need to be able to predict what will happen to the equilibrium constant when you change conditions.

If **Conditions Change** the **Position of Equilibrium** Will Move

1) If you **change** the **concentration**, **pressure** or **temperature** of a reversible reaction, you're going to **alter** the **position of equilibrium**. This just means you'll end up with **different amounts** of reactants and products at equilibrium.

2) If the change causes **more product** to form, then you say that the equilibrium shifts to the **right**. If **less product** forms, then the equilibrium has shifted to the **left**.

3) In Year 1, you met Le Chatelier's principle, which lets you predict how the **position of equilibrium** will change if a **condition changes**. Here it is again:

> If there's a change in **concentration**, **pressure** or **temperature**, the equilibrium will move to help **counteract** the change.

The removal of his dummy was a change that Maxwell always opposed.

4) So, basically, if you **raise the temperature**, the position of equilibrium will shift to try to **cool things down**. And if you **raise the pressure or concentration**, the position of equilibrium will shift to try to **reduce it again**.

5) The **size** of the equilibrium constant tells you where the equilibrium lies. The **greater** the value of K_c or K_p, the further to the **right** the equilibrium lies. **Smaller** values of K_c and K_p mean the equilibrium lies further to the **left**.

Temperature Changes **Alter** the Equilibrium Constant

1) From Le Chatelier's principle, you know that an **increase** in temperature causes more of the product of an **endothermic** reaction to form so that the extra heat is absorbed. Le Chatelier also states that a **decrease** in temperature causes more of the product of an **exothermic** reaction to form.

2) The equilibrium constant for a reaction depends on the **temperature**. Changing the temperature alters the position of equilibrium and the **value** of the equilibrium constant.

> **Example:** The reaction below is exothermic in the forward direction. If you increase the temperature, the equilibrium shifts to the left to absorb the extra heat. What happens to K_p?
>
> Exothermic $\longrightarrow$
> $$2SO_{2(g)} + O_{2(g)} \rightleftharpoons 2SO_{3(g)} \quad \Delta H = -197 \text{ kJ mol}^{-1}$$
> $\longleftarrow$ Endothermic
>
> *An exothermic reaction releases heat and has a negative ΔH. An endothermic reaction absorbs heat and has a positive ΔH.*
>
> If the equilibrium shifts to the left, then less product will form. By looking at the expression for the equilibrium constant, you can see that if there's less product, the value of K_p will decrease.
>
> *This reaction is between gases, so it's easiest to use K_p, but it's exactly the same for K_c and the other equilibrium constants you'll meet in the next few pages.*
>
> $$K_p = \frac{p(SO_3)^2}{p(SO_2)^2 p(O_2)}$$
>
> *There's less product and more reactant, so the number on the top gets smaller and the number on the bottom gets bigger. This means K_p must have decreased.*

3) The general rule for what happens to an equilibrium constant when you change the **temperature** of a reaction is that:

> - If changing the temperature causes **less product** to form, the equilibrium moves to the **left**, and the equilibrium constant **decreases**.
> - If changing the temperature causes **more product** to form, the equilibrium moves to the **right**, and the equilibrium constant **increases**.

More on Equilibrium Constants

Concentration and Pressure Changes Don't Affect the Equilibrium Constant

Concentration

The value of the equilibrium constant is fixed at a given temperature. So if the concentration of one thing in the equilibrium mixture changes then the concentrations of the others must change to keep the value of K_c the same.

E.g. $CH_3COOH_{(l)} + C_2H_5OH_{(l)} \rightleftharpoons CH_3COOC_2H_{5(l)} + H_2O_{(l)}$

If you increase the concentration of CH_3COOH then the equilibrium will move to the right to get rid of the extra CH_3COOH — so more $CH_3COOC_2H_5$ and H_2O are produced. This keeps the equilibrium constant the same.

Pressure

Increasing the pressure shifts the equilibrium to the side with fewer gas molecules — this reduces the pressure. Decreasing the pressure shifts the equilibrium to the side with more gas molecules. This raises the pressure again. K_p (or K_c) stays the same, no matter what you do to the pressure.

E.g. $2SO_{2(g)} + O_{2(g)} \rightleftharpoons 2SO_{3(g)}$

There are 3 moles on the left, but only 2 on the right.
So an increase in pressure would shift the equilibrium to the right.

So, to summarise, concentration and pressure don't affect the values of K_c or K_p, but they do change the amounts of products and reactants present at equilibrium. Changes in temperature not only alter the amounts of products and reactants present at equilibrium, but also change the value of the equilibrium constants.

Catalysts have NO EFFECT on the position of equilibrium or the value of K_c/K_p.
They can't increase yield — but they do mean equilibrium is approached faster.

Warm-Up Questions

Q1 If you raise the temperature of a reversible reaction, in which direction will the reaction move?

Q2 Does temperature change affect the equilibrium constant?

Q3 Why doesn't concentration affect the equilibrium constant?

Exam Questions

Q1 At temperature T_1, the equilibrium constant K_c for the following reaction is 0.67 mol^{-1} dm^3.

$2SO_{2(g)} + O_{2(g)} \rightleftharpoons 2SO_{3(g)}$ $\Delta H = -196$ kJmol^{-1}.

a) When equilibrium was established at a different temperature, T_2, the value of K_c increased. State which of T_1 or T_2 is the lower temperature and explain why.   [3 marks]

b) The experiment was repeated exactly the same in all respects at T_1, except a flask of smaller volume was used. How would this change affect the yield of sulfur trioxide and the value of K_c?   [2 marks]

Q2 The reaction between methane and steam is used to produce hydrogen. The forward reaction is endothermic.

$CH_{4(g)} + H_2O_{(g)} \rightleftharpoons CO_{(g)} + 3H_{2(g)}$

a) Write an equation for K_p for this reaction.   [1 mark]

b) Which of the following will cause the value of K_p to increase?

A Increasing the temperature.   B Using a catalyst

C Decreasing the pressure.   D Decreasing the temperature   [1 mark]

It's just a jump to the left, and then a step to the right...

Hmm, sounds like there's a song in there somewhere. I've now got a vision of chemists in lab coats dancing at a Xmas party... Let's not go there. Instead make sure you really get your head round this concept of changing conditions and the equilibrium shifting to compensate. Reread until you've definitely got it — it makes this topic much easier to learn.

Acids and Bases

Remember this stuff? Well, it's all down to Brønsted and Lowry — they've got a lot to answer for.

An Acid **Releases** Protons — a Base **Accepts** Protons

Brønsted-Lowry acids are **proton donors** — they release **hydrogen ions** (H^+) when they're mixed with water. You never get H^+ ions by themselves in water though — they're always combined with H_2O to form **hydroxonium ions, H_3O^+.**

$$HA_{(aq)} + H_2O_{(l)} \rightarrow H_3O^+_{(aq)} + A^-_{(aq)}$$

Brønsted-Lowry bases are **proton acceptors**. When they're in solution, they grab **hydrogen ions** from water molecules.

$$B_{(aq)} + H_2O_{(l)} \rightarrow BH^+_{(aq)} + OH^-_{(aq)}$$

HA is any old acid and B is just a random base.

Some Acids Can Release **More than One** Proton

1) Acids like **HCl** and **HNO_3** only have **one proton** that they can release into solution. These are **monobasic** acids.

2) But some acids, such as sulfuric acid (H_2SO_4) or phosphoric acid (H_3PO_4), have **more than one** proton that they can release into solution.

Monobasic acids are also known as monoprotic, dibasic as diprotic... etc.

3) **Sulfuric acid** can release **two protons** so it's a **dibasic acid**: $H_2SO_{4(aq)} \rightleftharpoons 2H^+_{(aq)} + SO_4^{2-}_{(aq)}$

4) **Phosphoric acid** is a **tribasic** acid. It can release **three protons** into solution: $H_3PO_{4(aq)} \rightleftharpoons 3H^+_{(aq)} + PO_4^{3-}_{(aq)}$

Acids and Bases form **Conjugate Pairs**

1) Conjugate pairs are species that are linked by the **transfer** of a **proton**. They're always on opposite sides of the reaction equation.

A species is just any type of chemical — it could be an atom, a molecule, an ion...

2) The species that has **lost** a proton is the **conjugate base** and the species that has **gained** a proton is the **conjugate acid**.

3) When Brønsted-Lowry acids and bases react together, the equilibrium below is set up.

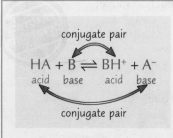

conjugate pair

$$\underset{\text{acid}}{HA} + \underset{\text{base}}{B} \rightleftharpoons \underset{\text{acid}}{BH^+} + \underset{\text{base}}{A^-}$$

conjugate pair

- In the forward reaction, HA acts as an acid as it donates a proton.
- In the reverse reaction, A⁻ acts as a base and accepts a proton from the BH⁺ ion to form HA.
- HA and A⁻ are called a conjugate pair — HA is the conjugate acid of A⁻ and A⁻ is the conjugate base of the acid, HA.
- Similarly, B and BH⁺ are a conjugate pair. The base B takes a proton to form BH⁺ — so B is the conjugate base of BH⁺, and BH⁺ is the conjugate acid of B.

4) **Water** is a special case — it reacts with acids to form a **conjugate acid** (H_3O^+), and reacts with **bases** to form a **conjugate base** (OH^-).

$$HA_{(aq)} + H_2O_{(l)} \rightleftharpoons A^-_{(aq)} + H_3O^+_{(aq)}$$

$$B_{(aq)} + H_2O_{(l)} \rightleftharpoons BH^+_{(aq)} + OH^-_{(aq)}$$

Acids React with **Metals** and **Bases**

You saw how acids can react in Year 1, but here's a quick recap:

1) **Reactive metals** react with acids releasing **hydrogen gas**. The metal atoms **donate electrons** to the **H^+ ions** in the acid solution. The metal atoms are **oxidised** and the H^+ ions are **reduced**.

E.g. $Ca_{(s)} + 2H^+_{(aq)} \rightarrow Ca^{2+}_{(aq)} + H_{2(g)}$

2) **Carbonates** react with acids to produce **carbon dioxide** and **water**.

$$CO_3^{2-}_{(aq)} + 2H^+_{(aq)} \rightarrow H_2O_{(l)} + CO_{2(g)}$$

3) **Alkalis** are bases that release **hydroxide ions** in water. They react with acids to form **water**.

$$H^+_{(aq)} + OH^-_{(aq)} \rightarrow H_2O_{(l)}$$

4) Most insoluble bases are **metal oxides**. Like alkalis, they react with acids to form **water**.

$$2H^+_{(aq)} + O^{2-}_{(s)} \rightarrow H_2O_{(l)}$$

These are ionic equations — they only include the reacting particles.

Module 5: Section 1 — Rates, Equilibrium & pH

Acids and Bases

Acid-Base Theory Took Time to Develop

Scientific theories can take **years** to develop. A scientist will come up with an idea, and then someone else will find holes in the theory and make changes to **improve** it. This is how the **Brønsted-Lowry theory** of acids and bases came about.

Lavoisier thought it was all to do with oxygen...

Lavoisier came up with the first theory of acids and bases in the 18th century. He didn't know the formulas of compounds like hydrochloric acid but he did know that sulfuric acid had the formula H_2SO_4 and nitric acid had the formula HNO_3. So he proposed that acids had to have **oxygen** in them. It was later shown that acids like hydrochloric acid (HCl) and hydrogen sulfide (H_2S) don't have any oxygen in them at all.

Arrhenius thought it was about H⁺ and OH⁻...

At the end of the 19th century, a chemist called Arrhenius suggested that acids **release protons** in aqueous solution, whilst bases release **hydroxide ions**. He said that when acids and bases react together they form **water** and a **salt**. This is true for loads of examples, but doesn't work for bases such as **ammonia** (NH_3), which don't contain any hydroxide ions.

The Brønsted-Lowry theory is based on Arrhenius' work...

Brønsted and Lowry came up with their definition of acids and bases independently of one another. It's clearly based on Arrhenius' theory, but broadens the definition of a base to be a **proton acceptor**. They also came up with the idea that acids and bases react to form **conjugate pairs**, rather than a salt and water. This definition currently explains most of our observations, so is one of the theories we still use today — around 100 years later.

Brønsted and Lowry were off to make holes in other people's theories.

Warm-Up Questions

Q1 Give the Brønsted-Lowry definitions of an acid and a base.
Q2 What's the difference between a monobasic, a dibasic and a tribasic acid?
Q3 What is the conjugate base of water? And the conjugate acid?
Q4 Write an ionic equation to show the reaction between copper(II) oxide and hydrochloric acid.

PRACTICE QUESTIONS

Exam Questions

Q1 Magnesium completely dissolves in aqueous sulfuric acid, $H_2SO_{4\ (aq)}$.

    a) Which ions are present in a solution of sulfuric acid? [1 mark]

    b) Write an ionic equation for the reaction of sulfuric acid and magnesium. [1 mark]

    c) What is the conjugate base of sulfuric acid? [1 mark]

Q2 a) Write an equation to show the equilibrium set up
       when the acid hydrogen cyanide, HCN, is added to water. [1 mark]

    b) From your equation, identify the two conjugate pairs formed. [2 marks]

    c) Which ion links conjugate pairs? [1 mark]

Q3 a) Write an equation to show the equilibrium set up when ammonia, a weak base, is dissolved in water. [1 mark]

    b) Is water behaving as an acid or a base in this equilibrium? Give a reason for your answer. [1 mark]

    c) What species forms a conjugate pair with water in this reaction? [1 mark]

I do like bases — they're just so accepting...

Make sure you can identify conjugate pairs. Remember — they're always on opposite sides of the equation, and you can switch between them by adding or removing protons. And have another read of how the Brønsted-Lowry theory was thought up — the way it was developed over time from other theories is a prime example of How Science Works.

pH

Just when you thought it was safe to turn the page — it's even more about acids and bases.
This page is positively swarming with calculations and constants...

The **pH Scale** is a Measure of **Hydrogen Ion Concentration**

pH is a measure of how **acidic** or **basic** something is. It measures the
concentration of **hydrogen** ions in solution. **Concentration of hydrogen ions**
can vary enormously so a **logarithmic scale** called the **pH scale** is used.
The pH scale goes from **0** (very acidic) to **14** (very alkaline). **pH 7** is **neutral**.

$$pH = -\log_{10}[H^+]$$

The stronger the acid, the lower the pH.

1) If you know the **hydrogen ion concentration** of a solution,
   you can calculate its **pH** by sticking the numbers into the **formula**.

> **Example:** A solution of hydrochloric acid has a hydrogen ion
> concentration of 0.01 mol dm^{-3}. What is the pH of the solution?
>
> *Use the 'log' button on your calculator for this.*
>
> $pH = -\log_{10}[H^+] = -\log_{10}[0.01] = 2$

Kelly's an expert at finding logs.

2) If you know the **pH** of a solution, and you want to find its
   hydrogen ion concentration, then you need the **inverse** of the pH formula: $[H^+] = 10^{-pH}$

> **Example:** A solution of sulfuric acid has a pH of 1.52.
> What is the hydrogen ion concentration of this solution?
>
> $[H^+] = 10^{-pH} = 10^{-1.52} = 0.0302$ mol dm^{-3} = **3.02 × 10^{-2} mol dm^{-3}**

For **Strong Monobasic Acids**, [H$^+$] = [Acid]

1) **Strong acids** such as hydrochloric acid and nitric acid **ionise fully** in solution.

2) They're also **monobasic**, which means **one mole of acid** produces **one mole of hydrogen ions**.
   So the H$^+$ concentration is the **same** as the acid concentration.

> **E.g.** For **0.10 mol dm^{-3} HCl**, [H$^+$] is also 0.10 mol dm^{-3}. So the **pH** = $-\log_{10}[H^+] = -\log_{10}0.10 =$ **1.00**.
> Or for **0.050 mol dm^{-3} HNO$_3$**, [H$^+$] is also 0.050 mol dm^{-3}, giving **pH** = $-\log_{10}0.050 =$ **1.30**.

The Ionic Product of Water, K_w, Depends on the Concentration of H$^+$ and OH$^-$

Water dissociates into **hydroxonium ions** and **hydroxide ions**. So the following equilibrium exists in water:

$$H_2O_{(l)} + H_2O_{(l)} \rightleftharpoons H_3O^+_{(aq)} + OH^-_{(aq)} \qquad \text{or more simply:} \qquad H_2O_{(l)} \rightleftharpoons H^+_{(aq)} + OH^-_{(aq)}$$

And, just like for any other equilibrium reaction, you can write an expression for the **equilibrium constant**.

It's such an important equilibrium constant, that it has it's own name — rather than K_c, the equilibrium
constant for the dissociation of water is called the **ionic product** of water, and has the symbol K_w.

The units of K_w are always mol^{2}dm^{-6}.

$$K_w = [H^+][OH^-]$$

It doesn't matter whether water is pure or part of a solution — this equilibrium is always happening, and K_w is always the same at the same temperature.

For **pure water**, there's a **1:1** ratio of H$^+$ and OH$^-$ ions due to dissociation. This means [H$^+$] = [OH$^-$] and $K_w = [H^+]^2$.
So if you know K_w of pure water at a certain temperature, you can calculate [H$^+$] and use this to find the pH.

K_w behaves like other equilibrium constants:

- Changing the **concentration** of [H$^+$] or [OH$^-$] in solution has no effect on the **value** of K_w as the equilibrium
  will shift, changing the concentration of the other substances to keep the value of K_w the same..

- Changing the **temperature** of the solution changes the value of K_w — dissociation of water is an **endothermic**
  process, so for example, warming the solution shifts the equilibrium to the **right** and K$_w$ increases.

The fact that K_w always has the **same value** for pure water or an aqueous solution
at a **given temperature** is really useful, as you're about to discover...

pH

Use K_w to Find the pH of a Strong Base

1) Sodium hydroxide (NaOH) and potassium hydroxide (KOH) are **strong bases** that **fully ionise** in water:

$$NaOH_{(s)} \rightarrow Na^+_{(aq)} + OH^-_{(aq)} \qquad KOH_{(s)} \rightarrow K^+_{(aq)} + OH^-_{(aq)}$$

2) They donate **one mole of OH⁻ ions** per mole of base.
   This means that the concentration of OH⁻ ions is the **same** as the **concentration of the base**.
   So for 0.02 mol dm⁻³ sodium hydroxide solution, [OH⁻] is also **0.02 mol dm⁻³**.

3) But to work out the **pH** you need to know **[H⁺]**
   — luckily this is linked to **[OH⁻]** through the **ionic product of water**, K_w:  $\boxed{K_w = [H^+][OH^-]}$

4) So if you know K_w and [OH⁻] for a **strong aqueous base** at a certain
   temperature, you can work out **[H⁺]** and then the **pH**.

> **Example:** Find the pH of 0.10 mol dm⁻³ NaOH at 298 K, given that K_w at 298 K is 1.0 × 10⁻¹⁴ mol² dm⁻⁶.
>
> 1) First put all the values you know into the expression for the ionic product of water, K_w:
>
> $$1.0 \times 10^{-14} = [H^+][0.10]$$
>
> 2) Now rearrange the expression to find [H⁺]:
>
> $$[H^+] = \frac{1.0 \times 10^{-14}}{0.10} = 1.0 \times 10^{-13} \text{ mol dm}^{-3}$$
>
> 3) Use your value of [H⁺] to find the pH of the solution:
>
> $$pH = -\log_{10}[H^+] = -\log_{10}(1.0 \times 10^{-13}) = \mathbf{13}$$

Warm-Up Questions

Q1 Write the formula for calculating the pH of a solution.
Q2 What can you assume about [H⁺] for a strong monobasic acid?
Q3 Write the expression for the ionic product of water.
Q4 What are the units of K_w?
Q5 Explain how you'd find the pH of a strong base.

Exam Questions

Q1 a) What's the pH of a solution of the strong acid, hydrobromic acid (HBr),
       if it has a concentration of 0.32 mol dm⁻³?   [1 mark]

    b) Hydrobromic acid is a stronger acid than hydrochloric acid.
       Explain what that means in terms of hydrogen ions and pH.   [1 mark]

Q2 A solution of sodium hydroxide contains 2.50 g dm⁻³. K_w at 298 K is 1.0 × 10⁻¹⁴ mol² dm⁻⁶.

    a) What is the molar concentration of the hydroxide ions in this solution?   [2 marks]

    b) Calculate the pH of this solution.   [2 marks]

Q3 Calculate the pH of a 0.0370 mol dm⁻³ solution of sodium hydroxide at 298 K.
    K_w, the ionic product of water, is 1.0 × 10⁻¹⁴ mol² dm⁻⁶ at 298 K.   [2 marks]

An ionic product — when your trousers have no creases in them...

You know things are getting serious when maths stuff like logs start appearing. It's fine really though, just practise a few questions and make sure you know how to use the log button on your calculator. And make sure you've learned the equation for K_w and both pH equations. And while you're up, go and make me a nice cup of tea, lots of milk, no sugar.

The Acid Dissociation Constant

More acid calculations to come, so you'll need to get that calculator warmed up... Either hold it for a couple of minutes in your armpit, or even better, warm it between your clenched buttocks. OK done that? Good stuff...

K_a is the **Acid Dissociation Constant**

1) Weak acids (like CH_3COOH) **don't** ionise fully in solution, so the $[H^+]$ **isn't** the same as the acid concentration. This makes it a **bit trickier** to find their pH. You have to use yet another **equilibrium constant**, K_a (the acid dissociation constant).

- For a weak aqueous acid, HA, you get the following equilibrium: $HA_{(aq)} \rightleftharpoons H^+_{(aq)} + A^-_{(aq)}$

- As only a **tiny amount** of HA dissociates, you can assume that $[HA_{(aq)}] \gg [H^+_{(aq)}]$ so $[HA_{(aq)}]_{start} \approx [HA_{(aq)}]_{equilibrium}$.

- So if you apply the equilibrium law, you get: $K_a = \dfrac{[H^+][A^-]}{[HA]_{start}}$

- You can also assume that dissociation of the **acid** is much greater than dissociation of **water**. This means you can assume that all the H^+ ions in solution come from the **acid**, so $[H^+_{(aq)}] \approx [A^-_{(aq)}]$.

  You can use this expression in calculations, but if you're asked to give an expression for K_a then make sure you write the one that includes $[A^-]$, don't use $[H^+]^2$.

  So $K_a = \dfrac{[H^+]^2}{[HA]}$ The units of K_a are $mol\ dm^{-3}$.

2) The assumptions made above to find K_a only work for **weak acids**. Stronger acids **dissociate more** in solution, so the difference between $[HA_{(aq)}]_{start}$ and $[HA_{(aq)}]_{equilibrium}$ becomes **significant**, and the assumption that $[HA_{(aq)}]_{start} = [HA_{(aq)}]_{equilibrium}$ is no longer **valid**.

To Find the **pH** of a **Weak Acid**, You Use K_a

K_a is an **equilibrium constant** just like K_c or K_w. It applies to a particular acid at a **specific temperature** regardless of the **concentration**. You can use this fact to find the **pH** of a known concentration of a weak acid.

Example: Calculate the hydrogen ion concentration and the pH of a $0.02\ mol\ dm^{-3}$ solution of propanoic acid (CH_3CH_2COOH). K_a for propanoic acid at this temperature is $1.30 \times 10^{-5}\ mol\ dm^{-3}$.

First, write down your expression for K_a and rearrange to find $[H^+]$.

$K_a = \dfrac{[H^+]^2}{[CH_3CH_2COOH]} \implies [H^+]^2 = K_a[CH_3CH_2COOH] = 1.30 \times 10^{-5} \times 0.02 = 2.60 \times 10^{-7}$

$\implies [H^+] = \sqrt{(2.60 \times 10^{-7})} = 5.10 \times 10^{-4}\ mol\ dm^{-3}$

You can now use your value for $[H^+]$ to find pH: $pH = -\log_{10} 5.10 \times 10^{-4} = 3.29$

You Might Have to Find the **Concentration** or K_a of a **Weak Acid**

You don't need to know anything new for this type of calculation. You usually just have to find **$[H^+]$** from the pH, then fiddle around with the **K_a expression** to find the missing bit of information.

Example: The pH of an ethanoic acid (CH_3COOH) solution was 3.02 at 298 K. Calculate the molar concentration of this solution. K_a of ethanoic acid is $1.75 \times 10^{-5}\ mol\ dm^{-3}$ at 298 K.

First, use the pH to find $[H^+]$: $[H^+] = 10^{-pH} = 10^{-3.02} = 9.55 \times 10^{-4}\ mol\ dm^{-3}$

Then rearrange the expression for K_a and plug in your values to find $[CH_3COOH]$:

$K_a = \dfrac{[H^+]^2}{[CH_3COOH]} \implies CH_3COOH = \dfrac{[H^+]^2}{K_a} = \dfrac{(9.55 \times 10^{-4})^2}{1.75 \times 10^{-5}} = 0.0521\ mol\ dm^{-3}$

This bunny may look cute, but he can't help Horace with his revision.

The Acid Dissociation Constant

$pK_a = -\log_{10} K_a$ and $K_a = 10^{-pK_a}$

pK_a is calculated from K_a in exactly the same way as pH is calculated from $[H^+]$ — and vice versa.

> **Example:** a) If an acid has a K_a value of 1.50×10^{-7} mol dm³, what is its pK_a?
>
> $pK_a = -\log_{10}(1.50 \times 10^{-7}) = \mathbf{6.82}$
>
> b) What is the K_a value of an acid if its pK_a is 4.32?
>
> $K_a = 10^{-4.32} = \mathbf{4.79 \times 10^{-5} \text{ mol dm}^{-3}}$

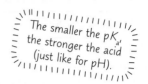

The smaller the pK_a, the stronger the acid (just like for pH).

Just to make things that bit more complicated, you might be given a **pK_a** value in a question to work out concentrations or pH. If so, you just need to convert it to K_a so that you can use the **K_a expression**.

> **Example:** Calculate the pH of 0.0500 mol dm⁻³ methanoic acid (HCOOH).
> Methanoic acid has a pK_a of 3.75 at this temperature.
>
> $K_a = 10^{-pK_a} = 10^{-3.75} = 1.78 \times 10^{-4}$ mol dm⁻³ ⟵ *First you have to convert the pK_a to K_a.*
>
> $K_a = \dfrac{[H^+]^2}{[COOH]}$ ⟹ $[H^+]^2 = K_a \times [HCOOH] = 1.78 \times 10^{-4} \times 0.0500 = 8.90 \times 10^{-6}$
>
> $[H^+] = \sqrt{(8.90 \times 10^{-6})} = 2.98 \times 10^{-3}$ mol dm⁻³
>
> pH = $-\log_{10} 2.98 \times 10^{-3} = \mathbf{2.53}$

You might also be asked to work out a **pK_a** value from concentrations or pH. In this case, you just work out the K_a value as usual and then convert it to **pK_a** — and Bob's a revision goat.

Bob the revision goat.

Warm-Up Questions

Q1 What are the units of K_a?

Q2 What assumptions do you have to make when calculating K_a for a weak acid?
Why aren't these assumptions true for a strong acid?

Q3 Describe how you would calculate the pH of a weak acid from its acid dissociation constant.

Q4 How is pK_a defined?

Q5 Would you expect strong acids to have higher or lower K_a values than weak acids?

Exam Questions

Q1 The value of K_a for the weak acid HA, at 298 K, is 5.60×10^{-4} mol dm⁻³.

a) Write an expression for K_a for HA. [1 mark]

b) Calculate the pH of a 0.280 mol dm⁻³ solution of HA at 298 K. [2 marks]

Q2 The pH of a 0.150 mol dm⁻³ solution of a weak monobasic acid, HX, is 2.65 at 298 K.

a) Calculate the value of K_a for the acid HX at 298 K. [2 marks]

b) Calculate pK_a for this acid. [1 mark]

Q3 Benzoic acid is a weak acid that is used as a food preservative. It has a pK_a of 4.2 at 298 K.
Find the pH of a 1.6×10^{-4} mol dm⁻³ solution of benzoic acid at 298 K. [3 marks]

Fluffy revision animals... aaawwwww...

Strong acids have high K_a values and weak acids have low K_a values. For pK_a values, it's the other way round — the stronger the acid, the lower the pK_a. If something's got p in front of it, like pH, pK_w or pK_a, it'll mean $-\log10$ of whatever. Oh and did you like the cute animals on this page? Did it really make your day? Good, I'm really pleased about that.

Buffers

I always found buffers a bit mind-boggling. How is it possible that a solution can resist becoming more acidic if you add acid to it? And why on earth would it want to? Here's where you find out...

Buffers Resist Changes in pH

> A **buffer** is a solution that **minimises** changes in pH when **small** amounts of acid or base are added.

A buffer **doesn't** stop the pH from changing completely — it does make the changes **very slight** though. Buffers only work for small amounts of acid or base — put too much in and they won't be able to cope. You can get **acidic buffers** and **basic buffers**, but you only need to know about acidic ones.

Acidic Buffers Contain a Weak Acid and its Conjugate Base

Acidic buffers have a pH of less than 7 — they're made by setting up an equilibrium between a **weak acid** and its **conjugate base**. This can be done in two ways:

1) **Mix a weak acid with the salt of its conjugate base.** e.g. ethanoic acid and sodium ethanoate:
- The salt **fully** dissociates into its ions when it dissolves: $CH_3COO^-Na^+_{(aq)} \rightarrow CH_3COO^-_{(aq)} + Na^+_{(aq)}$
- The **weak acid** only **slightly** dissociates: $CH_3COOH_{(aq)} \rightleftharpoons H^+_{(aq)} + CH_3COO^-_{(aq)}$

2) **Mix an excess of weak acid with a strong alkali.** e.g. ethanoic acid and sodium hydroxide:
- **All** the base reacts with the acid: $CH_3COOH_{(aq)} + OH^-_{(aq)} \rightarrow CH_3COO^- + H_2O$
- The weak acid was in **excess**, so there's still some left in solution once all the base has reacted. This acid **slightly dissociates**: $CH_3COOH_{(aq)} \rightleftharpoons H^+_{(aq)} + CH_3COO^-_{(aq)}$

In both cases, the following equilibrium is set up between the weak acid and its conjugate base:

Lots of undissociated weak acid ⟹ $CH_3COOH_{(aq)} \rightleftharpoons H^+_{(aq)} + CH_3COO^-_{(aq)}$ ⟸ Lots of CH_3COO^-

The equilibrium solution contains:
- Lots of undissociated acid (HA).
- Lots of the acid's conjugate base (A⁻).
- Enough H⁺ ions to make the solution acidic.

Conjugate Pairs Set Up an Equilibrium that Resists Changes in pH

It's the job of the conjugate pair to control the pH of a buffer solution. The **conjugate base** mops up an excess of **H⁺**, while the **conjugate acid releases** H⁺ if there's too much base around.

If you add a **small** amount of **acid** the **H⁺ concentration** increases. Most of the extra H⁺ ions combine with CH_3COO^- ions to form CH_3COOH. This shifts the equilibrium to the **left**, reducing the H⁺ concentration to close to its original value. So the **pH** doesn't change much.

The large number of CH_3COO^- ions make sure the buffer can cope with the addition of acid.

This isn't a problem as there's loads of spare CH_3COOH molecules.

If a **small** amount of **alkali** (e.g. NaOH) is added, the **OH⁻ concentration** increases. Most of the extra OH⁻ ions react with H⁺ ions to form water — removing H⁺ ions from the solution. This causes more CH_3COOH to **dissociate** to form H⁺ ions — shifting the equilibrium to the **right**. The H⁺ concentration increases until it's close to its original value, so the **pH** doesn't change much.

Buffer Solutions are Important in Blood

1) In our bodies, **blood** needs to be kept between pH 7.35 and 7.45. The pH is controlled using a **carbonic acid-hydrogen carbonate** buffer system. Two equilibrium reactions occur.

$$H_2CO_{3(aq)} \rightleftharpoons H^+_{(aq)} + HCO_3^-_{(aq)}$$
and $H_2CO_{3(aq)} \rightleftharpoons H_2O_{(l)} + CO_{2(aq)}$

2) The levels of **H_2CO_3** are controlled by **respiration**. By **breathing out CO₂** the level of H_2CO_3 is reduced as it moves this **equilibrium** to the **right**.

3) The levels of HCO_3^- are controlled by the **kidneys** with excess being **excreted** in the urine.

Module 5: Section 1 — Rates, Equilibrium & pH

Buffers

Here's How to Calculate the **pH** of a **Buffer Solution**

Calculating the **pH** of an acidic buffer isn't too tricky. You just need to know the K_a of the weak acid and the **concentrations** of the weak acid and its salt. Your calculation requires the following assumptions to be made:

- The salt of the conjugate base is fully dissociated, so assume that the equilibrium concentration of A^- is the same as the initial concentration of the salt.
- HA is only slightly dissociated, so assume that its equilibrium concentration is the same as its initial concentration.

The conjugate base doesn't only come from dissociation of the weak acid so $[H^+] \neq [A^-]$.

Here's how you calculate the pH of a buffer solution:

Example: A buffer solution contains 0.40 mol dm⁻³ methanoic acid, HCOOH, and 0.60 mol dm⁻³ sodium methanoate, HCOO⁻Na⁺. For methanoic acid, $K_a = 1.8 \times 10^{-4}$ mol dm⁻³. What is the pH of this buffer?

Firstly, write the expression for K_a of the weak acid:

Remember — these are all equilibrium concentrations.

$$HCOOH_{(aq)} \rightleftharpoons H^+_{(aq)} + HCOO^-_{(aq)} \implies K_a = \frac{[H^+][HCOO^-]}{[HCOOH]}$$

Then rearrange the expression and stick in the data to calculate $[H^+]$:

$$[H^+] = K_a \times \frac{[HCOOH]}{[HCOO^-]}$$

$$\implies [H^+] = 1.8 \times 10^{-4} \times \frac{0.4}{0.6} = 1.20 \times 10^{-4} \text{ mol dm}^{-3}$$

Finally, convert $[H^+_{(aq)}]$ to pH:

$$pH = -\log_{10}[H^+_{(aq)}] = -\log_{10}(1.20 \times 10^{-4}) = 3.92$$

And that's your answer.

Nobody's gonna change my pH.

Acids and bases didn't mess with Jeff after he became buffer.

Warm-Up Questions

Q1 What's a buffer solution?

Q2 Name two ways of preparing buffer solutions.

Q3 Describe how a mixture of ethanoic acid and sodium ethanoate act as a buffer.

Q4 Describe how the pH of the blood is buffered.

PRACTICE QUESTIONS

Exam Questions

Q1 A buffer solution contains 0.40 mol dm⁻³ benzoic acid, C_6H_5COOH, and 0.20 mol dm⁻³ sodium benzoate, $C_6H_5COO^-Na^+$. At 25 °C, K_a for benzoic acid is 6.4×10^{-5} mol dm⁻³.

a) Calculate the pH of the buffer solution. [2 marks]

b) Explain the effect on the buffer of adding a small quantity of dilute sulfuric acid. [1 mark]

Q2 A buffer was prepared by mixing solutions of butanoic acid, $CH_3(CH_2)_2COOH$, and sodium butanoate, $CH_3(CH_2)_2COO^-Na^+$, so that they had the same concentration.

a) Write a balanced chemical equation to show butanoic acid acting as a weak acid. [1 mark]

b) Given that K_a for butanoic acid is 1.5×10^{-5} mol dm⁻³ at 298 K, calculate the pH of the buffer solution. [2 marks]

Old buffers are often resistant to change...

So that's how buffers work. There's a pleasing simplicity and neatness about it that I find rather elegant. Like a fine glass of red wine with a nose of berry and undertones of raspberries, oak and... OK, I'll shut up now.

pH Curves and Titrations

If you add alkali to an acid, the pH changes in a squiggly sort of way.

You Can **Measure** the pH of a Solution Using a **pH Meter**

1) A **pH meter** does what it says on the tin — it's an electronic gadget you can use to tell you the **pH** of a solution.

2) pH meters have a **probe** that you put into your solution and a **digital display** that shows the reading. At the bottom of the probe is a bulb that's very **delicate**, so be careful when handling it.

3) Before you use a pH meter, you need to make sure it's **calibrated correctly**. To do this...

- Place the bulb of the pH meter into **distilled water** and allow the reading to settle. Now **adjust** the reading so that it reads **7.0**.
- Do the same with a standard solution of pH 4 and another of pH 10. Make sure you **rinse** the probe with **distilled water** in between each reading.

4) You're now ready to take your actual measurement. Place the probe in the liquid you're measuring and let the reading settle before you record the result. After each measurement, you should rinse the probe in **distilled water**.

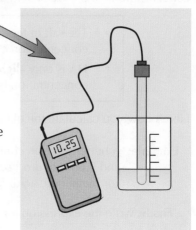

pH Curves Plot pH Against Volume of Acid or Base Added

1) **Titrations** let you find out **exactly** how much alkali is needed to **neutralise** a quantity of acid.

2) All you have to do is plot the **pH** of the titration mixture against the **amount of base** added as the titration goes on. The pH of the mixture can be measured using a pH meter and the scale on the burette can be used to see how much base has been added.

3) The **shape** of your plot looks a bit different depending on the **strengths** of the acid and base that are used.

4) Here are the graphs of the pH curves for the different combinations of strong and weak monobasic acids and bases:

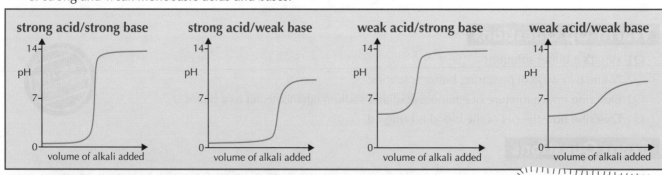

You can explain why each graph has a particular shape:

- The **initial** pH depends on the **strength** of the **acid**. So a strong acid titration will start at a much **lower** pH than a weak acid.

- To start with, addition of **small** amounts of base have **little impact** on the pH of the solution.

- All the graphs (apart from the weak acid/weak base graph) have a bit that's almost vertical — this is the **equivalence point** or **end point**. At this point $[H^+] \approx [OH^-]$ — it's here that all the acid is just **neutralised**. When this is the case, a tiny amount of base causes a sudden, big change in pH.

- You need to add **more weak base** than strong base to a **strong acid** to cause a pH change, and the change is less **pronounced**. On the other hand, you need to add **less strong base** to a **weak acid** to see a large change in pH.

- The **final** pH depends on the strength of the **base** — the **stronger** the base, the **higher** the final pH.

If you titrate a base with an acid instead, the shapes of the curves stay the same, but they're reversed.

pH Curves and Titrations

pH Curves can Help you Decide which Indicator to Use

1) You've met **titrations** before — they're experiments that let you work out the **concentrations** of different solutions.

2) You can use titrations instead of pH meters to work out the **concentration** of an acid or base. You'll need an **indicator** that changes **colour** to show you when your sample has been **neutralised**.

3) You need your indicator to change colour exactly at the **end point** of your titration. So you need to pick one that changes colour over a **narrow pH range** that lies entirely on the **vertical part** of the pH curve.

E.g. For this titration, the curve is vertical between **pH 8** and **pH 11** — so a very small amount of base will cause the pH to change from 8 to 11.

So you want an indicator that changes **colour** somewhere between pH 8 and pH 11.

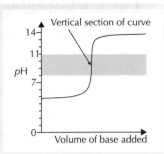

4) **Methyl orange** and **phenolphthalein** are **indicators** that are often used for acid-base titrations. They each change colour over a **different pH range**:

- For a **strong acid/strong base** titration, you can use **either** of these indicators — there's a rapid pH change over the range for **both** indicators.

- For a **strong acid/weak base** only **methyl orange** will do. The pH changes rapidly across the range for methyl orange, but not for phenolphthalein.

Name of indicator	Colour at low pH	Approx. pH of colour change	Colour at high pH
Methyl orange	red	3.1 – 4.4	yellow
Phenolphthalein	colourless	8.3 – 10	pink

- For a **weak acid/strong base**, **phenolphthalein** is the stuff to use. The pH changes rapidly over phenolphthalein's range, but not over methyl orange's.

- For **weak acid/weak base** titrations there's no sharp pH change, so **neither** of these indicators works. In fact, there aren't **any** indicators you can use in weak acid/weak base titrations, so you should just use a pH meter.

Indicators can be thought of as **weak acids**. They work because they have differently coloured **conjugate pairs**. As the pH of the solution changes during a titration, the equilibrium concentrations of the conjugate pairs will also change. The colour will **change** depending on whether the indicator is mainly **protonated** or **deprotonated**.

E.g.

$$\text{Phenolphthalein-H} \rightleftharpoons \text{Phenolphthalein}^- + H^+$$
colourless   pink

$$\text{Methylorange-H} \rightleftharpoons \text{Methylorange}^- + H^+$$
red   yellow

Warm-Up Questions

Q1 Sketch the pH curve for a weak acid/strong alkali titration.

Q2 What indicator should you use for a strong acid/weak alkali titration — methyl orange or phenolphthalein?

Q3 What colour is methyl orange at pH 2?

Exam Questions

Q1 1.0 mol dm^{-3} NaOH (a strong base) is added separately to 25 cm^3 samples of 1.0 mol dm^{-3} nitric acid (a strong acid) and 1.0 mol dm^{-3} ethanoic acid (a weak acid). Sketch the pH curves for each of these titrations.

[2 marks]

Q2 A sample of ethanoic acid (a weak acid) was titrated against potassium hydroxide (a strong base).

From the table on the right, select the best indicator for this titration, and explain your choice.

[2 marks]

Name of indicator	pH range
bromophenol blue	3.0 – 4.6
methyl red	4.2 – 6.3
bromothymol blue	6.0 – 7.6
thymol blue	8.0 – 9.6

I'll burette your bottom dollar that you're bored of pH by now...

Titrations involve playing with big bits of glassware that you're told not to break as they're really expensive — so you instantly become really clumsy. If you manage not to smash the burette, you'll find it easier to get accurate results if you use a dilute acid or alkali — drops of dilute acid and alkali contain fewer particles so you're less likely to overshoot.

Lattice Enthalpy and Born-Haber Cycles

On these pages you can learn about lattice enthalpy, not lettuce enthalpy, which is the enthalpy change when 1 mole consumes salad from a veggie patch. Bu–dum cha... (that was meant to be a drum — work with me here).

Lattice Enthalpy is a Measure of Ionic Bond Strength

Ionic compounds can form regular structures called **giant ionic lattices** where the positive and negative ions are held together by **electrostatic attractions**. When **gaseous ions** combine to make a solid lattice, energy is given out — this is called the **lattice enthalpy**.

Here's the definition of **standard lattice enthalpy** that you need to know:

> The standard lattice enthalpy, $\Delta_{LE}H^{\ominus}$, is the enthalpy change when 1 mole of an ionic lattice is formed from its gaseous ions under standard conditions.

Standard conditions are 298 K (25 °C) and 100 kPa.

Part of the sodium chloride lattice

The standard lattice enthalpy is a measure of **ionic bond strength**.
The more **negative** the lattice enthalpy, the **stronger** the bonding.
E.g. out of NaCl and MgO, MgO has stronger bonding.

$$Na^+_{(g)} + Cl^-_{(g)} \rightarrow NaCl_{(s)} \quad \Delta_{LE}H^{\ominus} = -787 \text{ kJ mol}^{-1}$$
$$Mg^{2+}_{(g)} + O^{2-}_{(g)} \rightarrow MgO_{(s)} \quad \Delta_{LE}H^{\ominus} = -3791 \text{ kJ mol}^{-1}$$

Ionic Charge and Size Affects Lattice Enthalpy

1) The **higher the charge** on the ions, the **more energy** is released when an ionic lattice forms. This is due to the **stronger electrostatic forces** between the ions.

2) More energy released means that the lattice enthalpy will be **more negative**. So the lattice enthalpies for compounds with **2+ or 2– ions** (e.g. Mg^{2+} or S^{2-}) are **more exothermic** than those with **1+ or 1– ions** (e.g. Na^+ or Cl^-).

> E.g. the lattice enthalpy of **NaCl** is only -787 kJ mol^{-1}, but the lattice enthalpy of **MgCl$_2$** is -2526 kJ mol^{-1}.
> **MgS** has an even **higher** lattice enthalpy (-3299 kJ mol^{-1}) because both Mg and S ions have **double charges**.

3) The **smaller** the **ionic radii** of the ions involved, the **more exothermic** (more negative) the **lattice enthalpy**. Smaller ions have a higher **charge density** and their **smaller ionic radii** mean that the ions can sit **closer together** in the lattice. Both these things mean that the attractions between the ions are **stronger**.

Born-Haber Cycles can be Used to Calculate Lattice Enthalpies

Hess's law says that the **total enthalpy change** of a reaction is always the **same**, no matter which route is taken — this is known as the conservation of energy.

You can't calculate a lattice enthalpy **directly**, so you have to use a **Born-Haber cycle** to figure out what the enthalpy change would be if you took **another, less direct, route**.

Here's a Born-Haber cycle you could use to calculate the lattice enthalpy of **NaCl**:

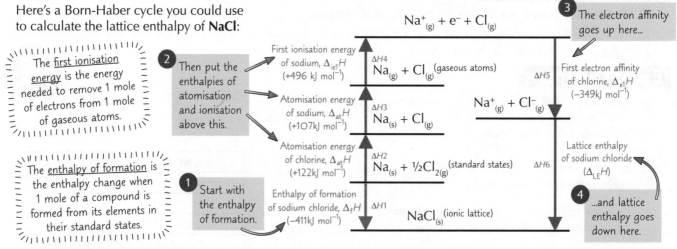

The first ionisation energy is the energy needed to remove 1 mole of electrons from 1 mole of gaseous atoms.

The enthalpy of formation is the enthalpy change when 1 mole of a compound is formed from its elements in their standard states.

① Start with the enthalpy of formation.

② Then put the enthalpies of atomisation and ionisation above this.

③ The electron affinity goes up here...

④ ...and lattice enthalpy goes down here.

$$Na^+_{(g)} + e^- + Cl_{(g)}$$

First ionisation energy of sodium, $\Delta_{ie1}H$ (+496 kJ mol^{-1}), $\Delta H4$

$Na_{(g)} + Cl_{(g)}$ (gaseous atoms)

Atomisation energy of sodium, $\Delta_{at}H$ (+107 kJ mol^{-1}), $\Delta H3$

$Na_{(s)} + Cl_{(g)}$

Atomisation energy of chlorine, $\Delta_{at}H$ (+122 kJ mol^{-1}), $\Delta H2$

$Na_{(s)} + \frac{1}{2}Cl_{2(g)}$ (standard states)

Enthalpy of formation of sodium chloride, $\Delta_f H$ (–411 kJ mol^{-1}), $\Delta H1$

$NaCl_{(s)}$ (ionic lattice)

First electron affinity of chlorine, $\Delta_{e1}H$ (–349 kJ mol^{-1}), $\Delta H5$

$Na^+_{(g)} + Cl^-_{(g)}$

Lattice enthalpy of sodium chloride ($\Delta_{LE}H$), $\Delta H6$

There are **two routes** you can follow to get from the elements in their **standard states** to the **ionic lattice**. The green arrow shows the **direct route** and the purple arrows show the **indirect route**. The enthalpy change for each is the **same**.

From Hess's law: $\Delta H6 = -\Delta H5 - \Delta H4 - \Delta H3 - \Delta H2 + \Delta H1$
$= -(-349) - (+496) - (+107) - (+122) + (-411) = \mathbf{-787 \text{ kJ mol}^{-1}}$

You need a minus sign if you go the wrong way along an arrow.

Lattice Enthalpy and Born-Haber Cycles

Calculations involving Group 2 Elements are a Bit Different

Born-Haber cycles for compounds containing **Group 2 elements** have a few **changes** from the one on the previous page. Make sure you understand what's going on so you can handle whatever compound they throw at you.

Here's the Born-Haber cycle for calculating the lattice enthalpy of **magnesium chloride** ($MgCl_2$):

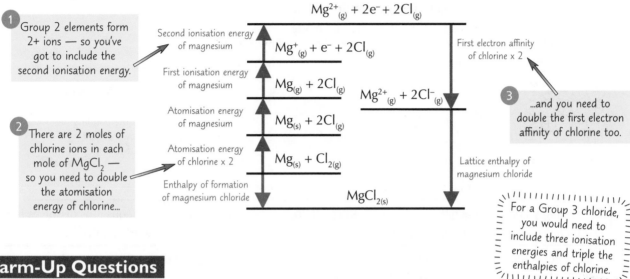

1 Group 2 elements form 2+ ions — so you've got to include the second ionisation energy.

2 There are 2 moles of chlorine ions in each mole of $MgCl_2$ — so you need to double the atomisation energy of chlorine...

Second ionisation energy of magnesium
First ionisation energy of magnesium
Atomisation energy of magnesium
Atomisation energy of chlorine x 2
Enthalpy of formation of magnesium chloride

$Mg^{2+}_{(g)} + 2e^- + 2Cl_{(g)}$
$Mg^+_{(g)} + e^- + 2Cl_{(g)}$
$Mg_{(g)} + 2Cl_{(g)}$
$Mg_{(s)} + 2Cl_{(g)}$
$Mg_{(s)} + Cl_{2(g)}$
$Mg^{2+}_{(g)} + 2Cl^-_{(g)}$
$MgCl_{2(s)}$

First electron affinity of chlorine x 2
Lattice enthalpy of magnesium chloride

3 ...and you need to double the first electron affinity of chlorine too.

For a Group 3 chloride, you would need to include three ionisation energies and triple the enthalpies of chlorine.

Warm-Up Questions

Q1 What is the definition of standard lattice enthalpy?

Q2 What does a large, negative lattice enthalpy mean, in terms of bond strength?

Q3 Why does magnesium chloride have a more negative lattice enthalpy than sodium chloride?

Q4 Why would lithium chloride have a more negative lattice enthalpy than sodium chloride?

PRACTICE QUESTIONS

Exam Questions

Q1 Using this data:

$\Delta_f H^{\ominus}$[potassium bromide] = –394 kJ mol^{-1} $\Delta_{at} H^{\ominus}$[bromine] = +112 kJ mol^{-1} $\Delta_{at} H^{\ominus}$[potassium] = +89 kJ mol^{-1}
$\Delta_{ie1} H^{\ominus}$[potassium] = +419 kJ mol^{-1} $\Delta_{e1} H^{\ominus}$[bromine] = –325 kJ mol^{-1}

a) Construct a Born-Haber cycle for potassium bromide (KBr). [3 marks]

b) Use your Born-Haber cycle to calculate the lattice enthalpy of potassium bromide. [2 marks]

Q2 Using this data:

$\Delta_f H^{\ominus}$[aluminium chloride] = –706 kJ mol^{-1} $\Delta_{at} H^{\ominus}$[chlorine] = +122 kJ mol^{-1} $\Delta_{at} H^{\ominus}$[aluminium] = +326 kJ mol^{-1}
$\Delta_{e1} H^{\ominus}$[chlorine] = –349 kJ mol^{-1} $\Delta_{ie1} H^{\ominus}$[aluminium] = +578 kJ mol^{-1}
$\Delta_{ie2} H^{\ominus}$[aluminium] = +1817 kJ mol^{-1} $\Delta_{ie3} H^{\ominus}$[aluminium] = +2745 kJ mol^{-1}

a) Construct a Born-Haber cycle for aluminium chloride ($AlCl_3$). [3 marks]

b) Use your cycle to calculate the lattice enthalpy of aluminium chloride. [2 marks]

Q3 Using this data:

$\Delta_f H^{\ominus}$[aluminium oxide] = –1676 kJ mol^{-1} $\Delta_{at} H^{\ominus}$[oxygen] = +249 kJ mol^{-1} $\Delta_{at} H^{\ominus}$[aluminium] = +326 kJ mol^{-1}
$\Delta_{ie1} H^{\ominus}$[aluminium] = +578 kJ mol^{-1} $\Delta_{ie2} H^{\ominus}$[aluminium] = +1817 kJ mol^{-1} $\Delta_{ie3} H^{\ominus}$[aluminium] = +2745 kJ mol^{-1}
$\Delta_{e1} H^{\ominus}$[oxygen] = –141 kJ mol^{-1} $\Delta_{e2} H^{\ominus}$[oxygen] = +844 kJ mol^{-1}

a) Construct a Born-Haber cycle for aluminium oxide (Al_2O_3). [3 marks]

b) Use your cycle to calculate the lattice enthalpy of aluminium oxide. [2 marks]

Using Born-Haber cycles — it's just like riding a bike...

All this energy going in and out can get a bit confusing. Remember these simple rules: 1) It takes energy to break bonds, but energy is given out when bonds are made. 2) A negative ΔH means energy is given out (it's exothermic). 3) A positive ΔH means energy is taken in (it's endothermic). 4) Never return to a firework once lit.

Enthalpies of Solution

Once you know what's happening when you stir sugar into your tea, your cuppa'll be twice as enjoyable.

Dissolving Involves Enthalpy Changes

When a solid **ionic lattice** dissolves in water these **two** things happen:

1) The bonds between the ions **break** to give gaseous ions — this is **endothermic**.
   The enthalpy change is the **opposite** of the **lattice enthalpy**.

2) Bonds between the gaseous ions and the water are **made** — this is **exothermic**.
   The enthalpy change here is called the **enthalpy change of hydration**.

The **enthalpy change of solution**, is the overall effect on the enthalpy of these two things.

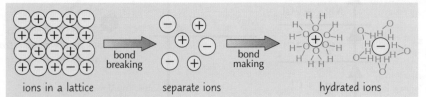

ions in a lattice   separate ions   hydrated ions

This effect happens because oxygen is more electronegative than hydrogen, so it draws the bonding electrons toward itself, creating a dipole.

So now, here are a couple more fancy **definitions** you need to know:

> The **enthalpy change of hydration**, $\Delta_{hyd}H^{\ominus}$, is the enthalpy change when 1 mole of gaseous ions dissolves in water.
> The **enthalpy change of solution**, $\Delta_{sol}H^{\ominus}$, is the enthalpy change when 1 mole of solute dissolves in water.

Substances generally **only** dissolve if the energy released is roughly the same, or **greater than** the energy taken in. So soluble substances tend to have **exothermic** enthalpies of solution.

Enthalpy Change of Solution can be Calculated

You can work out the enthalpy change of solution using a Born-Haber cycle — but one drawn a bit differently from those on pages 32 and 33.
You just need to know the **lattice enthalpy** of the compound and the **enthalpies of hydration** of the ions.

Here's how to draw the enthalpy cycle for working out the enthalpy change of solution for sodium chloride.

1 Put the ionic lattice and the dissolved ions on the top — connect them by the enthalpy change of solution. This is the direct route.

2 Connect the ionic lattice to the gaseous ions by the reverse of the lattice enthalpy.
The breakdown of the lattice has the opposite enthalpy change to the formation of the lattice.

$NaCl_{(s)}$ — Enthalpy change of solution $\Delta H3$ → $Na^+_{(aq)} + Cl^-_{(aq)}$

$\Delta H1$ — (lattice enthalpy) $-(-787 \text{ kJ mol}^{-1})$

$Na^+_{(g)} + Cl^-_{(g)}$

$\Delta H2$ Enthalpy of hydration of $Na^+_{(g)}$ (-406 kJ mol^{-1})
Enthalpy of hydration of $Cl^-_{(g)}$ (-364 kJ mol^{-1})

3 Connect the gaseous ions to the dissolved ions by the hydration enthalpies of **each** ion. This completes the indirect route.

From Hess's law: $\Delta H3 = \Delta H1 + \Delta H2 = +787 + (-406 + -364) = +17 \text{ kJ mol}^{-1}$

The enthalpy change of solution is slightly endothermic, but there are other factors at work that mean that sodium chloride still dissolves in water.

Here's another. This one's for working out the enthalpy change of solution for silver chloride:

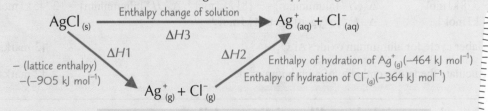

$AgCl_{(s)}$ — Enthalpy change of solution $\Delta H3$ → $Ag^+_{(aq)} + Cl^-_{(aq)}$

$\Delta H1$ — (lattice enthalpy) $-(-905 \text{ kJ mol}^{-1})$

$Ag^+_{(g)} + Cl^-_{(g)}$

$\Delta H2$ Enthalpy of hydration of $Ag^+_{(g)}$ (-464 kJ mol^{-1})
Enthalpy of hydration of $Cl^-_{(g)}$ (-364 kJ mol^{-1})

From Hess's law: $\Delta H3 = \Delta H1 + \Delta H2 = +905 + (-464 + -364) = +77 \text{ kJ mol}^{-1}$

This is much more endothermic than the enthalpy change of solution for sodium chloride. As such, silver chloride is insoluble in water.

As long as there's only one unknown enthalpy value, you can use these cycles to work out any value on the arrows. For example, if you know the enthalpy change of solution and the enthalpy changes of hydration, you can use those values to work out the lattice enthalpy.

Enthalpies of Solution

Ionic Charge and Ionic Radius Affect the Enthalpy of Hydration

The **two** things that can affect the lattice enthalpy (see page 32) can also affect the enthalpy of hydration.
They are the **size** and the **charge** of the ions.

Ions with a greater charge have a greater enthalpy of hydration.

Ions with a **higher charge** are better at **attracting** water molecules than those with lower charges — the electrostatic attraction between the ion and the water molecules is **stronger**. This means **more energy** is released when the bonds are **made** giving them a **more exothermic** enthalpy of hydration.

Smaller ions have a greater enthalpy of hydration.

Smaller ions have a **higher** charge density than bigger ions. They **attract** the water molecules **better** and have a **more exothermic** enthalpy of hydration.

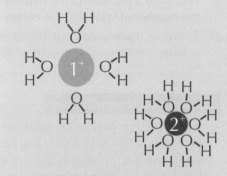

The higher charge and smaller size of the 2+ ion create a higher charge density than the 1+ ion. This creates a stronger attraction for the water molecules and gives a more exothermic enthalpy of hydration.

E.g. a magnesium ion is smaller and more charged than a sodium ion, which gives it a much bigger enthalpy of hydration.

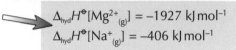

$\Delta_{hyd}H^{\ominus}[Mg^{2+}_{(g)}] = -1927 \text{ kJ mol}^{-1}$

$\Delta_{hyd}H^{\ominus}[Na^{+}_{(g)}] = -406 \text{ kJ mol}^{-1}$

Warm-Up Questions

Q1 Describe the two steps that occur when an ionic lattice dissolves in water.

Q2 Define the enthalpy change of solution.

Q3 Do soluble substances have exothermic or endothermic enthalpies of solution in general?

Q4 Sketch a Born-Haber cycle to calculate the enthalpy change of solution of silver chloride.

Q5 Name two factors that affect the enthalpy of hydration of an ion.

PRACTICE QUESTIONS

Exam Questions

Q1 a) Draw an enthalpy cycle for the enthalpy change of solution of $AgF_{(s)}$. Label each enthalpy change. [2 marks]

   b) Calculate the enthalpy change of solution for AgF from the following data: [2 marks]

   $\Delta_{LE}H^{\ominus}[AgF_{(s)}] = -960 \text{ kJ mol}^{-1}$, $\Delta_{hyd}H^{\ominus}[Ag^{+}_{(g)}] = -464 \text{ kJ mol}^{-1}$, $\Delta_{hyd}H^{\ominus}[F^{-}_{(g)}] = -506 \text{ kJ mol}^{-1}$.

Q2 a) Draw an enthalpy cycle for the enthalpy change of solution of $SrF_{2(s)}$. Label each enthalpy change. [2 marks]

   b) Calculate the enthalpy change of solution for SrF_2 from the following data: [2 marks]

   $\Delta_{LE}H^{\ominus}[SrF_{2(s)}] = -2492 \text{ kJ mol}^{-1}$, $\Delta_{hyd}H^{\ominus}[Sr^{2+}_{(g)}] = -1480 \text{ kJ mol}^{-1}$, $\Delta_{hyd}H^{\ominus}[F^{-}_{(g)}] = -506 \text{ kJ mol}^{-1}$.

Q3 Show that the enthalpy of hydration of $Cl^{-}_{(g)}$ is -364 kJ mol^{-1}, given that: [3 marks]

   $\Delta_{LE}H^{\ominus}[MgCl_{2(s)}] = -2526 \text{ kJ mol}^{-1}$, $\Delta_{hyd}H^{\ominus}[Mg^{2+}_{(g)}] = -1920 \text{ kJ mol}^{-1}$, $\Delta_{sol}H^{\ominus}[MgCl_{2(s)}] = -122 \text{ kJ mol}^{-1}$.

Q4 Which of these ions will have a greater enthalpy of hydration — Ca^{2+} or K^{+}?
Explain your answer. [3 marks]

Enthalpy change of solution of the Wicked Witch of the West = 939 kJ mol⁻¹...

Compared to the ones on the previous two pages, these enthalpy cycles are an absolute breeze. You've got to make sure the definitions are firmly fixed in your mind though. You only need to know the lattice enthalpy and the enthalpy of hydration of your lattice ions, and you're well on your way to finding out the enthalpy change of solution.

Entropy

If you were looking for some random chemistry pages, you've just found them.

Entropy Tells you How Much **Disorder** there is

1) Entropy is a measure of the **number of ways** that **particles** can be **arranged** and the **number of ways** that the **energy** can be shared out between the particles.

2) The more **disordered** the particles are, the higher the entropy is. A **large**, **positive** value of entropy shows a **high** level of disorder.

3) There are a few things that affect entropy:

Squirrels do not teach Chemistry. But if they did, this is what a demonstration of increasing entropy would look like.

Physical State affects Entropy

You have to go back to the good old **solid-liquid-gas** particle explanation thingy to understand this.

Solid particles just wobble about a fixed point — there's **hardly any** randomness, so they have the **lowest entropy**.

Gas particles whizz around wherever they like. They've got the most **random arrangements** of particles, so they have the **highest entropy**.

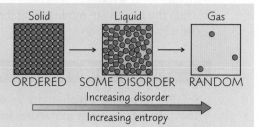

More Particles means More Entropy

It makes sense — the more particles you've got, the **more ways** they and their energy can be **arranged** — so in a reaction like $N_2O_{4(g)} \rightarrow 2NO_{2(g)}$, entropy increases because the **number of moles** increases.

More **Arrangements** Means More **Stability**

1) Substances really **like** disorder — they're actually more **energetically stable** when there's more disorder. So particles will move to try to **increase their entropy**.

2) This is why some reactions are **feasible** (they just happen by themselves — without the addition of energy) even when the enthalpy change is **endothermic**.

Example: The reaction of sodium hydrogencarbonate with hydrochloric acid is an **endothermic reaction** — but it is **feasible**. This is due to an **increase in entropy** as the reaction produces carbon dioxide gas and water. Liquids and gases are **more disordered** than solids and so have a **higher entropy**. This increase in entropy **overcomes** the change in enthalpy.

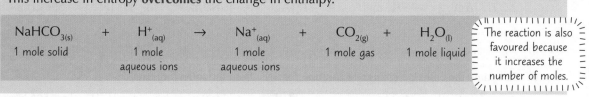

$NaHCO_{3(s)}$	+	$H^+_{(aq)}$	$\rightarrow$	$Na^+_{(aq)}$	+	$CO_{2(g)}$	+	$H_2O_{(l)}$
1 mole solid		1 mole aqueous ions		1 mole aqueous ions		1 mole gas		1 mole liquid

The reaction is also favoured because it increases the number of moles.

3) When a substance reaches its maximum entropy state (its lowest energy state), it's said to be **thermodynamically stable**. This means it won't react any further without the input of energy.

You Can **Calculate** the **Entropy Change** of a Reaction

You can calculate the **entropy change** of a reaction if you know the entropies of the **products** and of the **reactants**.

The units of entropy are $J K^{-1} mol^{-1}$.

$$\Delta S = S_{products} - S_{reactants}$$

Reactions with a positive value of ΔS are more likely to be feasible.

Entropy

Example: Calculate the entropy change for the reaction of ammonia and hydrogen chloride under standard conditions.

$$NH_{3(g)} + HCl_{(g)} \rightarrow NH_4Cl_{(s)}$$

$S^{\ominus}[NH_{3(g)}] = 192.3 \text{ J K}^{-1}\text{mol}^{-1}, \ S^{\ominus}[HCl_{(g)}] = 186.8 \text{ J K}^{-1}\text{mol}^{-1}, \ S^{\ominus}[NH_4Cl_{(s)}] = 94.60 \text{ J K}^{-1}\text{mol}^{-1}$

1) First find the entropy of the products:

$S^{\ominus}_{products} = S^{\ominus}[NH_4Cl] = 94.60 \text{ J K}^{-1}\text{mol}^{-1}$

2) Now find the entropy change of the reactants:

$S^{\ominus}_{reactants} = S^{\ominus}[NH_3] + S^{\ominus}[HCl] = 192.3 \text{ J K}^{-1}\text{mol}^{-1} + 186.8 \text{ J K}^{-1}\text{mol}^{-1} = 379.1 \text{ J K}^{-1}\text{mol}^{-1}$

3) Finally you can subtract the entropy of the reactants from the entropy of the products to find the entropy change for the reaction:

$\Delta S^{\ominus} = S^{\ominus}_{products} - S^{\ominus}_{reactants} = 94.60 - 379.1 = -284.5 \text{ J K}^{-1}\text{mol}^{-1}$

This shows a negative change in entropy. It's not surprising as 2 moles of gas have combined to form 1 mole of solid.

A positive entropy change of reaction means that a reaction is likely to be feasible, but a negative change in entropy of reaction **doesn't guarantee** the reaction **can't** happen — **enthalpy**, **temperature** and **kinetics** also play a part in whether or not a reaction occurs.

There's more about this on the next page...

Warm-Up Questions

Q1 What does the term 'entropy' mean?

Q2 In each of the following pairs choose the one with the greater entropy value.
   a) 1 mole of $NaCl_{(aq)}$ and 1 mole of $NaCl_{(s)}$
   b) 1 mole of $Br_{2(l)}$ and 1 mole of $Br_{2(g)}$
   c) 1 mole of $Br_{2(g)}$ and 2 moles of $Br_{2(g)}$

Q3 Write down the formula for the entropy change of a reaction.

PRACTICE QUESTIONS

Exam Questions

Q1 a) Based on just the equation below, predict whether the reaction is likely to be feasible. Give a reason for your answer.

$Mg_{(s)} + \frac{1}{2}O_{2(g)} \rightarrow MgO_{(s)}$ [2 marks]

b) Use the data on the right to calculate the entropy change for the reaction above. [2 marks]

c) Does the result of the calculation indicate that the reaction will be feasible? Give a reason for your answer. [1 mark]

Substance	Entropy — standard conditions (J K⁻¹ mol⁻¹)
$Mg_{(s)}$	32.7
$O_{2(g)}$	205.0
$MgO_{(s)}$	26.9

Q2 For the reaction $H_2O_{(l)} \rightarrow H_2O_{(s)}$:

$S^{\ominus}[H_2O_{(l)}] = 70 \text{ J K}^{-1}\text{mol}^{-1}, \qquad S^{\ominus}[H_2O_{(s)}] = 48 \text{ J K}^{-1}\text{mol}^{-1}$

a) Calculate the entropy change for this reaction. [2 marks]

b) Explain why this reaction might be feasible. [1 mark]

Being neat and tidy is against the laws of nature...

Well, there you go. Entropy in all its glory. You haven't seen the back of it yet though, oh no. There's more where this came from. Which is why, if random disorder has left you in a spin, I'd suggest reading it again and making sure you've got your head round this lot before you turn over. You'll thank me for it, you will... Chocolates are always welcome...

Free Energy

Free energy — I could do with a bit of that. My gas bill is astronomical.

For Feasible Reactions ΔG must be **Negative** or **Zero**

1) The tendency of a process to take place is dependent on three things — the **entropy**, ΔS, the **enthalpy**, ΔH, and the **temperature**, T. When you put all these things **together** you get the **free energy change**, ΔG. ΔG tells you if a reaction is **feasible** or not — the more negative the value of ΔG, the more feasible the reaction.

   Of course, there's a formula for it:

   $$\Delta G = \Delta H - T\Delta S$$

   ΔH = enthalpy change (in $J\,mol^{-1}$)
   T = temperature (in K)
   ΔS = entropy change (in $J\,K^{-1}mol^{-1}$)

   The units of ΔG are $J\,mol^{-1}$.

   > **Example:** Calculate the free energy change for the following reaction at 298 K.
   >
   > $MgCO_{3(g)} \rightarrow MgO_{(s)} + CO_{2(g)}$ $\Delta H^{\ominus} = +117\,000\,J\,mol^{-1}$, $\Delta S^{\ominus}_{system} = +175\,J\,K^{-1}\,mol^{-1}$
   >
   > $\Delta G = \Delta H - T\Delta S_{system} = +117\,000 - (298 \times (+175)) = \mathbf{+64\,900\,J\,mol^{-1}}$ (3 s.f.)
   >
   > *ΔG is positive — so the reaction isn't feasible at this temperature.*

2) When $\Delta G = 0$, the reaction is **just feasible**. So the temperature at which the reaction becomes feasible can be calculated by rearranging the equation like this:

   $$\Delta H - T\Delta S = 0, \text{ so } \boxed{T = \frac{\Delta H}{\Delta S}}$$

   > **Example:** At what temperature does the reaction $MgCO_{3(g)} \rightarrow MgO_{(s)} + CO_{2(g)}$ become feasible?
   >
   > $T = \dfrac{\Delta H}{\Delta S} = \dfrac{+117\,000}{+175} = \mathbf{669\,K}$

3) You can use ΔG to **predict** whether or not a reaction is **feasible**. By looking at the equation $\Delta G = \Delta H - T\Delta S$, you can see that:

   > When ΔH is **negative** and ΔS is **positive**, ΔG will always be **negative** and the reaction is **feasible**.
   > When ΔH is **positive** and ΔS is **negative**, ΔG will always be **positive** and the reaction is **not feasible**.

   In other situations, the feasibility of the reaction is dependent on the temperature.

Negative ΔG does not **Guarantee** a Reaction

The value of the free energy change doesn't tell you anything about the reaction's **rate**. Even if ΔG shows that a reaction is theoretically feasible, it might have a really high activation energy or happen so slowly that you wouldn't notice it happening at all. For example:

$H_{2(g)} + \frac{1}{2}O_{2(g)} \rightarrow H_2O_{(g)}$ $\Delta H^{\ominus} = -242\,000\,J\,mol^{-1}$, $\Delta S^{\ominus} = -44.4\,J\,K^{-1}\,mol^{-1}$

At 298 K, $\Delta G = -242\,000 - (298 \times (-44.4)) = \mathbf{-229\,000\,J\,mol^{-1}}$ (3 s.f.)

But this reaction is **not** feasible at 298 K — it needs a spark to start it off due to its **high activation energy**.

You Might Need to Work Out ΔH

Sometimes, to find ΔG for a reaction, you may first need to work out the **enthalpy change** of the reaction. You can calculate ΔH from the **temperature change** of a **known volume** of water (or solution) using this equation:

> energy change = mass × specific heat capacity × change in temperature

You may remember this equation from way back in Year 1.

More often, you'll probably see it written in symbols: $q = mc\Delta T$

q is the energy change in J (it's the same as ΔH (in $J\,mol^{-1}$) if the pressure is constant).
m is the mass of water or solution in g and ΔT is the temperature change in K or °C.
c is the specific heat capacity of the substance (usually the specific heat capacity of water, $4.18\,J\,g^{-1}\,K^{-1}$).

To find ΔH (the energy change per mole), just **divide** the value of q by the **number of moles** of reactant. Once you've worked out the enthalpy change, you can go on to work out ΔG...

Free Energy

Example: When 30.0 g of solid ammonium chloride ($NH_4Cl_{(s)}$) is dissolved in water, the temperature of the water decreases from 293 K to 291 K. The total mass of the solution is 980 g. What is the free energy change in $J\,mol^{-1}$ for this reaction at 25.0 °C? Assume the specific heat capacity of the solution is $4.18\ J\,g^{-1}K^{-1}$.

$$NH_4Cl_{(s)} \rightarrow NH_4^+{}_{(aq)} + Cl^-{}_{(aq)}$$

$S^{\ominus}[NH_4Cl_{(s)}] = 94.6\ J\,K^{-1}mol^{-1}$ $S^{\ominus}[NH_4^+{}_{(aq)}] = 113.4\ J\,K^{-1}mol^{-1}$ $S^{\ominus}[Cl^-] = 56.5\ J\,K^{-1}mol^{-1}$

1 First work out the enthalpy change, ΔH:

$q = mc\Delta T = 980 \times 4.18 \times (293 - 291) = 8192.8\ J$

$M_r(NH_4Cl) = 14.0 + (4 \times 1.0) + 35.5 = 53.5$

$30.0 \div 53.5 = 0.561$ moles of NH_4Cl ⟵ This is the number of moles of NH_4Cl that have dissolved to give q.

The balanced reaction involves 1 mole of NH_4Cl, so:

$\Delta H = 8192.8 \div 0.561 \approx +14\ 600\ J\,mol^{-1}$ ⟵ The reaction is endothermic, so ΔH is positive.

2 Then work out the entropy change, ΔS:

$\Delta S = \Delta S_{products} - \Delta S_{reactants} = (113.4 + 56.5) - 94.6 = 75.3\ J\,K^{-1}mol^{-1}$

3 Now you can find ΔG:

First, convert the temperature to Kelvin:

$T = 25.0 + 273 = 298\ K$

$\Delta G = \Delta H - T\Delta S = 14\ 600 - (298 \times 75.3)$

$\approx -7840\ J\,mol^{-1}$ (3 s.f.) ⟵ ΔG is negative, so the reaction is feasible at 25 °C.

Warm-Up Questions

Q1 What are the three things that determine the value of ΔG?

Q2 If the free energy change of a reaction is positive, what can you conclude about the reaction?

Q3 Why might a reaction with a negative ΔG value not always be feasible?

Q4 What equation links the energy change of a reaction with the specific heat capacity, temperature and mass?

Exam Questions

Q1 a) Use the equation below and the table on the right to calculate the free energy change for the complete combustion of methane at 298 K. [2 marks]

$CH_{4(g)} + 2O_{2(g)} \rightarrow CO_{2(g)} + 2H_2O_{(l)}$ $\Delta H^{\ominus} = -730\ kJ\,mol^{-1}$

b) Explain whether the reaction is feasible at 298 K. [1 mark]

c) What is the maximum temperature at which the reaction is feasible? [2 marks]

Substance	S ($J\,K^{-1}mol^{-1}$)
$CH_{4(g)}$	186
$O_{2(g)}$	205
$CO_{2(g)}$	214
$H_2O_{(l)}$	69.9
$C_3H_7OH_{(l)}$	193

Q2 In an experiment to determine ΔG for the complete combustion of propanol, the heat produced by burning 48.5 g of propanol raised the temperature of 100 ml of water by 3.50 °C.

The balanced equation for this reaction is: $C_3H_7OH_{(l)} + 4\frac{1}{2}O_{2(g)} \rightarrow 3CO_{2(g)} + 4H_2O_{(l)}$

Use the equation and the values in the table to calculate the free energy change of the combustion of propanol at 298 K. The specific heat capacity of water is $4.18\ J\,g^{-1}K^{-1}$. [5 marks]

ΔG for chemistry revision definitely has a positive value...

Okay, so ΔG won't tell you for definite whether a reaction will happen, but it will tell you if the reaction is at least theoretically feasible. Make sure you know the formula for ΔG, as well as how to work out the numbers to plonk in it. And I know I've said it before, but I'll say it again now... check your units, check your units, check your units.

Redox Equations

And now for something a bit different. Read on to learn more about redox...

In a **Redox Reaction,** Electrons are **Transferred**

In case you've forgotten all of that stuff you learnt about redox reactions in Year 1, here's a brief recap:

1) **Oxidation** is a **loss** of electrons. **Reduction** is a **gain** of electrons.

2) In a redox reaction, reduction and oxidation happen **simultaneously**.

3) An **oxidising agent accepts** electrons and gets **reduced**.

4) A **reducing agent donates** electrons and gets **oxidised**.

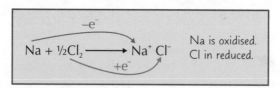

I couldn't find a red ox, so you'll have to make do with a multicoloured donkey instead.

You can Separate Redox Reactions into **Half-Reactions**

1) A redox reaction is made up of an **oxidation half-reaction** and a **reduction half-reaction**.

2) You can write an **ionic half-equation** for each of these **half-reactions**. For example, the half-equations for the oxidation of sodium and the reduction of chlorine look like this:

Sodium is oxidised — it donates electrons.

This is the electron donated by sodium.

$Na \rightarrow Na^+ + e^-$

$Cl_2 + 2e^- \rightarrow 2Cl^-$

Chlorine is reduced — it accepts electrons.

The chloride ion is negatively charged, so the half-equation balances.

Electrons are shown in half-equations so that the charges on each side of the equation balance.

3) An oxidation half-equation can be **combined** with a reduction half-equation to make a **full redox equation**.

Example: **Zinc metal** displaces **silver ions** from silver nitrate solution to form **zinc nitrate** and a deposit of **silver metal**.

The zinc atoms each lose 2 electrons (oxidation): $Zn_{(s)} \rightarrow Zn^{2+}_{(aq)} + 2e^-$

The silver ions each gain 1 electron (reduction): $Ag^+_{(aq)} + e^- \rightarrow Ag_{(s)}$

Two silver ions are needed to accept the **two electrons** released by each zinc atom. So you need to **double** the silver half-equation before the two half-equations can be combined:

$2Ag^+_{(aq)} + 2e^- \rightarrow 2Ag_{(s)}$

Now the number of electrons lost and gained **balance**, so the half-equations can be combined:

$Zn_{(s)} + 2Ag^+_{(aq)} + 2e^- \rightarrow Zn^{2+}_{(aq)} + 2e^- + 2Ag_{(s)}$

The electrons **cancel each other out**, so they aren't included in the full equation:

$Zn_{(s)} + 2Ag^+_{(aq)} \rightarrow Zn^{2+}_{(aq)} + 2Ag_{(s)}$

The charges on each side of the equation should be balanced — the charge on each side of this equation is +2.

4) Apart from multiplying up the reactants and products, **electrons**, **H+** ions and **water** are the **only** things that you're allowed to add to balance half-equations.

5) If your oxidising agent contains **oxygen**, you might have to add some H+ ions and H_2O to your half-equations to make them balance.

6) Once you've balanced the **atoms** in the half-equation, don't forget to also balance the **charges**. Read on to find out more...

Module 5: Section 2 — Energy

Redox Equations

Use e⁻, H⁺ and H₂O to Balance Half-Equations

Example: Acidified manganate(VII) ions (MnO_4^-) can be reduced to Mn^{2+} by Fe^{2+} ions.
Write the two half-equations for this reaction.

Iron is being oxidised. The half equation for this is: $\quad Fe^{2+}_{(aq)} \rightarrow Fe^{3+}_{(aq)} + e^-$

The second half-equation is a little bit trickier...

1) Manganate is being reduced. Start by writing this down: $\quad MnO_4^-{}_{(aq)} \rightarrow Mn^{2+}_{(aq)}$

2) To balance the **oxygens**, you need to add **water** to the right hand side of the equation:

$$MnO_4^-{}_{(aq)} \rightarrow Mn^{2+}_{(aq)} + 4H_2O_{(l)}$$

3) Now you need to add some **H⁺ ions** to the left hand side to balance the **hydrogens**:

$$MnO_4^-{}_{(aq)} + 8H^+_{(aq)} \rightarrow Mn^{2+}_{(aq)} + 4H_2O_{(l)}$$

This is why oxidising agents containing oxygen often have to be acidified — the oxygen needs those H+ ions for somewhere to go.

4) Finally, balance the **charges** by adding some **electrons**:

$$MnO_4^-{}_{(aq)} + 8H^+_{(aq)} + 5e^- \rightarrow Mn^{2+}_{(aq)} + 4H_2O_{(l)}$$

Charges: $\quad (-1) \quad\quad (+8) \quad\quad (-5) \quad (+2) \quad\quad\quad 0$

The charges on each side now add up to +2.

The transfer of 5e⁻ makes sense: Mn in manganate(VII) has an oxidation state of +7. It needs to gain five electrons for it to change to an oxidation state of +2.

Warm-Up Questions

Q1 Does an oxidising agent lose or gain electrons during a redox reaction?

Q2 Identify which species is being oxidised in this reaction: $\quad Zn + 2Ag^+ \rightarrow Zn^{2+} + 2Ag$

Q3 Which of these half-equations shows a reduction reaction? $\quad$ A $\quad Fe^{2+} \rightarrow Fe^{3+} + e^-$ $\quad$ B $\quad Cl_2 + 2e^- \rightarrow 2Cl^-$

PRACTICE QUESTIONS

Exam Questions

Q1 Give the two half-equations for this reaction: $Cl_2 + 2Fe^{2+} \rightarrow 2Cl^- + 2Fe^{3+}$ **[2 marks]**

Q2 The two half-equations for the reaction between aluminium and oxygen are:

$$Al \rightarrow Al^{3+} + e^- \quad\quad \text{and} \quad\quad O_2 + e^- \rightarrow O^{2-}$$

a) Balance these two half-equations. **[1 mark]**

b) Combine these half-equations to give the full redox equation for this reaction. **[1 mark]**

Q3 Acidified manganate(VII) ions will react with aqueous iodide ions to form iodine.
The two half-equations for the changes that occur are:

$$MnO_4^- + 8H^+ + 5e^- \rightarrow Mn^{2+} + 4H_2O \quad\quad \text{and} \quad\quad 2I^- \rightarrow I_2 + 2e^-$$

Write a balanced equation to show the reaction taking place. **[1 mark]**

Q4 Dichromate ions ($Cr_2O_7^{2-}$) are reduced to Cr^{3+} by zinc.
One of the half-equations for this reaction is: $Zn \rightarrow Zn^{2+} + 2e^-$.

a) Write the other half-equation. **[2 marks]**

b) Give the full redox equation for this reaction. **[1 mark]**

Sodium's lost an electron — it was an oxidant waiting to happen...

Just when you thought you knew all there is to know about redox, now you've got to figure out the equations too. Don't get all up in a tizzy about it, just make sure you've got the half-equations balanced before you stick them together — and remember to check the charges when you're done. The overall charge should be the same on both sides.

Redox Titrations

Redox titrations work like acid-base titrations but they're used to find out how much oxidising agent is needed to exactly react with a quantity of reducing agent (or vice versa). You don't need to use an indicator though...

Transition Elements are Used as Oxidising and Reducing Agents

Transition (d-block) elements are good at changing **oxidation state** (see p. 54). This makes them useful as oxidising and reducing agents as they'll readily **give out** or **receive** electrons. What's more, as they change oxidation state they often also change **colour**, so it's easy to spot when the reaction is finished. Here are a couple of examples:

Acidified **potassium manganate(VII)** solution, $KMnO_{4\,(aq)}$, is used as an **oxidising agent**.
It contains **manganate(VII) ions** (MnO_4^-), in which manganese has an oxidation state of +7.
They can be reduced to Mn^{2+} ions during a **redox reaction**.

> **Example:**   The oxidation of Fe^{2+} to Fe^{3+} by manganate(VII) ions in solution.
>
> Half equations: $MnO_4^- + 8H^+ + 5e^- \rightarrow Mn^{2+} + 4H_2O$ Manganese is reduced
>
> $5Fe^{2+} \rightarrow 5Fe^{3+} + 5e^-$ Iron is oxidised
>
> $\overline{MnO_4^- + 8H^+ + 5Fe^{2+} \rightarrow Mn^{2+} + 4H_2O + 5Fe^{3+}}$

*$MnO_4^-{}_{(aq)}$ is **purple**. $[Mn(H_2O)_6]^{2+}{}_{(aq)}$ is colourless. During this reaction, you'll see a colour change from **purple to colourless**.*

Acidified **potassium dichromate** solution, $K_2Cr_2O_{7\,(aq)}$, is another **oxidising agent**.
It contains **dichromate(VI) ions** ($Cr_2O_7^{2-}$) in which chromium has an oxidation state of **+6**.
They can be reduced to Cr^{3+} ions during a **redox reaction**.

> **Example:**   The oxidation of Zn to Zn^{2+} by dichromate(VI) ions in solution.
>
> Half equations: $Cr_2O_7^{2-} + 14H^+ + 6e^- \rightarrow 2Cr^{3+} + 7H_2O$ Chromium is reduced
>
> $\phantom{Cr_2O_7^{2-} + 14H^+ + 6e^-}$ $3Zn \rightarrow 3Zn^{2+} + 6e^-$ Zinc is oxidised
>
> $\overline{Cr_2O_7^{2-} + 14H^+ + 3Zn \rightarrow 2Cr^{3+} + 7H_2O + 3Zn^{2+}}$

*$Cr_2O_7^{2-}{}_{(aq)}$ is **orange**. $[Cr(H_2O)_6]^{3+}{}_{(aq)}$ is violet, but usually looks **green**. During this reaction, you'll see a colour change from **orange** to **green**.*

Titrations Using Transition Element Ions are Redox Titrations

To work out the **concentration** of a reducing agent, you just need to titrate a **known volume** of it against an oxidising agent of **known concentration**. This allows you to work out how much oxidising agent is needed to **exactly react** with your sample of reducing agent.

To find out how many **manganate(VII) ions** (MnO_4^-) are needed to react with a reducing agent:

You can also work out the concentration of an oxidising agent by titrating it with a reducing agent of known concentration.

1) First you measure out a quantity of the **reducing agent**, e.g. aqueous Fe^{2+} ions, using a pipette, and put it in a conical flask.

2) You then add some **dilute sulfuric acid** to the flask — this is an excess, so you don't have to be too exact.
The acid is added to make sure there are plenty of H^+ ions to allow the oxidising agent to be reduced.

3) Now you gradually add the aqueous MnO_4^- (the **oxidising agent**) to the reducing agent using a **burette**, **swirling** the conical flask as you do so.

4) You stop when the mixture in the flask **just** becomes tainted with the colour of the MnO_4^- (the **end point**) and record the volume of the oxidising agent added.

5) Run a few **titrations** and then calculate the **mean volume** of MnO_4^-.

Burette
Oxidising agent
Reducing agent and dilute sulphuric acid

You can also do titrations the **other way round** — adding the reducing agent to the oxidising agent. The rule tends to be that you add the substance of **known** concentration to the substance of **unknown** concentration.

Watch Out For the Sharp Colour Change

1) **Manganate(VII) ions** (MnO_4^-) in **aqueous potassium manganate(VII)** ($KMnO_4$) are **purple**. When they're added to the reducing agent, they start reacting. This reaction will continue until **all** of the reducing agent is used up.

2) The **very next drop** into the flask will give the mixture the **purple colour of the oxidising agent**. The trick is to spot **exactly** when this happens. *(You could use a coloured reducing agent and a colourless oxidising agent instead — then you'd be watching for the moment that the colour in the flask disappears.)*

3) Doing the reaction in front of a white surface can make colour changes easier to spot.

Redox Titrations

You Can **Calculate** the **Concentration** of a Reagent from the **Titration Results**

Example: 27.5 cm³ of 0.0200 mol dm⁻³ aqueous potassium manganate(VII) reacted with 25.0 cm³ of acidified iron(II) sulfate solution. Calculate the concentration of Fe^{2+} ions in the solution.

$$MnO_4^-{}_{(aq)} + 8H^+{}_{(aq)} + 5Fe^{2+}{}_{(aq)} \rightarrow Mn^{2+}{}_{(aq)} + 4H_2O_{(l)} + 5Fe^{3+}{}_{(aq)}$$

1) Work out the number of **moles of MnO_4^- ions** added to the flask.

> Number of moles MnO_4^- added $= \dfrac{\text{concentration} \times \text{volume}}{1000} = \dfrac{0.0200 \times 27.5}{1000} = 5.50 \times 10^{-4}$ moles

2) Look at the balanced equation to find how many moles of Fe^{2+} react with **one mole** of MnO_4^-. Then you can work out the **number of moles of Fe^{2+}** in the flask.

> 5 moles of Fe^{2+} react with 1 mole of MnO_4^-. So moles of $Fe^{2+} = 5.50 \times 10^{-4} \times 5 = 2.75 \times 10^{-3}$ moles.

3) Work out the **number of moles of Fe^{2+}** that would be in 1000 cm³ (1 dm³) of solution — this is the **concentration**.

> 25.0 cm³ of solution contained 2.75×10^{-3} moles of Fe^{2+}.
> 1000 cm³ of solution would contain $\dfrac{(2.75 \times 10^{-3}) \times 1000}{25.0} = 0.110$ moles of Fe^{2+}.
> So the concentration of Fe^{2+} is **0.110 mol dm⁻³**.

Warm-Up Questions

Q1 Write a half equation to show manganate(VII) ions acting as an oxidising agent.

Q2 Why is dilute acid added to the reaction mixture in redox titrations involving MnO_4^- ions?

Q3 If you carry out a redox titration by slowly adding aqueous MnO_4^- ions to aqueous Fe^{2+} ions, how can you tell that you've reached the end point?

Exam Questions

Q1 A 10 cm³ sample of $SnCl_2$ solution was titrated with acidified potassium manganate(VII) solution. Exactly 20 cm³ of 0.10 mol dm⁻³ potassium manganate(VII) solution was needed to fully oxidise the tin(II) chloride.

a) How many moles of potassium manganate(VII) were needed to fully oxidise the tin(II) chloride? [1 mark]

b) The equation for this reaction is: $2MnO_4^- + 16H^+ + 5Sn^{2+} \rightarrow 2Mn^{2+} + 8H_2O + 5Sn^{4+}$
How many moles of tin(II) chloride were present in the 10 cm³ sample? [1 mark]

c) Calculate the concentration of Sn^{2+} ions in the sample solution. [1 mark]

Q2 Steel wool contains a high percentage of iron, and a small amount of carbon.
A 1.30 g piece of steel wool was completely dissolved in 50.0 cm³ of aqueous sulfuric acid.
The resulting solution was titrated with 0.400 mol dm⁻³ of potassium manganate(VII) solution.
11.5 cm³ of the potassium manganate(VII) solution was needed to oxidise all of the iron(II) ions to iron(III).

a) Write a balanced equation for the reaction between the manganate(VII) ions and the iron(II) ions. [1 mark]

b) Calculate the concentration of iron(II) ions present in the original solution. [3 marks]

c) Calculate the percentage of iron present in the steel wool. Give your answer to one decimal place. [2 marks]

And how many moles does it take to change a light bulb...

...two, one to change the bulb, and another to ask "Why do we need light bulbs? We're moles — most of the time that we're underground, we keep our eyes shut. And the electricity costs a packet. We haven't thought this through..."

Iodine-Thiosulfate Titrations

This is another example of a redox titration — it's a nifty little reaction that you can use to find the concentration of an oxidising agent. And since it's a titration, that also means a few more calculations to get to grips with...

Iodine-Sodium Thiosulfate Titrations are Dead Handy

Iodine-sodium thiosulfate titrations are a way of finding the concentration of an **oxidising agent**.

The **more concentrated** an oxidising agent is, the **more ions will be oxidised** by a certain volume of it.
So here's how you can find out the concentration of a solution of the oxidising agent **potassium iodate(V)**:

STAGE 1: Use a sample of oxidising agent to oxidise as much iodide as possible.

1) Measure out a certain volume of **potassium iodate(V)** solution (**KIO₃**) (the oxidising agent) — say **25.0 cm³**.

2) Add this to an excess of acidified **potassium iodide** solution (**KI**).
The iodate(V) ions in the potassium iodate(V) solution
oxidise some of the **iodide ions** to **iodine**. $\longrightarrow$ $IO_3^-{}_{(aq)} + 5I^-{}_{(aq)} + 6H^+{}_{(aq)} \rightarrow 3I_{2(aq)} + 3H_2O_{(l)}$

STAGE 2: Find out how many moles of iodine have been produced.

You do this by **titrating** the resulting solution with **sodium thiosulfate** (**Na₂S₂O₃**).
(You need to know the concentration of the sodium thiosulfate solution.)

The iodine in the solution reacts
with **thiosulfate ions** like this: $\longrightarrow$ $I_{2\ (aq)} + 2S_2O_3^{2-}{}_{(aq)} \rightarrow 2I^-{}_{(aq)} + S_4O_6^{2-}{}_{(aq)}$

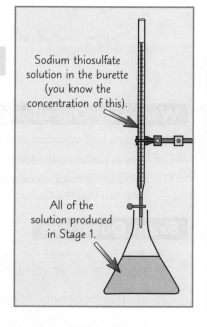

Sodium thiosulfate
solution in the burette
(you know the
concentration of this).

All of the
solution produced
in Stage 1.

Titration of Iodine with Sodium Thiosulfate

1) Take the flask containing the solution that was produced in Stage 1.

2) From a burette, add sodium thiosulfate solution to the flask **drop by drop**.

3) It's hard to see the end point, so when the iodine colour fades to a
pale yellow (this is close to the end point), add 2 cm³ of **starch solution**
(to detect the presence of iodine). The solution in the conical flask will go
dark blue, showing there's still some iodine there.

4) Add sodium thiosulfate **one drop at a time** until the blue colour disappears.

5) When this happens, it means all the iodine has **just** been reacted.

6) Now you can **calculate** the number of moles of iodine in the solution.

Here's how you'd do the titration calculation to find the **number of moles of iodine** produced in Stage 1.

Example: The iodine in the solution produced in Stage 1 reacted fully with 11.0 cm³ of 0.120 mol dm⁻³
thiosulfate solution. Work out the number of moles of iodine present in the starting solution.

$$I_2 + 2S_2O_3^{2-} \rightarrow 2I^- + S_4O_6^{2-}$$

11.0 cm³

0.120 mol dm⁻³

Number of moles of thiosulfate = $\dfrac{\text{concentration} \times \text{volume (cm}^3)}{1000} = \dfrac{0.120 \times 11.0}{1000} = 1.32 \times 10^{-3}$ moles

1 mole of iodine reacts with **2 moles** of thiosulfate.

So number of **moles of iodine** in the solution = $1.32 \times 10^{-3} \div 2 = \mathbf{6.60 \times 10^{-4}}$ **moles**

Iodine-Thiosulfate Titrations

STAGE 3: Calculate the concentration of the oxidising agent.

1) Now you look back at your original equation: $IO_3^-{}_{(aq)} + 5I^-{}_{(aq)} + 6H^+{}_{(aq)} \rightarrow 3I_{2(aq)} + 3H_2O_{(l)}$

2) 25.0 cm^3 of potassium iodate(V) solution produced **6.60×10^{-4} moles of iodine**.
   The equation shows that **one mole** of iodate(V) ions will produce **three moles** of iodine.

3) That means there must have been **$6.60 \times 10^{-4} \div 3 = 2.20 \times 10^{-4}$ moles of iodate(V) ions** in the original solution.
   So now it's straightforward to find the **concentration** of the potassium iodate(V) solution, which is what you're after:

$$\text{number of moles} = \frac{\text{concentration} \times \text{volume (cm}^3)}{1000} \quad \Rightarrow \quad 2.20 \times 10^{-4} = \frac{\text{concentration} \times 25.0}{1000}$$

$$\Rightarrow \text{concentration of potassium iodate(V) solution} = \textbf{0.00880 mol dm}^{-3}$$

Warm-Up Questions

Q1 How can an iodine-sodium thiosulfate titration help you to work out the concentration of an oxidising agent?

Q2 How many moles of thiosulfate ions react with one mole of iodine molecules?

Q3 What is added during an iodine-sodium thiosulfate titration to make the end point easier to see?

Q4 Describe the colour change at the end point of the iodine-sodium thiosulfate titration.

Exam Questions

Q1 10.0 cm^3 of potassium iodate(V) solution was reacted with excess acidified potassium iodide solution.
All of the resulting solution was titrated with $0.150 \text{ mol dm}^{-3}$ sodium thiosulfate solution.
It fully reacted with 24.0 cm^3 of the sodium thiosulfate solution.

    a) Write an equation showing how iodine is formed in the reaction
between iodate(V) ions and iodide ions in acidic solution. [1 mark]

    b) How many moles of thiosulfate ions were there in 24.0 cm^3 of the sodium thiosulfate solution? [1 mark]

    c) In the titration, iodine reacted with sodium thiosulfate according to this equation:

$$I_{2(aq)} + 2Na_2S_2O_{3(aq)} \rightarrow 2NaI_{(aq)} + Na_2S_4O_{6(aq)}$$

    Calculate the number of moles of iodine that reacted with the sodium thiosulfate solution. [1 mark]

    d) How many moles of iodate(V) ions produce 1 mole of iodine from potassium iodide? [1 mark]

    e) What was the concentration of the potassium iodate(V) solution? [2 marks]

Q2 An 18.0 cm^3 sample of potassium manganate(VII) solution was reacted with an excess of acidified potassium
iodide solution. The resulting solution was titrated with $0.300 \text{ mol dm}^{-3}$ sodium thiosulfate solution.
12.5 cm^3 of sodium thiosulfate solution were needed to fully react with the iodine.

When they were mixed, the manganate(VII) ions reacted with the iodide ions according to this equation:

$$2MnO_4^-{}_{(aq)} + 10I^-{}_{(aq)} + 16H^+ \rightarrow 5I_{2(aq)} + 8H_2O_{(aq)} + 2Mn^{2+}{}_{(aq)}$$

During the titration, the iodine reacted with sodium thiosulfate according to this equation:

$$I_{2(aq)} + 2Na_2S_2O_{3(aq)} \rightarrow 2NaI_{(aq)} + Na_2S_4O_{6(aq)}$$

Calculate the concentration of the potassium manganate(VII) solution. [4 marks]

Two vowels went out for dinner — they had an iodate...

This might seem like quite a faff — you do a redox reaction to release iodine, titrate the iodine solution, do a sum to find the iodine concentration, write an equation, then do another sum to work out the concentration of something else.
It does work though, and you do have to know how. If you're rusty on the calculations, look back at your Year 1 notes.

Electrochemical Cells

There are electrons toing and froing in redox reactions. And when electrons move, you get electricity.

Electrochemical Cells Make Electricity

Electrochemical cells can be made from **two different metals** dipped in salt solutions of their **own ions** and connected by a wire (the **external circuit**).

There are always **two** reactions within an electrochemical cell — one's an oxidation and one's a reduction — so it's a **redox process** (see page 40).

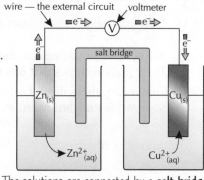

Here's what happens in the **zinc/copper** electrochemical cell on the right:

1) Zinc **loses electrons** more easily than copper. So in the half-cell on the left, zinc (from the zinc electrode) is **oxidised** to form $Zn^{2+}_{(aq)}$ ions. This releases electrons into the external circuit.

2) In the other half-cell, the **same number of electrons** are taken from the external circuit, **reducing** the Cu^{2+} ions to copper atoms.

The solutions are connected by a **salt bridge** made from filter paper soaked in $KNO_{3(aq)}$. This allows ions to flow through and balance out the charges.

So **electrons** flow through the wire from the most reactive metal to the least.

A voltmeter in the external circuit shows the **voltage** between the two half-cells. This is the **cell potential** or **e.m.f.**, E_{cell}.

You can also have half-cells involving **solutions of two aqueous ions of the same element**, such as $Fe^{2+}_{(aq)}/Fe^{3+}_{(aq)}$. The conversion from Fe^{2+} to Fe^{3+}, or vice versa, happens on the surface of a platinum **electrode**.

Electrochemical cells can also be made from **non-metals**. For systems involving a **gas** (e.g. chlorine), the gas can be **bubbled over** a platinum electrode sitting in a solution of its **aqueous ions** (e.g. Cl^-).

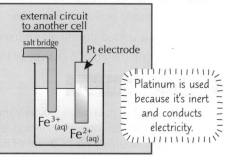

Platinum is used because it's inert and conducts electricity.

The Reactions at Each Electrode are Reversible

1) The **reactions** that occur at each electrode in the **zinc/copper cell** above are:

2) The **reversible arrows** show that both reactions can go in **either direction**. **Which direction** each reaction goes in depends on **how easily** each metal **loses electrons** (i.e. how easily it's **oxidised**).

$$Zn^{2+}_{(aq)} + 2e^- \rightleftharpoons Zn_{(s)}$$
$$Cu^{2+}_{(aq)} + 2e^- \rightleftharpoons Cu_{(s)}$$

3) How easily a metal is oxidised is measured using **electrode potentials**. A metal that's **easily oxidised** has a very **negative electrode potential**, while one that's harder to oxidise has a less negative or **a positive electrode potential**.

Half-cell	Electrode potential $E^{\ominus}$ (V)
$Zn^{2+}_{(aq)}/Zn_{(s)}$	−0.76
$Cu^{2+}_{(aq)}/Cu_{(s)}$	+0.34

4) The table on the left shows the electrode potentials for the copper and zinc half-cells. The **zinc half-cell** has a **more negative** electrode potential, so **zinc is oxidised** (the reaction goes **backwards**), while **copper is reduced** (the reaction goes **forwards**). Remember, the little ⊖ symbol next to the E means it's under standard conditions — 298 K and 100 kPa.

There's a Convention for Drawing Electrochemical Cells

It's a bit of a faff drawing pictures of electrochemical cells. There's a **shorthand** way of representing them though — for example, this is the **Zn/Cu cell**:

There are a couple of important **conventions** when drawing cells:

1) The **half-cell** with the **more negative** potential goes on the **left**.

2) The **oxidised forms** go in the **centre** of the cell diagram.

If you follow the conventions, you can use the electrode potentials to calculate the overall cell potential.

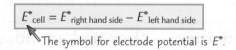

$$E^{\ominus}_{cell} = E^{\ominus}_{right\ hand\ side} - E^{\ominus}_{left\ hand\ side}$$

The symbol for electrode potential is $E^{\ominus}$.

Zn_{(s)}	Zn^{2+}_{(aq)}	Cu^{2+}_{(aq)}	Cu_{(s)}
reduced form	oxidised form	oxidised form	reduced form

Changes go in this direction

The cell potential will always be a **positive voltage**, because the more negative $E^{\ominus}$ value is being subtracted from the more positive $E^{\ominus}$ value. For example, the cell potential for the Zn/Cu cell = +0.34 − (−0.76) = **+1.1 V**.

Electrochemical Cells

Electrode Potentials are Measured Against Standard Hydrogen Electrodes

You measure the electrode potential of a half-cell against a **standard hydrogen electrode**.

> The **standard electrode potential**, $E^{\ominus}$, of a half-cell is the **voltage measured** under **standard conditions** when the **half-cell** is connected to a **standard hydrogen electrode**.

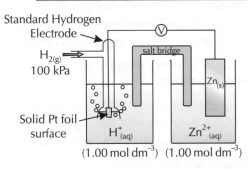

Standard Hydrogen Electrode

$H_{2(g)}$
100 kPa

salt bridge

$Zn_{(s)}$

Solid Pt foil surface

$H^+_{(aq)}$ $Zn^{2+}_{(aq)}$
$(1.00 \text{ mol dm}^{-3})$ $(1.00 \text{ mol dm}^{-3})$

Standard conditions are:

1) Any solutions must have a concentration of **1.00 mol dm⁻³** or be **equimolar** (i.e. contain the same number of moles of ions).

2) The temperature must be **298 K (25 °C)**.

3) The pressure must be **100 kPa**.

1) The **standard hydrogen electrode** is always shown on the **left** — it doesn't matter whether or not the other half-cell has a more positive value. The standard hydrogen electrode half-cell has a value of **0.00 V**.

2) The whole cell potential = $E^{\circ}_{\text{right hand side}} - E^{\circ}_{\text{left hand side}}$.
$E^{\circ}_{\text{left hand side}} = 0.00$ V, so the **voltage reading** will be equal to $E^{\circ}_{\text{right hand side}}$.
This reading could be **positive** or **negative**, depending which way the **electrons flow**.

Conditions Affect the Value of the Electrode Potential

Just like any other reversible reaction, the **equilibrium position** in a half-cell is affected by changes in **temperature**, **pressure** and **concentration**. Changing the equilibrium position changes the **cell potential**.
To get around this, **standard conditions** are used to measure electrode potentials — using these conditions means you always get the **same value** for the electrode potential and you can **compare values** for different cells.

Warm-Up Questions

Q1 $Zn^{2+}_{(aq)} + 2e^- \rightleftharpoons Zn_{(s)}$ $E^{\circ} = -0.76$ V $Cu^{2+}_{(aq)} + 2e^- \rightleftharpoons Cu_{(s)}$ $E^{\circ} = +0.34$ V
Draw a diagram to show the set up of a zinc/copper electrochemical cell, including the direction of electrons.

Q2 What's the definition of standard electrode potential?

Q3 What is the voltage of the standard hydrogen electrode half-cell?

Exam Questions

Q1 A cell is made up of a lead and an iron plate, dipped in solutions of lead(II) nitrate and iron(II) nitrate respectively and connected by a salt bridge. The electrode potentials for the two electrodes are:

$Fe^{2+}_{(aq)} + 2e^- \rightleftharpoons Fe_{(s)}$ $E^{\ominus} = -0.44$ V $Pb^{2+}_{(aq)} + 2e^- \rightleftharpoons Pb_{(s)}$ $E^{\ominus} = -0.13$ V

a) Which metal becomes oxidised in the cell? Explain your answer.   [2 marks]

b) Find the standard cell potential of this cell.   [1 mark]

Q2 An electrochemical cell containing a zinc half-cell and a silver half-cell was set up using a potassium nitrate salt bridge. The cell potential at 25 °C was measured to be 1.40 V.

$Zn^{2+}_{(aq)} + 2e^- \rightleftharpoons Zn_{(s)}$ $E^{\ominus} = -0.76$ V $Ag^+_{(aq)} + e^- \rightleftharpoons Ag_{(s)}$ $E^{\ominus} = +0.80$ V

a) Use the standard electrode potentials given to calculate the standard cell potential for a zinc-silver cell. [1 mark]

b) Suggest two possible reasons why the actual cell potential was different from the value calculated in part (a).   [2 marks]

Cells aren't just for Biologists, you know...

You've just got to think about this stuff. The metal on the left-hand electrode disappears off into the solution, leaving its electrons behind. This makes the left-hand electrode the negative one. So the right-hand electrode's got to be the positive one. It makes sense if you think about it. This electrode gives up electrons to turn the positive ions into atoms.

The Electrochemical Series

The electrochemical series is like a pop chart of the most reactive metals – except without the pop so it's really just a chart.

The **Electrochemical Series** Shows You What's **Reactive** and What's Not

1) The **more reactive** a **metal** is, the **more** it wants to **lose electrons** to form a **positive ion**.
   More reactive metals have **more negative standard electrode potentials**.

> **Example:** Magnesium is **more reactive** than zinc — so it's more eager to form 2+ ions than zinc is.
> The list of standard electrode potentials shows that Mg^{2+}/Mg has a **more negative** value than Zn^{2+}/Zn.
> In terms of oxidation and reduction, magnesium would **reduce** Zn^{2+} (or Zn^{2+} would **oxidise** Mg).

2) The more reactive a **non-metal** is, the **more** it wants to **gain electrons** to form a **negative ion**.
   More reactive non-metals have **more positive standard electrode potentials**.

> **Example:** Chlorine is **more reactive** than bromine — so it's more eager to form a negative ion than bromine is.
> The list of standard electrode potentials shows that $\frac{1}{2}Cl_2/Cl^-$ is **more positive** than $\frac{1}{2}Br_2/Br^-$.
> In terms of oxidation and reduction, chlorine would **oxidise** Br^- (or Br^- would **reduce** Cl).

3) Here's an **electrochemical series** showing some standard electrode potentials:

More positive electrode potentials mean that:
1. The left-hand substances are more easily reduced.
2. The right-hand substances are more stable.

Half-reaction	$E^{\ominus}$/V
$Mg^{2+}_{(aq)} + 2e^- \rightleftharpoons Mg_{(s)}$	−2.37
$Zn^{2+}_{(aq)} + 2e^- \rightleftharpoons Zn_{(s)}$	−0.76
$H^+_{(aq)} + e^- \rightleftharpoons \frac{1}{2}H_{2(g)}$	0.00
$Cu^{2+}_{(aq)} + 2e^- \rightleftharpoons Cu_{(s)}$	+0.34
$Fe^{3+}_{(aq)} + e^- \rightleftharpoons Fe^{2+}_{(aq)}$	+0.77
$\frac{1}{2}Br_{2(aq)} + e^- \rightleftharpoons Br^-_{(aq)}$	+1.07
$\frac{1}{2}Cl_{2(aq)} + e^- \rightleftharpoons Cl^-_{(aq)}$	+1.36

More negative electrode potentials mean that:
1. The right-hand substances are more easily oxidised.
2. The left-hand substances are more stable.

Use **Electrode Potentials** to **Predict** Whether a Reaction Will Happen

To figure out if a metal will react with the aqueous ions of another metal, you can use their E° values.

> **Example:** Predict whether:
> a) Zinc reacts with aqueous copper ions.
>
> First you write the two **half-equations** down as reduction reactions:
> $$Zn^{2+}_{(aq)} + 2e^- \rightleftharpoons Zn_{(s)} \qquad E^{\circ} = -0.76 \text{ V}$$
> $$Cu^{2+}_{(aq)} + 2e^- \rightleftharpoons Cu_{(s)} \qquad E^{\circ} = +0.34 \text{ V}$$

The half-reactions are written as reduction reactions but one will always have to move in the direction of oxidation. Zn^{2+}/Zn has a more negative electrode potential than Cu^{2+}/Cu, so the zinc will be oxidised.

> Then you look at the standard electrode potentials.
> The half-equation with the **more negative** electrode potential will move to the **left**: $Zn_{(s)} \rightarrow Zn^{2+}_{(aq)} + 2e^-$
> The half-equation with the **more positive** electrode potential will move to the **right**: $Cu^{2+}_{(aq)} + 2e^- \rightarrow Cu_{(s)}$
>
> The two half-equations combine to give: $Zn_{(s)} + Cu^{2+}_{(aq)} \rightarrow Zn^{2+}_{(aq)} + Cu_{(s)}$
>
> This is the **feasible** direction of the two half-reactions and it matches the reaction described in the question.
> So zinc **will** react with aqueous copper ions.
>
> b) Copper reacts with dilute sulfuric acid.
>
> Again, write the two **half-equations** down: $Cu^{2+}_{(aq)} + 2e^- \rightleftharpoons Cu_{(s)} \qquad E^{\circ} = +0.34 \text{ V}$ — For the acid, use the hydrogen half-equation.
> $$2H^+_{(aq)} + 2e^- \rightleftharpoons H_{2(g)} \qquad E^{\circ} = 0.00 \text{ V}$$
>
> The hydrogen half-equation has the **more negative** E°, so it will move to the **left**: $H_{2(g)} \rightarrow 2H^+_{(aq)} + 2e^-$
>
> The two half-equations combine to give: $H_{2(g)} + Cu^{2+}_{(aq)} \rightarrow 2H^+_{(aq)} + Cu_{(s)}$
>
> This equation shows the **feasible** direction of the two half-equations but shows gaseous hydrogen reacting with copper ions, not solid copper reacting with sulfuric acid. So copper **won't** react with sulfuric acid.

The Electrochemical Series

Sometimes the Prediction is Wrong

A **prediction** using E° only states if a reaction is **possible** under **standard conditions**. The prediction might be **wrong if...**

...the conditions are not standard.

1) Changing the concentration (or temperature) of the solution can cause the electrode potential to change.

2) For example the zinc/copper cell has these half equations in equilibrium...

$$Zn_{(s)} \rightleftharpoons Zn^{2+}_{(aq)} + 2e^- \quad E^\circ = -0.76\,V$$
$$Cu^{2+}_{(aq)} + 2e^- \rightleftharpoons Cu_{(s)} \quad E^\circ = +0.34\,V$$

$$Zn_{(s)} + Cu^{2+}_{(aq)} \rightleftharpoons Zn^{2+}_{(aq)} + Cu_{(s)} \quad E_{cell} = +1.10\,V$$

3) ...if you increase the concentration of Zn^{2+}, the equilibrium will shift to the left, reducing the ease of electron loss. The electrode potential of Zn/Zn^{2+} becomes less negative and the whole cell potential will be lower.

4) ...if you increase the concentration of Cu^{2+}, the equilibrium will shift to the right, increasing the ease of electron gain. The electrode potential of Cu^{2+}/Cu becomes more positive and the whole cell potential will be higher.

...the reaction kinetics are not favourable.

1) The rate of a reaction may be so slow that the reaction might not appear to happen.

2) If a reaction has a high activation energy, this may stop it happening.

Warm-Up Questions

Q1 Cu is less reactive than Pb. Predict which of these half-reactions has the more negative standard electrode potential: A $Pb^{2+} + 2e^- \rightleftharpoons Pb$ B $Cu^{2+} + 2e^- \rightleftharpoons Cu$

Q2 Use electrode potentials to show that magnesium will reduce Zn^{2+}.

Q3 Use the table on the opposite page to predict whether or not Zn^{2+} ions can oxidise Fe^{2+} ions to Fe^{3+} ions.

Exam Questions

Q1 Use the $E^\ominus$ values in the table on the right and on the previous page to determine the outcome of mixing the following solutions. If there is a reaction, determine the $E^\ominus$ value and write the equation. If there isn't a reaction, state this and explain why.

Half-reaction	E°/V
$MnO_4^-{}_{(aq)} + 8H^+{}_{(aq)} + 5e^- \rightleftharpoons Mn^{2+}{}_{(aq)} + 4H_2O_{(l)}$	+1.51
$Cr_2O_7^{2-}{}_{(aq)} + 14H^+{}_{(aq)} + 6e^- \rightleftharpoons 2Cr^{3+}{}_{(aq)} + 7H_2O_{(l)}$	+1.33
$Sn^{4+}{}_{(aq)} + 2e^- \rightleftharpoons Sn^{2+}{}_{(aq)}$	+0.14
$Ni^{2+}{}_{(aq)} + 2e^- \rightleftharpoons Ni_{(s)}$	−0.25

a) Zinc metal and Ni^{2+} ions. [2 marks]

b) Acidified MnO_4^- ions and Sn^{2+} ions. [2 marks]

c) $Br_{2(aq)}$ and acidified $Cr_2O_7^{2-}$ ions. [2 marks]

Q2 Potassium manganate(VII), $KMnO_4$, and potassium dichromate $K_2Cr_2O_7$, are both used as oxidising agents. From their electrode potentials (given in the table above), which would you predict is the stronger oxidising agent? Explain why. [2 marks]

Q3 A cell is set up with copper and nickel electrodes in $1\,mol\,dm^{-3}$ solutions of their ions, Cu^{2+} and Ni^{2+}, connected by a salt bridge.

a) Write equations for the reactions that occur in each half-cell. [2 marks]

b) Find the voltage of the cell. Use the $E^\ominus$ values in the table above and on the previous page. [1 mark]

c) What is the overall equation for this reaction? [1 mark]

d) How would the voltage of the cell change if a more dilute copper solution was used? [1 mark]

My mam always said I had potential...

To see if a reaction will happen, you basically find the two half-equations in the electrochemical series and check that the one you are predicting to go backwards is the one with the more negative electrode potential. Alternatively, you could calculate the cell potential for the reaction — if it's negative, it's never going to happen.

Storage and Fuel Cells

Yet more electrochemical reactions on these pages, but you're nearly at the end of the section so keep going...

Energy Storage Cells are Like Electrochemical Cells

Energy storage cells (fancy name for a battery) have been around for ages and modern ones **work** just like an **electrochemical cell**. For example the nickel-iron cell was developed way back at the start of the 1900s and is often used as a back-up power supply because it can be repeatedly charged and is very robust. You can work out the **voltage** produced by these **cells** by using the **electrode potentials** of the substances used in the cell.

There are **lots** of different cells and you **won't** be asked to remember the E° for the reactions, but you might be **asked** to work out the **cell potential** or **cell voltage** for a given cell... so here's an example I prepared earlier.

Example: The nickel-iron cell has a nickel oxide hydroxide (NiO(OH)) cathode and an iron (Fe) anode with potassium hydroxide as the electrolyte. Using the half equations given:

    a) write out the full equation for the reaction.

    b) calculate the cell voltage produced by the nickel-iron cell.

$$Fe + 2OH^- \rightleftharpoons Fe(OH)_2 + 2e^- \qquad E^\circ = -0.44V$$
$$NiO(OH) + H_2O + e^- \rightleftharpoons Ni(OH)_2 + OH^- \qquad E^\circ = +0.76V$$

You have to double everything in the second equation so that the electrons balance those in the first equation.

For the first part you have to **combine** the two half-equations together. The e^- and the OH^- are not shown because they get cancelled out.

The **overall** reaction is...
$$2NiO(OH) + 2H_2O + Fe \rightarrow 2Ni(OH)_2 + Fe(OH)_2$$

To calculate the **cell voltage** you use the **same formula** for working out the **cell potential** (page 46).

So the cell voltage $= E^\circ_{\text{right hand side}} - E^\circ_{\text{left hand side}}$
$$= +0.76 - (-0.44)$$
$$= 1.2V$$

Remember, $E^\circ_{\text{left hand side}}$ is the more negative electrode potential.

Fuel Cells Generate Electricity from Reacting a Fuel with an Oxidant

A **fuel cell** produces electricity by reacting a **fuel**, usually hydrogen, with an **oxidant**, which is most likely to be oxygen.

1) At the **anode** the platinum catalyst **splits** the H_2 into protons and electrons.

2) The **polymer electrolyte membrane** (PEM) **only** allows the H^+ across and this **forces** the e^- to travel **around** the circuit to get to the cathode.

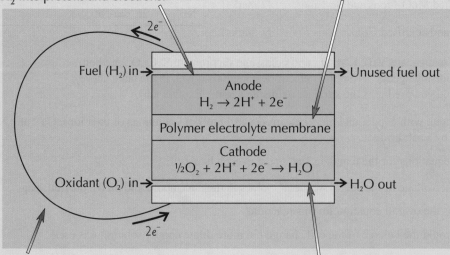

Fuel (H_2) in → Anode $H_2 \rightarrow 2H^+ + 2e^-$ → Unused fuel out

Polymer electrolyte membrane

Cathode $\frac{1}{2}O_2 + 2H^+ + 2e^- \rightarrow H_2O$

Oxidant (O_2) in → → H_2O out

3) An **electric current** is created in the circuit, which is used to **power** something like a car or a bike or a dancing Santa.

4) At the **cathode**, O_2 **combines** with the H^+ from the anode and the e^- from the circuit to make H_2O. This is the only waste product.

Storage and Fuel Cells

Electrochemical Cells Have Some **Important Advantages**

- They are more efficient at producing energy than conventional combustion engines. This is because energy is wasted during combustion as heat.
- They produce a lot less pollution (such as CO_2).
  For hydrogen fuel cells, the only waste product is water.

However, there are also drawbacks to using electrochemical cells for energy:

1) The production of the cells involves the use of **toxic chemicals**, which need to be **disposed of** once the cell has reached the end of its life span.

2) The chemicals used to make the cells are also often very **flammable**. E.g. lithium (commonly used in rechargeable batteries), is **highly reactive** and will catch fire if a fault causes it to overheat.

Cuteness is an important advantage of electrochemical seals.

Warm-Up Questions

Q1 How does a fuel cell produce electricity?

Q2 What particle travels through the electrolyte in a hydrogen-oxygen fuel cell?

Q3 Give one advantage and one disadvantage of electrochemical cells over conventional combustion engines.

Exam Questions

Q1 The diagram below shows the structure of a hydrogen-oxygen fuel cell.

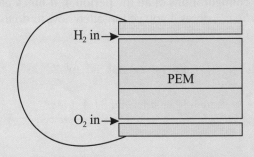

a) i) Label the site of oxidation and the site of reduction on the diagram. [2 marks]

   ii) Draw an arrow to show the direction of the flow of electrons. [1 mark]

b) Write a half-equation for the reaction at each electrode. [2 marks]

c) Explain the purpose of the polymer electrolyte membrane (PEM) in the fuel cell. [2 marks]

Q2 The two half-equations for the reaction that happen in a nickel/cadmium battery are shown below.

$$Cd(OH)_{2(s)} + 2e^- \rightleftharpoons Cd_{(s)} + 2OH^-_{(aq)} \qquad E^{\ominus} = -0.88 \text{ V}$$

$$NiO(OH)_{(s)} + H_2O_{(l)} + e^- \rightleftharpoons Ni(OH)_{2(s)} + OH^-_{(aq)} \qquad E^{\ominus} = +0.52 \text{ V}$$

a) Calculate the cell voltage for a nickel/cadmium cell. [1 mark]

b) Write an equation for the overall reaction occurring in this cell. [1 mark]

In the past they used donkey-powered mills. They were called...wait for it...

...mule cells. Buddum tish. Oh dear, I'm really struggling today. Anyway, the hydrogen future is not upon us yet. It may have some advantages over the oil we use today but there are a few things to overcome first. So maybe it will happen and maybe it won't. All we really know is it's the end of the section and that's got to be a good thing. Hurrah!!

The d-block

The d-block can be found slap bang in the middle of the periodic table. It's here you'll find the transition elements. The most precious metals in the world are found in the d-block. That's got to make it worth a look...

Transition Elements are Found in the d-Block

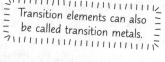

Transition elements can also be called transition metals.

1) The **d-block** is the block of elements in the middle of the periodic table.

2) Most of the elements in the d-block are **transition elements**.

3) You only need to know about the transition elements in the first row of the d-block (period 4) — the ones from **titanium to copper**.

Group 1	Group 2												Group 3	Group 4	Group 5	Group 6	Group 7	Group 0
					1 H Hydrogen 1													4 He 2
7 Li 3	9 Be 4												11 B 5	12 C 6	14 N 7	16 O 8	19 F 9	20 Ne 10
23 Na 11	24 Mg 12				← d-block →								27 Al 13	28 Si 14	31 P 15	32 S 16	35.5 Cl 17	40 Ar 18
39 K 19	40 Ca 20	45 Sc 21	48 Ti 22	51 V 23	52 Cr 24	55 Mn 25	56 Fe 26	59 Co 27	59 Ni 28	64 Cu 29	65 Zn 30		70 Ga 31	73 Ge 32	75 As 33	79 Se 34	80 Br 35	84 Kr 36
86 Rb 37	88 Sr 38	89 Y 39	91 Zr 40	93 Nb 41	96 Mo 42	99 Tc 43	101 Ru 44	103 Rh 45	106 Pd 46	108 Ag 47	112 Cd 48		115 In 49	119 Sn 50	122 Sb 51	128 Te 52	127 I 53	131 Xe 54
133 Cs 55	137 Ba 56	57-71 Lanthanides	179 Hf 72	181 Ta 73	184 W 74	186 Re 75	190 Os 76	192 Ir 77	195 Pt 78	197 Au 79	201 Hg 80		204 Tl 81	207 Pb 82	209 Bi 83	210 Po 84	210 At 85	222 Rn 86
223 Fr 87	226 Ra 88	89-103 Actinides																

"A'm tellin' ya boy — there's gold in that thar d-block."

You Need to Know the Electron Configurations of the Transition Elements

1) Make sure you can write down the **electron configurations** of **all** the **period 4, d-block elements** in sub-shell notation. Have a look back at you Year 1 notes if you've forgotten how to do this. Here are a couple of examples:

$$V = 1s^2\ 2s^2\ 2p^6\ 3s^2\ 3p^6\ 3d^3\ 4s^2 \qquad Co = 1s^2\ 2s^2\ 2p^6\ 3s^2\ 3p^6\ 3d^7\ 4s^2$$

The 4s electrons fill up before the 3d electrons. But chromium and copper are a trifle odd — see below.

2) Here's the definition of a transition element:

> A **transition element** is a d-block element that can form **at least one stable ion** with an **incomplete d sub-shell**.

3) A d sub-shell can hold **10** electrons. So transition elements must form **at least one ion** that has **between 1 and 9 electrons** in the d sub-shell. All the period 4 d-block elements are transition elements apart from **scandium** and **zinc**. The diagram below shows the 3d and 4s sub-shells of these elements:

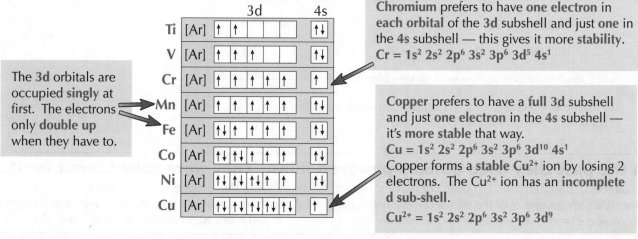

The **3d** orbitals are occupied **singly** at first. The electrons only **double up** when they have to.

Chromium prefers to have **one electron** in **each orbital** of the 3d subshell and just **one** in the 4s subshell — this gives it more **stability**.
$Cr = 1s^2\ 2s^2\ 2p^6\ 3s^2\ 3p^6\ 3d^5\ 4s^1$

Copper prefers to have a **full 3d** subshell and just **one electron** in the 4s subshell — it's **more stable** that way.
$Cu = 1s^2\ 2s^2\ 2p^6\ 3s^2\ 3p^6\ 3d^{10}\ 4s^1$
Copper forms a **stable Cu^{2+} ion** by losing 2 electrons. The Cu^{2+} ion has an **incomplete d sub-shell**.
$Cu^{2+} = 1s^2\ 2s^2\ 2p^6\ 3s^2\ 3p^6\ 3d^9$

The d-block

When **Ions** are Formed, the **s Electrons** are Removed First

When transition elements form **positive** ions, the **s electrons** are removed **first**, then the d electrons.

1) Iron can form Fe^{2+} ions and Fe^{3+} ions.

2) When it forms 2+ ions, it loses both its 4s electrons.
$Fe = 1s^2\,2s^2\,2p^6\,3s^2\,3p^6\,3d^6\,4s^2 \rightarrow Fe^{2+} = 1s^2\,2s^2\,2p^6\,3s^2\,3p^6\,3d^6$

3) Only once the 4s electrons are removed can a 3d electron be removed.
E.g. $Fe^{2+} = 1s^2\,2s^2\,2p^6\,3s^2\,3p^6\,3d^6 \rightarrow Fe^{3+} = 1s^2\,2s^2\,2p^6\,3s^2\,3p^6\,3d^5$

Scandium and Zinc **Aren't** Transition Elements

Scandium and zinc can't form **stable ions** with **incomplete d sub-shells**.
So neither of them fits the definition of a **transition element**.

Scandium only forms one ion, **Sc^{3+}**, which has an **empty d sub-shell**.
Scandium has the electron configuration $1s^2\,2s^2\,2p^6\,3s^2\,3p^6\,3d^1\,4s^2$.
It loses three electrons to form Sc^{3+}, which has the electron configuration $1s^2\,2s^2\,2p^6\,3s^2\,3p^6$.

Zinc only forms one ion, **Zn^{2+}**, which has a **full d sub-shell**.
Zinc has the electron configuration $1s^2\,2s^2\,2p^6\,3s^2\,3p^6\,3d^{10}\,4s^2$.
When it forms Zn^{2+} it loses 2 electrons, both from the 4s sub-shell — so it keeps its full 3d sub-shell.

Warm-Up Questions

Q1 Name two transition elements in period 4 of the periodic table.

Q2 What's the definition of a transition element?

Q3 Name two period 4 elements that aren't transition elements.

Exam Questions

Q1 Which of the following shows an incorrect electron configuration for the transition element atom?

A vanadium: $1s^2\,2s^2\,2p^6\,3s^2\,3p^6\,3d^3\,4s^2$

B chromium: $1s^2\,2s^2\,2p^6\,3s^2\,3p^6\,3d^5\,4s^1$

C manganese: $1s^2\,2s^2\,2p^6\,3s^2\,3p^6\,3d^6\,4s^1$

D iron: $1s^2\,2s^2\,2p^6\,3s^2\,3p^6\,3d^6\,4s^2$ [1 mark]

Q2 Write electron configurations using sub-shell notation for the following atoms and ions.

a) Ni   b) Fe^{2+} c) Cu^{2+} d) Mn^{6+} [4 marks]

Q3 How many unpaired electrons are there in each of the following atoms and ions?

a) Co   b) Cr   c) Cr^{3+} d) V^{5+} [4 marks]

Q4 A student states that scandium and titanium are both period 4 transition elements.

Comment on the student's statement. [2 marks]

Scram Sc and Zn — we don't take kindly to your types round these parts...

As long as you're up to speed with your electron configuration rules, these pages are a bit of a breeze. Chromium and copper do throw a couple of spanners in the works (those banterous scamps), so make sure you don't get complacent.

Properties of Transition Elements

Thanks to their interesting electronic structures, the transition elements make pretty coloured solutions and get involved in all sorts of fancy reactions. Some of them make pretty good catalysts too. What a great bunch of lads.

Transition Elements have **Special Chemical Properties**

1) Transition elements can exist in **variable oxidation states**.
   For example, iron can exist in the **+2** oxidation state as **Fe^{2+}** ions and in the **+3** oxidation state as **Fe^{3+}** ions.

2) They also form **coloured ions**. E.g. Fe^{2+} ions are **pale green** and Fe^{3+} ions are **yellow**.

   Some common **coloured** ions and **oxidation states** are shown below. The colours refer to the **aqueous ions**.

Oxidation state	+7	+6	+5	+4	+3	+2
Titanium					Ti^{3+} (purple)	Ti^{2+} (violet)
Vanadium			VO_2^{+} (yellow)	VO^{2+} (blue)	V^{3+} (green)	V^{2+} (violet)
Chromium		$Cr_2O_7^{2-}$ (orange)			Cr^{3+} (violet)	
Manganese	MnO_4^{-} (purple)	MnO_4^{2-} (green)				Mn^{2+} (pale pink)
Iron					Fe^{3+} (yellow)	Fe^{2+} (pale green)
Cobalt						Co^{2+} (pink)
Nickel						Ni^{2+} (green)
Copper						Cu^{2+} (pale blue)

$Cr^{3+}_{(aq)}$ is technically violet, but in practice aqueous solutions that contain Cr^{3+} ions usually look green.

These elements show **variable** oxidation states because the **energy levels** of the 4s and the 3d sub-shells are **very close** to one another. So different numbers of electrons can be gained or lost using fairly **similar** amounts of energy.

Transition Elements and their Compounds make **Good Catalysts**

1) Transition elements and their compounds make **good catalysts** because they can **change oxidation states** by gaining or losing electrons within their **d orbitals**. This means they can **transfer electrons** to **speed up** reactions.

2) Transition **metals** are also good at **adsorbing** substances onto their **surfaces** to lower the activation energy of reactions.

   Here are a few examples of transition element catalysts:

   - **$CuSO_4$** (oxidation state of copper = +2) catalyses the reaction of **zinc** with **acids**. $\longrightarrow$ $Zn_{(s)} + H_2SO_{4(aq)} \xrightarrow{CuSO_{4(s)}} ZnSO_{4(aq)} + H_{2(g)}$

   - **MnO_2** (oxidation state of manganese = +4) catalyses the **decomposition of hydrogen peroxide**. $\Rightarrow$ $2H_2O_{2(aq)} \xrightarrow{MnO_{2(s)}} 2H_2O_{(l)} + O_{2(g)}$

   - **Iron** (oxidation state = 0) is the catalyst in the **Haber process** to produce **ammonia**. $\longrightarrow$ $N_{2(g)} + 3H_{2(g)} \xrightarrow{Fe_{(s)}} 2NH_{3(g)}$

3) Catalysts are good for **industry** and for the **environment** as they allow reactions to happen **faster** and at **lower temperatures** and pressures, **reducing energy usage**.

4) Using transition element catalysts can pose health **risks** as many of the metals and their compounds are **toxic**. For example, long term exposure to **copper** can damage the **liver** and **kidneys**, and exposure to **manganese** can cause **psychiatric problems**.

Properties of Transition Elements

Transition Element Hydroxides are Brightly Coloured Precipitates

1) When you mix an aqueous solution of **transition element ions** with aqueous **sodium hydroxide** (NaOH) or aqueous **ammonia** (NH_3) you get a **coloured hydroxide precipitate**.

2) In **aqueous solutions**, transition elements take the form $[M(H_2O)_6]^{n+}$. They can also be written as $M^{n+}_{(aq)}$, as long as the metal ion is **only** bonded to **water**. If it's bonded to anything else you need to write out the whole formula.

3) You need to know the **equations** for the following reactions, and the **colours** of the hydroxide precipitates:

copper(II): $[Cu(H_2O)_6]^{2+}_{(aq)} + 2OH^-_{(aq)} \rightarrow [Cu(OH)_2(H_2O)_4]_{(s)} + 2H_2O_{(l)}$

this can also be written as: $Cu^{2+}_{(aq)} + 2OH^-_{(aq)} \rightarrow Cu(OH)_{2(s)}$

$[Cu(H_2O)_6]^{2+}_{(aq)} + 2NH_{3(aq)} \rightarrow [Cu(OH)_2(H_2O)_4]_{(s)} + 2NH_4^+_{(aq)}$

In excess NH_3, $[Cu(OH)_2(H_2O)_4]_{(s)}$ reacts further to form $[Cu(NH_3)_4(H_2O)_2]^{2+}_{(aq)}$ which is a **dark blue** colour.

This goes from a pale blue solution to a blue precipitate.

iron(II): $[Fe(H_2O)_6]^{2+}_{(aq)} + 2OH^-_{(aq)} \rightarrow [Fe(OH)_2(H_2O)_4]_{(s)} + 2H_2O_{(l)}$

$[Fe(H_2O)_6]^{2+}_{(aq)} + 2NH_{3(aq)} \rightarrow [Fe(OH)_2(H_2O)_4]_{(s)} + 2NH_4^+_{(aq)}$

This goes from a pale green solution to a green precipitate, which darkens on standing.

iron(III): $[Fe(H_2O)_6]^{3+}_{(aq)} + 3OH^-_{(aq)} \rightarrow [Fe(OH)_3(H_2O)_3]_{(s)} + 3H_2O_{(l)}$

$[Fe(H_2O)_6]^{3+}_{(aq)} + 3NH_{3(aq)} \rightarrow [Fe(OH)_3(H_2O)_3]_{(s)} + 3NH_4^+_{(aq)}$

This goes from a yellow solution to an orange precipitate, which darkens on standing.

manganese(II): $[Mn(H_2O)_6]^{2+}_{(aq)} + 2OH^-_{(aq)} \rightarrow [Mn(OH)_2(H_2O)_4]_{(s)} + 2H_2O_{(l)}$

$[Mn(H_2O)_6]^{2+}_{(aq)} + 2NH_{3(aq)} \rightarrow [Mn(OH)_2(H_2O)_4]_{(s)} + 2NH_4^+_{(aq)}$

This goes from a pale pink solution to a pink/buff precipitate, which darkens on standing.

chromium(III): $[Cr(H_2O)_6]^{3+}_{(aq)} + 3OH^-_{(aq)} \rightarrow [Cr(OH)_3(H_2O)_3]_{(s)} + 3H_2O_{(l)}$

In excess NaOH, $[Cr(OH)_3(H_2O)_3]_{(s)}$ reacts further to form $Cr(OH)_6^{3-}_{(aq)}$ which is a **dark green** colour.

$[Cr(H_2O)_6]^{3+}_{(aq)} + 3NH_{3(aq)} \rightarrow [Cr(OH)_3(H_2O)_3]_{(s)} + 3NH_4^+_{(aq)}$

In excess NH_3, $[Cr(OH)_3(H_2O)_3]_{(s)}$ reacts further to form $[Cr(NH_3)_6]^{3+}_{(aq)}$ which is a **purple** colour.

This goes from a green solution to a grey-green precipitate.

If you know which **transition element** ion produces which **colour** precipitate, you can use these reactions to **identify** a transition element ion solution (see page 61).

Warm-Up Questions

Q1 State three chemical properties which are characteristic of transition elements.

Q2 Write an equation for the reaction of iron(II) ions with hydroxide ions. Describe the colour change that occurs during this reaction.

Exam Question

Q1 Identify the following transition elements from the descriptions below:

a) Forms a yellow aqueous solution when its ions have an oxidation state of +3. [1 mark]

b) A grey-green precipitate is formed when aqueous ammonia is added to an aqueous solution of its 3+ ions. [1 mark]

c) One of its oxides catalyses the decomposition of hydrogen peroxide. [1 mark]

Oi you — get off my property...

Learning the colour changes and equations on this page might seem like a pain in the neck but there's a decent chance you'll have to recall some of the stuff here in the exam. So it's worth spending a bit of time memorising them...

Ligands and Complex Ions

Transition elements are always forming complex ions. These aren't as complicated as they sound, though. Honest.

Complex Ions are Metal Ions Surrounded by Ligands

1) Transition elements can form **complex ions**. E.g, iron forms a **complex ion with water** — $[Fe(H_2O)_6]^{2+}$.

> A **complex ion** is a **metal ion** surrounded by **coordinately bonded ligands**.

2) A **coordinate bond** (or dative covalent bond) is a covalent bond in which **both electrons** in the shared pair come from the **same atom**.

3) So a **ligand** is an atom, ion or molecule that **donates a pair of electrons** to a central metal atom or ion.

4) The **coordination number** is the **number** of **coordinate bonds** that are formed with the central metal atom/ion.

5) In most of the complex ions that you need to know about, the coordination number will be **4** or **6**. If the ligands are **small**, like H_2O, CN^- or NH_3, **6** can fit around the central metal atom/ion. But if the ligands are **larger**, like Cl^-, **only 4** can fit around the central metal atom/ion.

6 coordinate bonds mean an octahedral shape

Here are a few examples:

> The different types of bond arrow show that the complex is 3-D. The wedge-shaped arrows represent bonds coming towards you and the dashed arrows represent bonds sticking out behind the molecule.

> The ligands don't always have to be the same.

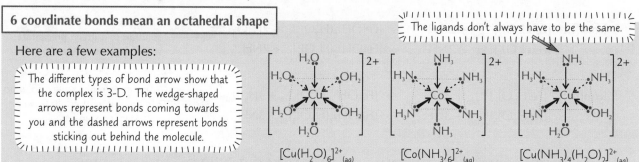

$[Cu(H_2O)_6]^{2+}_{(aq)}$ $[Co(NH_3)_6]^{2+}_{(aq)}$ $[Cu(NH_3)_4(H_2O)_2]^{2+}_{(aq)}$

4 coordinate bonds usually mean a tetrahedral shape...

E.g. $[CoCl_4]^{2-}$, which is blue, and $[CuCl_4]^{2-}$, which is yellow and shown here.

...but not always

In a **few** complexes, **4 coordinate bonds** form a **square planar** shape. E.g. $[NiCl_2(NH_3)_2]$ — see the next page.

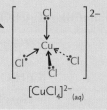

$[CuCl_4]^{2-}_{(aq)}$

A Ligand Must Have at Least One Lone Pair of Electrons

A ligand must have **at least one lone pair of electrons**, or it won't have anything to form a **coordinate bond** with.

- Ligands that have one lone pair available for bonding are called monodentate — e.g. $H_2\ddot{O}$, $\ddot{N}H_3$, $\ddot{C}l^-$, $\ddot{C}N^-$.
- Ligands with two lone pairs are called bidentate — e.g. ethane-1,2-diamine: $\ddot{N}H_2CH_2CH_2\ddot{N}H_2$ Bidentate ligands can each form two coordinate bonds with a metal ion.
- Ligands that form two or more coordinate bonds are called multidentate.

> You might see ethane-1,2-diamine abbreviated to "en".

Complex Ions Can Show Optical Isomerism

Optical isomerism is a type of stereoisomerism. With complex ions, it happens when an ion can exist in **two non-superimposable mirror images**.

This happens in octahedral complexes when **three bidentate ligands**, are attached to the central ion. E.g $[Ni(NH_2CH_2CH_2NH_2)_3]^{2+}$.

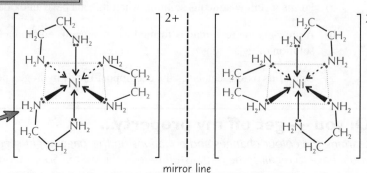

mirror line

Ligands and Complex Ions

Complex Ions Can Show Cis/Trans Isomerism

E/Z is another type of stereoisomerism. In stereoisomerism, the atoms are joined together in the same way, but they have different orientations in space.

Cis/trans isomerism is a special case of **E/Z isomerism** (you met this in Year 1). When there are only **two different groups** involved, you can use the cis/trans naming system. **Square planar** and **octahedral** complex ions that have at least **two pairs** of ligands show cis/trans isomerism. Cis isomers have the **same groups** on the **same side**, trans have the **same groups opposite** each other. Here are a couple of examples:

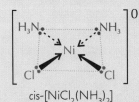 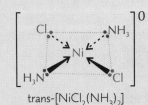 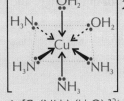 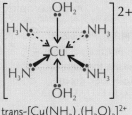

cis-[NiCl$_2$(NH$_3$)$_2$] trans-[NiCl$_2$(NH$_3$)$_2$] cis-[Cu(NH$_3$)$_4$(H$_2$O)$_2$]$^{2+}$ trans-[Cu(NH$_3$)$_4$(H$_2$O)$_2$]$^{2+}$

Cis-platin Can Bind to DNA in Cancer Cells

Cis-platin is a complex of platinum(II) with two chloride ions and two ammonia molecules in a square planar shape. It is used as an **anti-cancer** drug.

This is how it works:

1) The two **chloride ligands** are very easy to displace. So the cis-platin loses them, and bonds to two **nitrogen atoms** on the DNA molecule inside the **cancerous cell** instead.

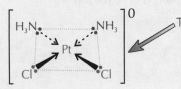

The two chloride ions are **next to each other**, so this complex is **cis-platin**. If they were **opposite** each other you would have **trans-platin**, which has different biological effects.

2) This **block** on its DNA prevents the cancerous cell from **reproducing** by division. The cell will **die**, since it is unable to repair the damage.

3) The downside is that cis-platin also prevents **normal cells** from reproducing, including blood, which can suppress the **immune system** and increase the risk of infection. Cis-platin may also cause **damage** to the **kidneys**.

Warm-Up Questions

Q1 Explain what the term 'coordination number' means in relation to a complex ion.
Q2 Draw the shape of the complex ion [Co(NH$_3$)$_6$]$^{2+}$. Name the shape.
Q3 What is meant by the term 'bidentate ligand'? Give an example of one.
Q4 Draw the cis and trans isomers of the complex [NiCl$_2$(NH$_3$)$_2$].

Exam Questions

Q1 Iron(III) can form the complex ion [Fe(C$_2$O$_4$)$_3$]$^{3-}$ with three ethanedioate ions. The ethanedioate ion is a bidentate ligand. Its structure is shown on the right.

a) Draw a diagram to show a possible structure of the [Fe(C$_2$O$_4$)$_3$]$^{3-}$ complex ion. [1 mark]

b) The [Fe(C$_2$O$_4$)$_3$]$^{3-}$ complex displays optical isomerism. Explain what optical isomerism is. [1 mark]

Q2 Cis-platin is a platinum-based complex ion that is used as an anti-cancer drug.

a) Draw the structure of cis-platin. [1 mark]

b) Explain how cis-platin works as a cancer treatment. [2 marks]

Put your hands up — we've got you surrounded...

You'll never get transition element ions floating around by themselves in a solution — they'll always be surrounded by other molecules. It's kind of like what'd happen if you put a dish of sweets in a room of eight (or eighteen) year-olds. When you're drawing complex ions, you should always include some wedge-shaped bonds to show that it's 3-D.

Substitution Reactions

There are more substitutions on this page than the number of elephants you can fit in a mini.

Ligands can Exchange Places with One Another

One ligand can be **swapped** for another ligand — this is **ligand substitution**. It usually causes a **colour change**.

1) If the ligands are of **similar size**, e.g. H_2O, NH_3 or CN^-, then the **coordination number** of the complex ion **doesn't change**, and neither does the **shape**.

> $[Cr(H_2O)_6]^{3+}$ is violet but, in practice, solutions containing this complex usually look green.

$$[Cr(H_2O)_6]^{3+}_{(aq)} + 6NH_{3(aq)} \rightleftharpoons [Cr(NH_3)_6]^{3+}_{(aq)} + 6H_2O_{(l)}$$

octahedral   octahedral
violet   purple

2) If the ligands are **different sizes**, e.g. H_2O and Cl^-, there's a **change of coordination number** and a **change of shape**.

$$[Cu(H_2O)_6]^{2+}_{(aq)} + 4Cl^-_{(aq)} \rightleftharpoons [CuCl_4]^{2-}_{(aq)} + 6H_2O_{(l)}$$

octahedral   tetrahedral
pale blue   yellow

3) Sometimes the substitution is only **partial**.

$$[Cu(H_2O)_6]^{2+}_{(aq)} + 4NH_{3(aq)} \rightleftharpoons [Cu(NH_3)_4(H_2O)_2]^{2+}_{(aq)} + 4H_2O_{(l)}$$

octahedral   octahedral
pale blue   deep blue

> As it's in solution and contains ligands that aren't water, you need to include all the water ligands when writing the formula of a complex like $[Cu(NH_3)_4(H_2O)_2]^{2+}$. But if you're writing out the formula of a precipitate, such as $[Cu(H_2O)_4(OH)_2]$, you can leave out the water ligands and just write $Cu(OH)_2$.

> This reaction only happens when you add an excess of ammonia — if you just add a bit, you get a blue precipitate of $[Cu(H_2O)_4(OH)_2]$ instead (see page 55).

You Might be Asked to Predict the Products of Unfamiliar Substitution Reactions

Example: A student has a solution of $[Co(H_2O)_6]^{2+}$ ions. She adds excess $KCN_{(aq)}$ to a sample of the solution. Write an equation for this ligand substitution reaction and predict the shape of the complex ion formed.

The CN^- ligand is of a similar size to the H_2O ligand so CN^- replaces H_2O with **no change** in coordination number or shape of the complex ion.

$$[Co(H_2O)_6]^{2+}_{(aq)} + 6CN^-_{(aq)} \rightleftharpoons [Co(CN)_6]^{4-}_{(aq)} + 6H_2O_{(l)}$$

The original complex is octahedral so $[Co(CN)_6]^{4-}$ is **octahedral**.
The H_2O ligand has **no charge** and CN^- has a 1– charge, so the **overall charge** of the complex **changes**.

Example continued: The student then adds excess $HCl_{(aq)}$ to a sample of the $[Co(H_2O)_6]^{2+}$ solution. Write an equation for this ligand substitution reaction and predict the shape of the complex ion formed.

The Cl^- ligand is larger than the H_2O ligand so when Cl^- replaces H_2O it results in a **change** in coordination number and shape of the complex ion.

$$[Co(H_2O)_6]^{2+}_{(aq)} + 4Cl^-_{(aq)} \rightleftharpoons [CoCl_4]^{2-}_{(aq)} + 6H_2O_{(l)}$$

$[Co(Cl)_4]^{2-}$ is **tetrahedral**.

Substitution Reactions

Haem is a multidentate ligand.

Fe²⁺ in **Haemoglobin** Allows **Oxygen** to be Carried in the Blood

1) Haemoglobin contains Fe^{2+} ions. The Fe^{2+} ions form **6 coordinate bonds**.
   Four of the **lone pairs** come from nitrogen atoms within a circular part of a molecule called 'haem'.
   A fifth lone pair comes from a nitrogen atom on a protein (globin).
   The last position is the important one — this has a **water ligand** attached to the **iron**.

2) In the lungs the oxygen concentration is high, so the water ligand is **substituted** for an
   oxygen molecule (O_2), forming **oxyhaemoglobin**. This is carried around the body and when it gets
   to a place where oxygen is needed, the oxygen molecule is exchanged for a water molecule again.

3) If **carbon monoxide** (CO) is inhaled, the **haemoglobin** swaps its **water** ligand for a
   carbon monoxide ligand, forming **carboxyhaemoglobin**. This is bad news because
   carbon monoxide is a **strong** ligand and **doesn't** readily exchange with oxygen or
   water ligands, meaning the haemoglobin **can't transport oxygen** any more.

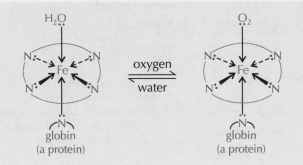

Gary thinks he's a haemoglobin molecule. This is him carrying 'O_2' around. He takes his job quite seriously. Just don't mention carbon monoxide to him.

Warm-Up Questions

Q1 Give an example of a ligand substitution reaction that involves a change of coordination number.

Q2 What is the coordination number of the Fe^{2+} ion in the haemoglobin complex?

PRACTICE QUESTIONS

Exam Questions

Q1 A sample of copper(II) sulfate powder is dissolved in pure water, giving a pale blue solution.

   a) Give the formula of the complex ion that is present in the pale blue solution.   [1 mark]

   b) An excess of ammonia is added to the solution.

      i) Write a balanced equation for the ligand substitution reaction that takes place.   [2 marks]

      ii) Give the colour of the new solution.   [1 mark]

      iii) What shape is the new complex ion formed?   [1 mark]

Q2 Haemoglobin is a complex ion that is found in the blood. It consists of an Fe^{2+} ion bonded to four
nitrogen atoms from a haem ring, one nitrogen atom from a protein called globin, and one water molecule.

   a) When blood passes through the lungs, a ligand substitution reaction occurs.

      i) Which of the ligands in the haemoglobin complex is replaced, and by what?   [1 mark]

      ii) Why is this ligand substitution reaction important?   [1 mark]

   b) Explain how inhaling carbon monoxide can damage the human body.   [2 marks]

There's no hard work for substitution — well, not that much anyway ...

Three things to do with this page — One: learn what a ligand substitution reaction is and how to predict their products.
Two: learn why haemoglobin's an important example of one. Three: fold it into a mad-looking origami chimp.

Reactions of Ions

Transition elements love to swap electrons around, so they're always getting involved in redox reactions.

Transition Elements Take Part in Redox Reactions

1) Transition elements can exist in many different **oxidation states** (see page 54).

2) They can **change** oxidation state by **gaining** or **losing electrons** in **redox reactions**.

3) For complex ions in solution, a change in oxidation state is often accompanied by a **colour change**.

Here are a few examples:

If it's been a while since you've looked at redox reactions, now might be a good time to flick back through your Year 1 notes and brush up a bit.

Interconversion between Fe^{2+} and Fe^{3+}

$Fe^{2+}_{(aq)}$ (pale green) is oxidised to $Fe^{3+}_{(aq)}$ (yellow) by **acidified potassium manganate(VII)** solution, $KMnO_{4(aq)}$.

Half equations:
$$MnO_4^- + 8H^+ + 5e^- \rightarrow Mn^{2+} + 4H_2O \qquad \text{Manganese is reduced.}$$
$$Fe^{2+} \rightarrow Fe^{3+} + e^- \qquad \text{Iron is oxidised.}$$

Full equation:
$$MnO_4^- + 8H^+ + 5Fe^{2+} \rightarrow Mn^{2+} + 4H_2O + 5Fe^{3+}$$

$Fe^{3+}_{(aq)}$ (yellow) is **reduced** to $Fe^{2+}_{(aq)}$ (pale green) by **iodide** ions, $I^-_{(aq)}$.

Half equations:
$$2I^- \rightarrow I_2 + 2e^- \qquad \text{Iodide is oxidised.}$$
$$Fe^{3+} + e^- \rightarrow Fe^{2+} \qquad \text{Iron is reduced.}$$

Full equation:
$$2I^- + 2Fe^{3+} \rightarrow 2Fe^{2+} + I_2$$

The top half-equation has 5 electrons and the bottom one just has 1. So, to get the balanced full equation, you need to multiply the top half-equation by 1 and the bottom half-equation by 5.

Interconversion between Cr^{3+} and $Cr_2O_7^{2-}$

$[Cr(OH)_6]^{3-}$ is formed by adding excess $NaOH_{(aq)}$ to $[Cr(H_2O)_6]^{3+}$.

The Cr^{3+} ion in $[Cr(OH)_6]^{3-}$ (dark green) is oxidised to the yellow chromate(VI) solution, $CrO_4^{2-}_{(aq)}$, by warming with **hydrogen peroxide** solution, $H_2O_{2(aq)}$, in **alkaline** conditions.

Half equations:
$$H_2O_2 + 2e^- \rightarrow 2OH^- \qquad \text{Oxygen is reduced.}$$
$$2Cr(OH)_6^{3-} + 4OH^- \rightarrow 2CrO_4^{2-} + 8H_2O + 6e^- \qquad \text{Chromium is oxidised.}$$

Full equation:
$$3H_2O_2 + 2Cr(OH)_6^{3-} \rightarrow 2OH^- + 2CrO_4^{2-} + 8H_2O$$

Adding dilute sulfuric acid to the chromate(VI) solution produces the orange dichromate(VI) solution, $Cr_2O_7^{2-}_{(aq)}$.

$$2CrO_4^{2-} + 2H^+ \rightarrow Cr_2O_7^{2-} + H_2O$$

$Cr_2O_7^{2-}_{(aq)}$ (orange) is reduced to $Cr^{3+}_{(aq)}$ (green) by **acidified zinc**.

Half equations:
$$Zn \rightarrow Zn^{2+} + 2e^- \qquad \text{Zinc is oxidised.}$$
$$Cr_2O_7^{2-} + 14H^+ + 6e^- \rightarrow 2Cr^{3+} + 7H_2O \qquad \text{Chromium is reduced.}$$

Full equation:
$$Cr_2O_7^{2-} + 14H^+ + 3Zn \rightarrow 2Cr^{3+} + 7H_2O + 3Zn^{2+}$$

You don't need to memorise the equations on this page — if you're asked to construct a full equation you'll be given the half-equations.

Reduction of Cu^{2+} and disproportionation of Cu^+

$Cu^{2+}_{(aq)}$ (pale blue) is reduced to the off-white precipitate copper(I) iodide by **iodide ions**, $I^-_{(aq)}$.

$$2Cu^{2+}_{(aq)} + 4I^-_{(aq)} \rightarrow 2CuI_{(s)} + I_{2(aq)}$$

$Cu^+_{(aq)}$ is unstable and **spontaneously disproportionates** (oxidises and reduces itself) to produce $Cu_{(s)}$ and $Cu^{2+}_{(aq)}$.

$$2Cu^+_{(aq)} \rightarrow Cu_{(s)} + Cu^{2+}_{(aq)}$$

Reactions of Ions

Transition Element Ions can be Identified Using Sodium Hydroxide

1) Many transition element ions form **coloured precipitates** when **aqueous sodium hydroxide** is added (see page 55).

2) This is a good way to **identify** which transition element ions might be in a **mixture**.

3) Add $NaOH_{(aq)}$ solution, dropwise from a pipette, to a test tube containing the unknown solution and **record the colour** of any precipitate formed.

4) The table on the right shows some of the ions that can be identified using this method.

ION	OBSERVATION
Cu^{2+}	blue precipitate
Fe^{2+}	green precipitate
Fe^{3+}	orange precipitate
Mn^{2+}	pink/buff precipitate
Cr^{3+}	grey-green precipitate

Some Ligands can be Identified Using Simple Tests

1) The tests for some common ligands can be carried out using simple apparatus in the lab.

2) The tests for these ions were covered in more detail in Year 1.

But here's a quick summary of the tests and results for some common ligands:

ION	TEST	OBSERVATION
CO_3^{2-} (carbonate)	Add nitric acid to the test compound. Bubble any gas given off through limewater.	Limewater turns from clear to cloudy if carbonate is present, due to $CO_{2(g)}$.
Cl^- (chloride)	add silver nitrate to test compound	white precipitate forms
Br^- (bromide)	add silver nitrate to test compound	cream precipitate forms
I^- (iodide)	add silver nitrate to test compound	pale yellow precipitate forms
SO_4^{2-} (sulfate)	add barium nitrate or barium chloride to test compound	white precipitate forms
NH_4^+ (ammonium)	Add cold NaOH to the test compound and warm. Hold damp, red litmus paper over the solution.	Red litmus paper turns blue in presence of ammonia.

You need to be careful what reagents you add so that you don't introduce ions that could interfere with any later tests. E.g. in the test for CO_3^{2-} ions you could use $HCl_{(aq)}$ instead of $HNO_{3(aq)}$, but doing this would add chloride ions to the sample, so you wouldn't be able to find out whether or not the initial solution contained chloride ions — you'd definitely get a white ppt. with silver nitrate.

Warm-Up Questions

Q1 Write a half equation showing $Cr_2O_7^{2-}$ being reduced to Cr^{3+}.

Q2 Describe a test to determine whether or not a mixture contains carbonate ions.

Exam Questions

Q1 Manganate(VII) ions, MnO_4^-, oxidise the oxygen in H_2O_2 to oxygen gas in a redox reaction. The half equations for this reaction are:

$$MnO_4^- + 8H^+ + 5e^- \rightarrow Mn^{2+} + 4H_2O \qquad \text{and} \qquad H_2O_2 \rightarrow O_2 + 2H^+ + 2e^-$$

Give the balanced full equation for the reaction. [1 mark]

Q2 A student is given a sample of an unknown solution containing a transition element complex. The student carries out two tests:

1. Acidified silver nitrate is added to the compound. A pale yellow precipitate forms.

2. Aqueous sodium hydroxide is added to a sample of the solution and a blue precipitate forms.

Give a likely formula of the unknown transition element complex. [1 mark]

If only all tests were as simple as adding a few drops of NaOH...

Make sure you know how to interpret unfamiliar redox reactions and reserve a little space in the old dome for those ion tests. Heaven forbid you should lose marks in the exam for confusing your white and pale yellow precipitates.

Extra Exam Practice

Hurrah — you've reached the end of <u>Module 5</u>. In your exams, the questions can bring together a range of topics from across the course. For now though, let's see how much of this module has sunk in...

- Have a look at this example of how to answer a tricky exam question.
- Then check how much you've understood from Module 5 by having a go at the questions on the next page.

There's a load of synoptic questions on p.110-116 that will test your knowledge of the whole course.

---

1 Propanoic acid (C_2H_5COOH) has a K_a of 1.26×10^{-5}.
A buffer solution was made by mixing 150 cm³ of a 0.250 mol dm⁻³ solution of propanoic acid with 50.0 cm³ of 0.0500 mol dm⁻³ potassium propanoate solution (C_2H_5COOK).

Calculate the pH of the resulting buffer solution.

(5 marks)

A big part of answering calculation questions like this is working out the steps you need to take to get the final answer. Writing down expressions you'll need first can help you stay on track with your working.

You want this formula to calculate the pH. But to use it, you'll need to find out the concentration of H^+ ions.

You can use this formula to find the concentration of H^+ ions, but you'll need the concentrations of the acid and the salt to use it — so start by finding these.

The HA and A⁻ shorthand is used to make your workings quicker later on.

If you leave 1.26×10^{-5} in standard form, your workings will be clearer.

1

buffer equilibrium: $C_2H_5COOH \rightleftharpoons C_2H_5COO^- + H^+$

$pH = -\log_{10}[H^+]$

$K_a = \dfrac{[H^+][A^-]}{[HA]}$

Volume of the buffer solution = 150 + 50.0 = 200 cm³ = **0.200 dm³**

Moles = concentration × volume

Moles of propanoic acid added = 0.250 × (150 ÷ 1000) = 0.0375 mol

Final concentration of propanoic acid, [HA] = 0.0375 ÷ 0.200
= **0.1875 mol dm⁻³**

Moles of potassium propanoate added = 0.0500 × (50.0 ÷ 1000)
= 0.00250 mol

Final concentration of potassium propanoate, [A⁻] = 0.00250 ÷ 0.200
= **0.0125 mol dm⁻³**

$[H^+] = K_a \times \dfrac{[HA]}{[A^-]}$

$[A^-] = [C_2H_5COO^-]_{equilibrium} = [C_2H_5COO^- K^+]_{start}$

$[HA] = [C_2H_5COOH]_{equilibrium} = [C_2H_5COOH]_{start}$

$[H^+] = \mathbf{1.26 \times 10^{-5}} \times \dfrac{0.1875}{0.0125} = 1.89 \times 10^{-4}$

$pH = -\log[H^+]$
$= -\log(1.89 \times 10^{-4})$
$= 3.723... = \mathbf{3.72 \ (3 \ s.f.)}$

To calculate the concentration of the acid and salt, you need to find the final volume of the solution. Don't forget to convert into dm³.

Two solutions have been added together so the final concentrations of the acid and salt will be lower than the values given in the question.

$C_2H_5COO^- K^+$ is fully dissociated and C_2H_5COOH is only slightly dissociated, so you can use this information to assume the values of [A⁻] and [HA].

You'd get 5 marks for the correct answer, but if your answer was wrong, you'd get some marks for showing your working. You'd get 1 mark for calculating the moles of propanoic acid, 1 mark for calculating the moles of potassium propanoate, 1 mark for rearranging the K_a equation and 1 mark for calculating [H⁺].

Check that the answer seems sensible — pH 3.72 is reasonable for a weak acid of this concentration.

Extra Exam Practice

2 A student carried out an investigation to find the activation energy for the reaction between acidified bromide and bromate(V) ions.

$$5Br^-_{(aq)} + BrO_3^-{}_{(aq)} + 6H^+_{(aq)} \rightarrow 3Br_{2(aq)} + 3H_2O_{(l)}$$

A fixed amount of indicator was added to the reaction mixture and the time taken for the indicator to decolourise due to the presence of bromine was measured.

(a) Give the two half-equations for the reaction between acidified bromide and bromate(V) ions.

(2 marks)

(b) The student weighed out 0.05 g of KBr for the reaction, using a balance that measures to the nearest 0.01 g. Explain why the student's choice of apparatus was not appropriate.

(1 mark)

(c) The student had previously carried out an investigation to find the rate equation for the reaction. Outline a method that the student could use to determine the activation energy of the reaction. Explain how the student would find E_a. Refer to the equation below:

$$\ln k = -\frac{E_a}{RT} + \ln A$$

(5 marks)

(d) At 25.0 °C, the student determined the rate constant was 353 mol^{-4} dm^{12} s^{-1}, and the pre-exponential factor was 3.07×10^{12} mol^{-4} dm^{12} s^{-1}. Use the equation in **(c)** to determine the activation energy of this reaction. Give your answer in kJ mol^{-1}. (R = 8.314 J K^{-1} mol^{-1})

(2 marks)

3 Hydrogen is reacted with carbon dioxide at 298 K to produce carbon monoxide and water.

$$H_{2(g)} + CO_{2(g)} \rightleftharpoons CO_{(g)} + H_2O_{(g)} \quad \Delta H^\ominus = +41.2 \text{ kJ mol}^{-1}$$

Entropy data for the species involved in the reaction are shown in **Table 1**.

Table 1

Compound	$H_{2(g)}$	$CO_{2(g)}$	$CO_{(g)}$	$H_2O_{(g)}$
$S^\ominus$ / J K^{-1} mol^{-1}	130.6	213.7	197.9	188.7

(a) Use the data provided to calculate the free energy change of the reaction at 298 K. Give your answer in kJ mol^{-1}.

(4 marks)

(b) 1.6 mol of H_2 and 1.6 mol of CO_2 are sealed in a vessel at a certain temperature and left to react. The equilibrium mixture contains 0.6 mol of CO. The total pressure of the mixture is 101 kPa. Calculate the gas equilibrium constant for this reaction and show that it does not require units.

(5 marks)

(c) If carbon monoxide is inhaled, a reaction can occur in the body that can be fatal. Describe the complex ion involved in this reaction and outline what happens to this complex when carbon monoxide is inhaled.

(3 marks)

(d) Hydrogen and carbon dioxide can also be reacted with one another at higher temperatures in the presence of a nickel catalyst to produce methane and water. Suggest one property of nickel that makes it a good catalyst.

(1 mark)

Benzene and Aromatic Compounds

We begin this section with a fantastical tale of the discovery of the magical rings of Benzene.
Our story opens in a shire where four hobbits are getting up to mischief... Actually no, that's something else.

Benzene has a **Ring Of Carbon Atoms**

Benzene has the formula C_6H_6. It has a cyclic structure, with its six carbon atoms joined together in a ring. There are two ways of representing it — the **Kekulé model** and the **delocalised model**.

The **Kekulé Model** Came First

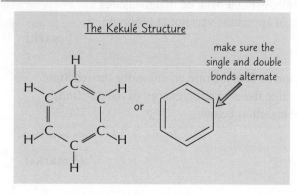

The Kekulé Structure

make sure the single and double bonds alternate

or

1) In 1865, the German chemist Friedrich August Kekulé proposed that **benzene** was made up of a **planar** (flat) **ring** of **carbon** atoms with **alternating single** and **double** bonds between them.

2) In Kekulé's model, each carbon atom is also bonded to **one hydrogen** atom.

3) He later adapted the model to say that the benzene molecule was constantly **flipping** between two forms (**isomers**) by switching over the double and single bonds.

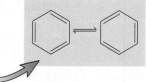

4) If the Kekulé model was correct, you'd expect there to always be three bonds with the length of a **C–C bond** (154 pm) and three bonds with the length of a **C=C bond** (134 pm).

5) However **X-ray diffraction studies** have shown that all the carbon-carbon bonds in benzene have the **same length** of 140 pm — i.e. they are **between** the length of a single bond and a double bond.

6) So the Kekulé structure **can't** be completely right. Chemists still **draw** the Kekulé structure of benzene though, as it's useful when drawing **reaction mechanisms**.

Apparently Kekulé imagined benzene as a snake catching its own tail. So here's a picture of a man charming some snakes.

The **Delocalised Model** Replaced Kekulé's Model

The bond-length observations are explained with the **delocalised** model.

1) The delocalised model says that the **p-orbitals** of all six carbon atoms **overlap** to create a **π-system**.

2) The π-system is made up of two **ring-shaped** clouds of electrons — one above and one below the plane of the six carbon atoms.

3) All the bonds in the ring are the **same length** because all the bonds are the same.

4) The electrons in the rings are said to be **delocalised** because they don't belong to a **specific** carbon atom. They are represented as a **circle** inside the ring of carbons rather than as double or single bonds.

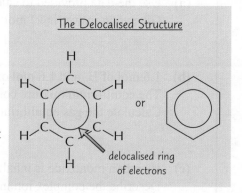

The Delocalised Structure

or

delocalised ring of electrons

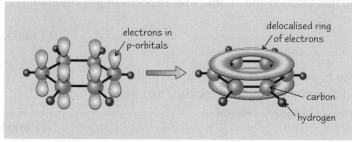

electrons in p-orbitals

delocalised ring of electrons

carbon

hydrogen

Benzene is a planar (flat) molecule — it's got a ring of carbon atoms with their hydrogens sticking out all on a flat plane.

Benzene and Aromatic Compounds

Enthalpy Changes of Hydrogenation Give More Evidence for Delocalisation

1) If you react an **alkene** with **hydrogen gas**, two atoms of hydrogen add across the **double bond**. This is called **hydrogenation**, and the enthalpy change of the reaction is the **enthalpy change of hydrogenation**.

2) Cyclohexene has **one** double bond. When it's hydrogenated, the enthalpy change is **–120 kJ mol⁻¹**. If benzene had three double bonds (as in the Kekulé structure), you'd expect the enthalpy of hydrogenation to be (3 × 120) = –360 kJ mol⁻¹.

3) But the **experimental** enthalpy of hydrogenation of benzene is **–208 kJ mol⁻¹** — far **less exothermic** than expected.

4) Energy is put in to break bonds and released when bonds are made. So **more energy** must have been put in to break the bonds in benzene than would be needed to break the bonds in the Kekulé structure.

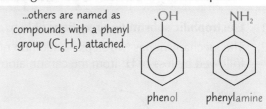

5) This difference indicates that benzene is **more stable** than the Kekulé structure would be. Benzene's **resistance to reaction** gives more evidence for it being **more stable** than the Kekulé structure suggests (see page 66). The stability is thought to be due to the **delocalised ring of electrons**.

Aromatic Compounds are Derived from Benzene

1) Compounds containing a **benzene ring** are called **arenes** or 'aromatic compounds'. There are **two** ways of **naming** arenes, but there's no easy rule to know which name to give them. Here are some examples:

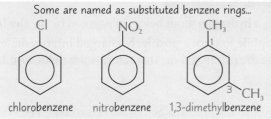

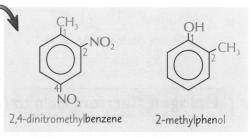

2) If there's **more than one** functional group attached to the benzene ring you have to **number** the **carbons** to show where the groups are.

- If all the functional groups are the **same**, pick any group to start from and count round the way that gives the **smallest** numbers.

- If the functional groups are **different**, start from whichever functional group gives the molecule its **suffix** (e.g. the –OH group for a phenol) and continue counting round the way that gives the **smallest** numbers.

Warm-Up Questions

Q1 Draw the Kekulé and delocalised models of benzene.

Q2 What are the two ways of naming aromatic compounds? Give an example of each.

Exam Question

Q1 a) In 1865, Friedrich Kekulé proposed the structure for benzene shown on the right. What does this model imply about the C–C bond lengths in the molecule? **[1 mark]**

C–C longer than C=C

b) How was it shown that the bond lengths suggested by the Kekulé structure are incorrect? **[1 mark]**

X-ray diffraction studies = all c-c same length

c) Describe another piece of evidence that shows that the Kekulé structure is incorrect. **[2 marks]**

∆H hydrogenation for benzene is less exothermic than expected

---

Everyone needs a bit of stability in their life... *benzene is more stable*

The structure of benzene is bizarre — even top scientists struggled to find out what its molecular structure looked like. Make sure you can draw all the different representations of benzene given on this page, including the ones showing the Cs and Hs. Yes, and don't forget there's a hydrogen at every point on the ring — it's easy to forget they're there.

Electrophilic Substitution

Benzene is an alkene but it often doesn't behave like one — whenever this is the case, you can pretty much guarantee that our kooky friend Mr Delocalised Electron Ring is up to his old tricks again...

Alkenes usually like Addition Reactions, but Not Benzene

1) **Alkenes** react easily with **bromine** water at room temperature. This **decolourises** the orange bromine water. It's an **electrophilic addition reaction** — the bromine atoms are added across the double bond of the alkene. For example:

$$H_2C=CH_2 \text{ (ethene)} + Br-Br \text{ (bromine)} \longrightarrow H-\underset{\underset{H}{|}}{\overset{\overset{Br}{|}}{C}}-\underset{\underset{H}{|}}{\overset{\overset{Br}{|}}{C}}-H \text{ (1,2-dibromoethane)}$$

Remember — electrophiles are positively charged ions, or polar molecules, that are attracted to areas of negative charge.

2) If the Kekulé structure (see page 64) were correct, you'd expect a **similar reaction** between benzene and bromine. In fact, to make it happen you need **hot benzene** and **ultraviolet light** — and it's still a real **struggle**.

3) This difference between benzene and other alkenes is explained by the π-system in benzene — the **delocalised electron rings** above and below the plane of carbon atoms. They **spread out** the negative charge and make the benzene ring very **stable**. So benzene is **unwilling** to undergo **addition reactions** which would destroy the stable ring. The **reluctance** of benzene to undergo addition reactions is **more evidence** supporting the **delocalised model**.

4) In alkenes, the π-**bond** in the C=C double bond is an area of localised **high electron density** which strongly attracts **electrophiles**. In benzene, this attraction is reduced due to the negative charge being spread out.

5) So benzene prefers to react by **electrophilic substitution**.

Arenes Undergo Electrophilic Substitution Reactions

1) **Electrophilic substitution reactions** of benzene result in a **hydrogen** atom being substituted by an **electrophile**.

2) The mechanism has two steps — addition of the **electrophile** to form a **positively charged intermediate**, followed by loss of **H⁺** from the carbon atom attached to the electrophile. This **reforms** the delocalised ring.

Benzene reacts with the electrophile, breaking the delocalised ring.   An unstable intermediate forms.   H⁺ is lost, and the delocalised ring is reformed.

E is any electrophile.

Halogen Carriers Help to Make Good Electrophiles

An electrophile has to have a pretty strong **positive charge** to be able to attack the stable benzene ring. Most compounds **aren't polarised enough** — but some can be made into **stronger electrophiles** using a catalyst called a **halogen carrier**.

A halogen carrier accepts a **lone pair of electrons** from a **halogen** atom on an **electrophile**. As the lone pair of electrons is pulled away, the **polarisation** in the molecule **increases** and sometimes a **carbocation** forms. This makes the electrophile **stronger**. Halogen carriers include **aluminium halides**, **iron halides** and **iron**.

$$\overset{\delta+}{R}-\overset{\delta-}{Cl:}\dashrightarrow AlCl_3 \longrightarrow R^+ \ AlCl_4^-$$
haloalkane   halogen carrier   carbocation

Although R⁺ gets shown as a free ion, it probably remains associated with AlCl₄⁻ — this doesn't affect how R⁺ reacts though.

Halogen Carriers Help Halogens Substitute into the Benzene Ring

1) Benzene will react with **halogens** (e.g. Br₂) in the presence of an **aluminium chloride catalyst**, AlCl₃.

2) The catalyst **polarises** the halogen, allowing one of the halogen atoms to act as an **electrophile**.

3) During the reaction, a halogen atom is **substituted** in place of a H atom — this is called **halogenation**.

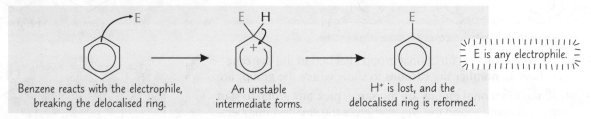

benzene → + AlCl₃Br⁻ → bromobenzene + HBr + AlCl₃

Electrophilic Substitution

Friedel-Crafts Reactions Form C–C Bonds

Friedel-Crafts reactions are really useful for forming C–C bonds in organic synthesis. They are carried out by refluxing benzene with a halogen carrier and either a **haloalkane** or an **acyl chloride**. There are two types:

1) **Friedel-Crafts alkylation** puts **any alkyl group** onto a benzene ring using a **haloalkane** and a halogen carrier. The general reaction is:

$$C_6H_6 + R\text{-}X \xrightarrow[\text{Reflux}]{AlCl_3} C_6H_5R + HX$$

Example: To make methylbenzene:

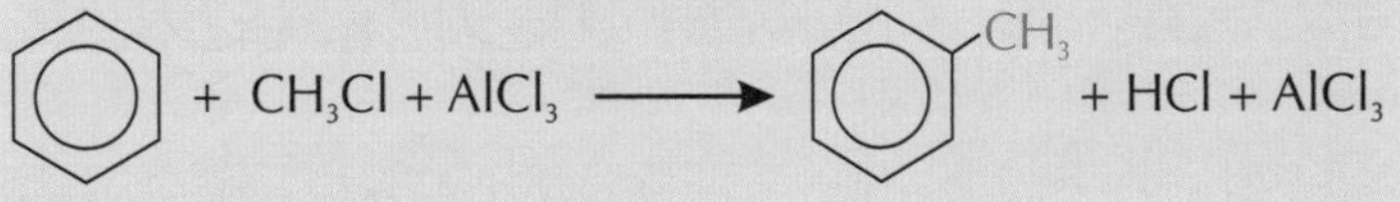

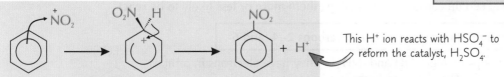

2) **Friedel-Crafts acylation** substitutes an **acyl group** for an H atom on benzene. You have to reflux benzene with an **acyl chloride** instead of a chloroalkane. This produces **phenylketones** (unless R = H, in which case an aldehyde called benzenecarbaldehyde, or benzaldehyde, is formed). The general reaction is:

Acyl groups contain a C=O double bond.

$$C_6H_6 + RCOCl \xrightarrow[\text{Reflux}]{AlCl_3} C_6H_5COR + HCl$$

Example: To make phenylethanone:

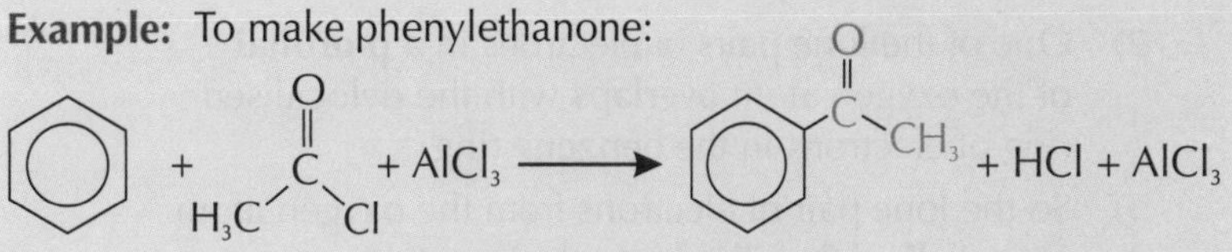

Nitric Acid Acts as an Electrophile with a Sulfuric Acid Catalyst

When you warm **benzene** with **concentrated nitric acid** and **concentrated sulfuric acid**, you get nitrobenzene.
Sulfuric acid is a **catalyst** — it helps make the nitronium ion, NO_2^+, which is the **electrophile**. It's then regenerated at the end of the reaction mechanism.

$$HNO_3 + H_2SO_4 \rightarrow H_2NO_3^+ + HSO_4^-$$
$$H_2NO_3^+ \rightarrow NO_2^+ + H_2O$$

This H^+ ion reacts with HSO_4^- to reform the catalyst, H_2SO_4.

If you only want one NO_2 group added (**mononitration**), you need to keep the temperature **below 55 °C**. Above this temperature you'll get lots of substitutions.

Warm-Up Questions

Q1 What type of reaction does benzene tend to undergo?
Q2 Name two substances that are used as halogen carriers in substitution reactions of benzene.
Q3 Describe two ways of making C–C bonds with benzene.
Q4 Which two acids are used in the production of nitrobenzene?

Exam Question

Q1 a) A student takes two test tubes, each containing bromine water. He adds cyclohexene to one of the test tubes and benzene to the other. Describe and explain what the student will see. [3 marks]

b) To make bromine and benzene react, they are heated together with iron(III) chloride.

i) What is the function of the iron(III) chloride? [1 mark]

ii) Draw a mechanism for this reaction. [3 marks]

Shhhh... Don't disturb The Ring...

Arenes really like Mr Delocalised Electron Ring and they won't give him up for nobody, at least not without a fight. They'd much rather get tangled up in an electrophilic substitution — anything not to bother The Ring.

Substituted Benzene Rings

On its own benzene is quite reluctant to react — you have to use catalysts and often high temperatures for anything to happen. But substituted benzene rings have other functional groups on them, and this changes their reactivity.

Phenols Have Benzene Rings with **–OH** Groups Attached

Phenol has the formula **C₆H₅OH**.
Other phenols have various groups attached to the benzene ring:

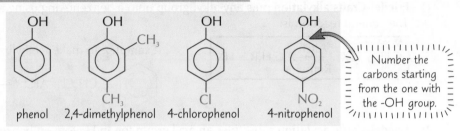

phenol   2,4-dimethylphenol   4-chlorophenol   4-nitrophenol

> Number the carbons starting from the one with the -OH group.

Phenol is More **Reactive** than **Benzene**

1) The -OH group means that phenol is more likely to undergo **electrophilic substitution** than benzene.

2) One of the lone pairs of electrons in a **p-orbital** of the oxygen atom **overlaps** with the delocalised ring of electrons in the benzene ring.

3) So the lone pair of electrons from the oxygen atom is **partially delocalised** into the π-system.

4) This increases the **electron density** of the ring, making it more likely to be attacked by electrophiles.

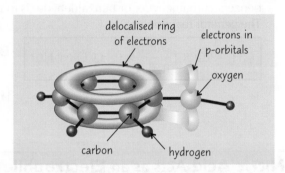

delocalised ring of electrons — electrons in p-orbitals — oxygen — carbon — hydrogen

Functional Groups Can Affect the **Position** of **Substitution**

1) In an unsubstituted **benzene** ring, all the carbon atoms are the **same** so electrophiles can react with **any** of them.

2) If you have a **substituted** benzene ring, such as **phenol**, the functional group can change the **electron density** at certain carbon atoms, making them **more** or **less** likely to be **react**.

Electron donating groups direct substitution to carbons 2-,4- and 6-.

Electron-donating groups include -OH and -NH₂ — they have electrons in orbitals that **overlap** with the delocalised ring and increase its **electron density**.

In particular, they increase the electron density at carbons **2-**, **4-** and **6-**, so electrophiles are **most likely** to react at these positions.

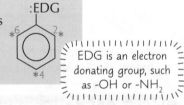

> EDG is an electron donating group, such as -OH or -NH₂

Electron withdrawing groups direct substitution to carbons 3- and 5-.

-NO₂ is an **electron withdrawing group**. It doesn't have any orbitals that can overlap with the delocalised ring and it's **electronegative**, so it **withdraws** electron density from the ring.

In particular, it withdraws electron density at carbons 2-,4- and 6-, so electrophiles are **unlikely** to react at these positions. This has the effect of **directing** electrophilic substitution to the **3-** and **5-** positions.

3) So you can **predict** the products of electrophilic substitution reactions.

Example: Predict the product of the following reaction:

$$NO_2$$
+ AlCl₃ + CH₃CH₂Cl ⟶ ?

> The benzene ring's only substituted once, so it doesn't matter whether you number the carbons clockwise or anticlockwise. This means the 3- and the 5- positions are the same.

-NO₂ is **electron withdrawing**, so directs electrophilic substitution to **carbon 3**.

The product is **3-ethylnitrobenzene**:

Angela and Sue weren't entirely sure of their direction

Substituted Benzene Rings

Phenol Reacts with **Bromine Water**

1) Phenol is **more reactive** than **benzene**, so if you shake phenol with orange bromine water, it will **react**, **decolourising** it.

2) The -OH group is **electron donating** so directs substitution to carbons 2-, 4- and 6-. The product is called **2,4,6-tribromophenol** — it's insoluble in water and **precipitates** out of the mixture. It smells of antiseptic.

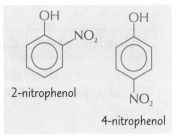

2,4,6-tribromophenol

Phenol Can be **Nitrated** Using **Dilute Nitric Acid**

1) Phenol reacts with **dilute nitric acid** to give two **isomers** of **nitrophenol**, and water.

2) Nitrating phenol is much **easier** than nitrating benzene — that requires **concentrated** nitric acid and a concentrated sulfuric acid **catalyst**.

3) The difference is due to the **activating** effect of the **OH group** again — and that's also why you're most likely to get NO_2 groups at positions 2 and 4 on the carbon ring.

2-nitrophenol

4-nitrophenol

Phenol reacts with **Bases** and **Sodium** to form **Salts**

Phenol is weakly acidic, so will undergo typical acid-base reactions.

1) Phenol reacts with **sodium hydroxide solution** at room temperature in a **neutralisation reaction** to form **sodium phenoxide** and **water**.

2) It **doesn't react** with **sodium carbonate** solution though — phenol is not a **strong enough** acid.

phenol   sodium phenoxide

Warm-Up Questions

Q1 What is the formula and structure of phenol?

Q2 Which of the carbon atoms in phenol are electrophiles most likely to react with?

Q3 Write a balanced equation for the reaction between phenol and bromine (Br_2).

Q4 Write a balanced equation for the reaction between phenol and sodium hydroxide solution.

PRACTICE QUESTIONS

Exam Questions

Q1 a) Draw the structure of 2-methylphenol. [1 mark]

   b) When 2-methylphenol reacts with dilute nitric acid, two isomers are formed. Draw both these isomers and give their systematic names. [2 marks]

Q2 a) Bromine water can be used to distinguish between benzene and phenol. Describe what you would observe in each case and name any products formed. [2 marks]

   b) Explain why phenol reacts differently from benzene. [2 marks]

   c) Name the type of reaction that occurs between phenol and bromine. [1 mark]

Phenol Destination 4 — more compounds, more equations, more horror...

The reactions of phenol are all pretty similar to benzene — phenol's just more reactive so the reaction conditions can be a bit milder. Of course there's the added confusion of predicting which carbon the electrophilic substitution will happen at, so have another look at that bit and make sure you've got it completely under your belt.

Module 6: Section 1 — Aromatic Compounds and Carbonyls

Aldehydes and Ketones

Aldehydes and ketones are both carbonyl compounds. You met them in Year 1 — they're made from oxidising alcohols. Well now you get to learn a whole load more reactions and mechanisms. I bet you can't wait to get started...

Aldehydes and Ketones Contain a Carbonyl Group

1) Aldehydes and ketones are **carbonyl compounds** — they contain the **carbonyl** functional group, **C=O**.

2) **Aldehydes** have their carbonyl group at the **end** of the carbon chain. Their names end in **–al**.

3) **Ketones** have their carbonyl group in the **middle** of the carbon chain. Their names end in **–one**, and often have a number to show which **carbon** the carbonyl group is on.

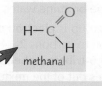
methanal

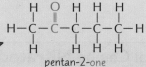
pentan-2-one

Aldehydes and Carboxylic Acids are Made by Oxidising Primary Alcohols

You can use **acidified dichromate(VI) ions** ($Cr_2O_7^{2-}$) to **mildly** oxidise alcohols.
Acidified **potassium dichromate(VI)** ($K_2Cr_2O_7$ / H_2SO_4) is often used.

$$R-CH_2-OH + [O] \longrightarrow R-C\overset{O}{\underset{H}{\big<}} + [O] \xrightarrow{\text{reflux}} R-C\overset{O}{\underset{OH}{\big<}}$$

$+ H_2O$

primary alcohol   aldehyde   carboxylic acid

[O] = oxidising agent

The orange dichromate(VI) ion is reduced to the green chromium(III) ion, Cr^{3+}.

You can control how **far** the alcohol is oxidised by controlling the **reaction conditions**:

- If you gently heat a primary alcohol with acidified potassium dichromate(VI) in a **distillation apparatus**, then you will form the **aldehyde**.
- If you **reflux** a primary alcohol (or an aldehyde) with acidified potassium dichromate(VI), then you'll oxidise the aldehyde further and form a **carboxylic acid**.

Ketones are made by oxidising secondary alcohols with acidified potassium dichromate(VI). They can't be oxidised any further.

You Can Reduce Aldehydes and Ketones Back to Alcohols

Using a **reducing agent** [H] you can:

1) reduce an aldehyde to a primary alcohol.

$$R-C\overset{O}{\underset{H}{\big<}} + 2[H] \longrightarrow R-CH_2-OH$$

2) reduce a ketone to a secondary alcohol.

$$R-C\overset{O}{\underset{R'}{\big<}} + 2[H] \longrightarrow R-\overset{H}{\underset{R'}{\overset{|}{\underset{|}{C}}}}-OH$$

The reducing agent is normally **NaBH$_4$** (sodium tetrahydriborate(III) or sodium borohydride) dissolved in water with methanol.

It's a **nucleophilic addition reaction** — a **nucleophile** attacks the molecule, and an extra group is **added** to it.

The reducing agent, e.g. NaBH$_4$, supplies **hydride ions**, H$^-$. H$^-$ has a **lone pair** of electrons, so it's a **nucleophile** and can attack the δ+ carbon on the **carbonyl group** of an aldehyde or ketone:

Addition of water then gives...

Nucleophiles are electron pair donors. They react with atoms that don't have enough electrons

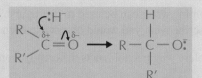

Aldehydes and Ketones

Hydrogen Cyanide will React with Carbonyls by Nucleophilic Addition

Hydrogen cyanide reacts with carbonyl compounds to produce **hydroxynitriles** (molecules with a CN and OH group). It's a **nucleophilic addition reaction**.

Hydrogen cyanide is a **weak acid** — it partially dissociates in water to form H^+ and CN^- ions. $HCN \rightleftharpoons H^+ + CN^-$

1) The CN^- ion **attacks** the slightly positive carbon atom and **donates** a pair of electrons to it. Both electrons from the double bond transfer to the oxygen.

2) H^+ (from hydrogen cyanide or water) bonds to the oxygen to form the **hydroxyl group** (OH).

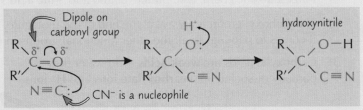

Hydrogen cyanide is a **highly toxic** gas. When this reaction is done in the laboratory, a solution of **acidified sodium cyanide** is used instead, to reduce the risk. Even so, the reaction should be done in a **fume cupboard**.

2,4-dinitrophenylhydrazine Tests for Aldehydes and Ketones

1) When **2,4-dinitrophenylhydrazine** (2,4-DNP or Brady's reagent) is dissolved in methanol and concentrated sulfuric acid it will react with **carbonyl groups** to form a **bright orange precipitate**. This only happens with **C=O groups**, not with ones like COOH, so it only tests for **aldehydes** and **ketones**.

2) The orange precipitate is a **derivative** of the carbonyl compound. Each different carbonyl compound produces a crystalline derivative with a **different melting point**. So if you measure the melting point of the crystals and compare it against the **known** melting points of the derivatives, you can **identify** the carbonyl compound.

Use Tollens' Reagent to Test for an Aldehyde

This test lets you distinguish between an aldehyde and a ketone. It uses the fact that an **aldehyde** can be **easily oxidised** to a carboxylic acid, but a ketone can't.

- Tollens' reagent is a colourless solution of silver nitrate dissolved in aqueous ammonia.
- When heated together in a test tube, the aldehyde is oxidised and the silver ions in the Tollens' reagent are reduced to silver causing a silver mirror to form.

$$Ag(NH_3)_2^+{}_{(aq)} + e^- \rightarrow Ag_{(s)} + 2NH_{3(aq)}$$
colourless → silver

Tollens' reagent can also be called ammoniacal silver nitrate.

- The test tube should be heated in a beaker of hot water, rather than directly over a flame.

Warm-Up Questions

Q1 Give the reagents and conditions for oxidising an aldehyde to a carboxylic acid.
Q2 Draw the reaction mechanism for reducing a ketone to an alcohol.
Q3 Describe how you could determine the identity of an aldehyde or ketone using 2,4-dinitrophenylhydrazine.

Exam Question

Q1 Compounds X and Y are unknown compounds both with the molecular formula C_3H_6O.
When compounds X and Y are reacted separately with 2,4-dinitrophenylhydrazine, both form an orange precipitate.
When heated gently with Tollens' reagent, compound Y forms a silver mirror. No change is observed for compound X.

a) Identify, with reasoning, compounds X and Y. [3 marks]

b) Draw a mechanism to show how compound X reacts with HCN. [2 marks]

c) Which of the compounds would oxidise to form a carboxylic acid? [1 mark]

Silver mirror, silver mirror on the wall, who's the fairest carbonyl of them all...

You've got to be a pro at recognising different functional groups from a mile off. Make sure you know how aldehydes differ from ketones and what happens if you try to oxidise them. And how to reduce them. And don't forget the details of those pesky tests. Phew, it's hard work some of this chemistry. Don't worry, it'll only make you stronger.

Carboxylic Acids and Acyl Chlorides

Carboxylic acids — the clue's in the name. They're weak acids, so expect some acid-base reactions to come your way...

Carboxylic Acids contain -COOH

1) **Carboxylic acids** contain the **carboxyl** functional group **-COOH**. To name them, you find and name the longest alkane chain, take off the 'e' and add **'–oic acid'**.

ethanoic acid   4-hydroxy-2-methylbutanoic acid

2) The carboxyl group is always at the **end** of the molecule. It's more important than other functional groups (when it comes to naming) so all the other functional groups in the molecule are numbered starting from this carbon.

3) Carboxylic acids are **weak acids** — in water they partially dissociate into **carboxylate ions** and **H⁺ ions**.

This equilibrium lies to the left because most of the molecules don't dissociate.

carboxylic acid   carboxylate ion

Carboxylic Acids Form Hydrogen Bonds

Carboxylic acids are polar molecules, since electrons are drawn towards the O atoms. **Hydrogen bonds** are able to form between the **highly polarised** $H^{\delta+}$ atom and $O^{\delta-}$ atoms on other molecules. This makes small carboxylic acids **very soluble** in water — they form hydrogen bonds with the water molecules.

···· Hydrogen bond

Carboxylic Acids React with Metals, Carbonates and Bases

1) Carboxylic acids react with the more **reactive metals** in a **redox reaction** to form a **salt** and **hydrogen gas**.

$$2CH_3COOH_{(aq)} + Mg_{(s)} \rightarrow (CH_3COO)_2Mg_{(aq)} + H_{2(g)}$$
ethanoic acid   magnesium ethanoate

Salts of carboxylic acids are called carboxylates and their names end with –oate.

2) Carboxylic acids react with **carbonates** CO_3^{2-} to form a **salt**, **carbon dioxide** and **water**.

$$2CH_3COOH_{(aq)} + Na_2CO_{3(s)} \rightarrow 2CH_3COONa_{(aq)} + H_2O_{(l)} + CO_{2(g)}$$
ethanoic acid   sodium ethanoate

In reactions 1 and 2, the gas fizzes out of the solution.

3) Carboxylic acids are neutralised by other **bases** to form **salts** and **water**.

With **alkalis**: $CH_3COOH_{(aq)} + NaOH_{(aq)} \rightarrow CH_3COONa_{(aq)} + H_2O_{(l)}$

With **metal oxides**: $2CH_3COOH_{(aq)} + MgO_{(s)} \rightarrow (CH_3COO)_2Mg_{(aq)} + H_2O_{(l)}$

Acyl Chlorides are Formed by Reacting Carboxylic Acids with SOCl₂

Acyl (or **acid**) **chlorides** have the functional group **-COCl** — their general formula is $C_nH_{2n-1}OCl$.

All their names end in '**–oyl chloride**', e.g.:

The carbon atoms are numbered from the end with the acyl functional group. (This is the same as with carboxylic acids.)

ethanoyl chloride   4-hydroxy-2,3-dimethylpentanoyl chloride

They're made by reacting **carboxylic acids** with **SOCl₂** (thionyl chloride) — the **-OH** group in the acid is replaced by **-Cl**. For example:

propanoic acid   + SOCl₂ ⟶   propanoyl chloride   + SO₂ + HCl

Carboxylic Acids and Acyl Chlorides

Acyl Chlorides Easily **Lose** Their **Chlorine**

This irreversible reaction is a much easier, faster way to produce an ester than reacting an alcohol with a carboxylic acid (see page 74).

Acyl chlorides react with...

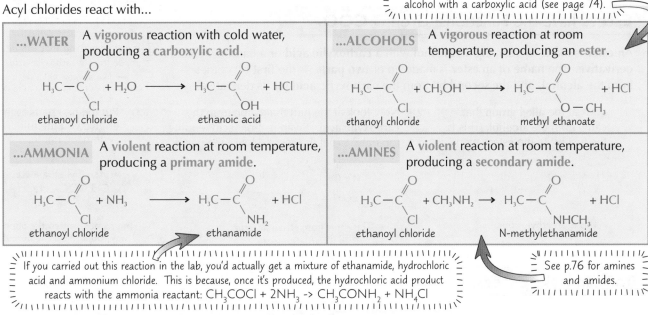

...WATER A **vigorous** reaction with cold water, producing a **carboxylic acid**.

H_3C-C (O, Cl) $+ H_2O \longrightarrow H_3C-C$ (O, OH) $+ HCl$

ethanoyl chloride — ethanoic acid

...ALCOHOLS A **vigorous** reaction at room temperature, producing an **ester**.

H_3C-C (O, Cl) $+ CH_3OH \longrightarrow H_3C-C$ (O, $O-CH_3$) $+ HCl$

ethanoyl chloride — methyl ethanoate

...AMMONIA A **violent** reaction at room temperature, producing a **primary amide**.

H_3C-C (O, Cl) $+ NH_3 \longrightarrow H_3C-C$ (O, NH_2) $+ HCl$

ethanoyl chloride — ethanamide

...AMINES A **violent** reaction at room temperature, producing a **secondary amide**.

H_3C-C (O, Cl) $+ CH_3NH_2 \rightarrow H_3C-C$ (O, $NHCH_3$) $+ HCl$

ethanoyl chloride — N-methylethanamide

If you carried out this reaction in the lab, you'd actually get a mixture of ethanamide, hydrochloric acid and ammonium chloride. This is because, once it's produced, the hydrochloric acid product reacts with the ammonia reactant: $CH_3COCl + 2NH_3 \rightarrow CH_3CONH_2 + NH_4Cl$

See p.76 for amines and amides.

Each time, **Cl** is **substituted** by an oxygen or nitrogen group and **hydrogen chloride** fumes are given off — they're **nucleophilic addition-elimination** reactions.

Acyl Chlorides React with **Phenol** to Form **Esters**

You can normally make **esters** by reacting an **alcohol** with a **carboxylic acid**. Phenols react **very** slowly with carboxylic acids, so it's faster to use an **acyl chloride**, such as ethanoyl chloride.

Ethanoyl chloride reacts slowly with phenol at room temperature, producing the ester **phenyl ethanoate** and **hydrogen chloride** gas.

H_3C-C (O, Cl) $+ HO-$⬡ $\rightleftharpoons H_3C-C$ (O, O-⬡) $+ HCl$

ethanoyl chloride — phenyl ethanoate

Warm-Up Questions

Q1 Draw an equilibrium to show the dissociation of a carboxylic acid in water.
Q2 Explain why small carboxylic acids are soluble in water.

PRACTICE QUESTIONS

Exam Question

Q1 The reaction scheme below shows some of the reactions of an acyl chloride and its derivatives.

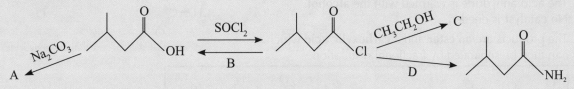

a) What is the systematic name for organic product A? [1 mark]

b) Give the reagent(s) in reaction B. [1 mark]

c) Give the skeletal formula of organic product C. [1 mark]

d) Give the reagent(s) in reaction D. [1 mark]

Acyl Chlorides — ace by name, ace by nature....

Acyl chlorides are really reactive — they'll react with most nucleophiles and the chlorine atom gets replaced. This is really useful in organic synthesis. So make sure you've got all those reactions learnt. You should know them so well that you're able to recite them backwards while standing on your head and trying to solve a 1000 piece jigsaw puzzle.

Esters

Esther's a sweet girl. Her favourite colour's green and she's got a weakness for hob nobs. That's all you need to know. Esters, however, are yet another type of organic compound. You need to know how to make 'em and how to break 'em.

Esters have the Functional Group –COO–

An **ester** is made by reacting an **alcohol** with a **carboxylic acid** or a carboxylic acid **derivative**. The **name** of an **ester** is made up of **two parts** — the **first** bit comes from the **alcohol**, and the **second** bit from the carboxylic acid (or its derivative).

> A carboxylic acid derivative is just something that can be made from a carboxylic acid — like an acyl chloride.

1) Look at the **alkyl group** that came from the **alcohol**. This is the first bit of the ester's name.

This is an **ethyl** group.

2) Now look at the part that came from the carboxylic acid. Swap its '-oic acid' ending for 'oate' to get the second bit of the name.

This came from ethanoic acid, so it's an **ethanoate**.

3) Put the two parts together to give you the full systematic name.

It's **ethyl** ethanoate
$CH_3COOCH_2CH_3$

The name's written the opposite way round from the formula.

You can make Esters...

1) From Alcohols and Carboxylic Acids

1) If you heat a **carboxylic acid** with an **alcohol** in the presence of an **acid catalyst**, you get an ester.

2) Concentrated sulfuric acid is usually used as the acid catalyst. It's called an **esterification** reaction.

$$R-C(=O)(O-H) \;+\; R-O-H \;\rightleftharpoons\; R-C(=O)(O-R) \;+\; H_2O$$

carboxylic acid   alcohol   ester   water

This oxygen comes from the alcohol.

3) The reaction is **reversible**, so you need to separate out the product **as it's formed**.

4) For small esters, you can warm the mixture and just **distil off** the ester, because it's more volatile than the other compounds.

5) Larger esters are harder to form so it's best to heat them under **reflux** and use **fractional distillation** to separate the ester from the other compounds.

> It's an example of a condensation reaction — where molecules combine by releasing a small molecule.

2) From Alcohols and Acid Anhydrides

An **acid anhydride** is made from two carboxylic acid molecules.

Acid anhydrides can be reacted with alcohols to make **esters** too.

1) The acid anhydride is warmed with the **alcohol**. **No catalyst** is needed.

2) The products are an **ester** and a **carboxylic acid** which can then be separated by fractional distillation.

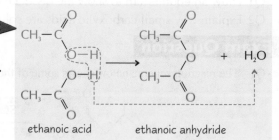

ethanoic acid   ethanoic anhydride

acid anhydride   + $R-O-H$ (alcohol)   →   ester   +   carboxylic acid

3) From Alcohols and Acyl Chlorides

When alcohols react with acyl chlorides, an ester is formed along with hydrogen chloride gas.

> There's more about acyl chlorides on p.72-73.

$R-C(=O)(Cl)$ (acyl chloride)   + $R-O-H$ (alcohol)   → $R-C(=O)(O-R)$ (ester)   + $H-Cl$ (hydrogen chloride)

Esters

Esters are **Hydrolysed** to Form **Alcohols**

There are two ways to hydrolyse esters — using **acid hydrolysis** or **base hydrolysis**.
With both types you get an **alcohol**, but the second product in each case is different.

Acid Hydrolysis

Acid hydrolysis splits the ester into a **carboxylic acid** and an **alcohol**.
You have to **reflux** the ester with a **dilute acid**, such as hydrochloric or sulfuric.

As it's a reversible reaction, you need to use lots of water to push the equilibrium over to the right.

ethyl ethanoate   ethanoic acid   ethanol

Base Hydrolysis

This time you have to **reflux** the ester with a **dilute alkali**, such as sodium hydroxide.
You get a **carboxylate salt** and an **alcohol**.

ethyl ethanoate   sodium ethanoate   ethanol

We are never, ever, ever getting back together

Like, ever?

Esther's break up was completely irreversible.

Warm-Up Questions

Q1 What is the functional group of an ester?

Q2 Give two ways of making esters using an alcohol.

Q3 What are the products when you hydrolyse an ester in acidic conditions?

Q4 Under what conditions is the hydrolysis of an ester a reversible reaction?

PRACTICE QUESTIONS

Exam Questions

Q1 Propyl ethanoate is a pear-scented oil. It is used as a solvent and as a flavouring.

a) Name the alcohol that it can be made from.   [1 mark]

b) Name and draw two different organic substances that could be
    added to the alcohol to produce the propyl ethanoate.   [2 marks]

Q2 a) Choose the two compounds that will react together under acidic conditions
        to form the ester 2-methylpropylpentanoate:

    A   **B**   OH   **C** HO   **D** HO   [1 mark]

b) What are the products when this ester is warmed with aqueous sodium hydroxide?   [1 mark]

Esters están terminando...

*Those two ways of hydrolysing esters are just similar enough that it's easy to get in a muddle. Remember — hydrolysis
in acidic conditions is reversible, and you get a carboxylic acid as well as an alcohol. Hydrolysis with a base is a one
way reaction that gives you an alcohol and a carboxylate salt. Now we've got that sorted, I think it's time for a cuppa.*

Amines and Amides

We start this section with a few more types of compounds for you to learn about — these ones all contain nitrogen.

Amines are Organic Derivatives of **Ammonia**

If one or more of the **hydrogens** in **ammonia** (NH_3) is replaced with an organic group, you get an **amine**.
Amines can be **primary**, **secondary** or **tertiary** depending on how many **alkyl** groups the nitrogen atom is bonded to.
If the nitrogen atom is bonded to **four** alkyl groups, you get a **positively** charged **quaternary ammonium** ion.

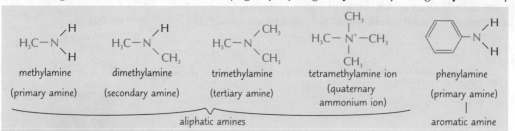

methylamine
(primary amine)

dimethylamine
(secondary amine)

trimethylamine
(tertiary amine)

tetramethylamine ion
(quaternary
ammonium ion)

phenylamine
(primary amine)

aliphatic amines

aromatic amine

> 'Aliphatic' is a term
> for compounds
> without any benzene
> ring structures.

Amines Are **Bases**

1) There's a **lone pair of electrons** on the **nitrogen** atom of an amine that's able to accept **protons** (H^+ ions). This means that amines are **bases**.

2) Amines are **neutralised** by **acids** to make **ammonium salts**.
For example, **ethylamine** reacts with **hydrochloric acid** to form ethylammonium chloride:

> Acids are proton donors, and bases
> are proton acceptors. It's all there
> on page 22 if you need a reminder.

$$CH_3CH_2NH_2 + HCl \rightarrow CH_3CH_2NH_3^+Cl^-$$

Aliphatic Amines can be Made From **Haloalkanes**

Amines can be made by heating a **haloalkane** with an excess of **ethanolic ammonia** (ammonia dissolved in ethanol).

You'll get a **mixture** of primary, secondary and tertiary amines, and quaternary ammonium salts, as more than one hydrogen is likely to be substituted. You can separate the products using **fractional distillation**.

For example, bromoethane will react with ammonia to form ethylamine:

$$2 \overset{H}{\underset{H}{N}}{-}H + CH_3CH_2Br \longrightarrow CH_3CH_2\overset{H}{\underset{H}{N}} + NH_4Br$$

ammonia   ethylamine

> This is a
> nucleophilic
> substitution
> reaction.

Ethylamine can also react with bromoethane to form diethylamine:

$$NH_3 + CH_3CH_2\overset{H}{\underset{H}{N}} + CH_3CH_2Br \longrightarrow CH_3CH_2\overset{CH_2CH_3}{\underset{H}{N}} + NH_4Br$$

ethylamine   diethylamine

And so on.

Aromatic Amines are Made by **Reducing** a **Nitro Compound**

Nitro compounds, such as **nitrobenzene**, are reduced in two steps:

1) Heat a mixture of a **nitro compound**, **tin metal** and **concentrated hydrochloric acid** under **reflux** — this makes a **salt**.

2) To get the **aromatic amine**, you have to add **sodium hydroxide**.

$$\underset{nitrobenzene}{\overset{NO_2}{\bigcirc}} + 6[H] \xrightarrow[\text{(2) NaOH}]{\overset{\text{(1) tin, conc. HCl}}{\text{reflux}}} \underset{phenylamine}{\overset{NH_2}{\bigcirc}} + 2H_2O$$

Amides are Carboxylic Acid Derivatives

Amides contain the functional group **–CONH$_2$**.

The **carbonyl group** pulls electrons away from the rest of the -CONH$_2$ group, so amides behave differently from amines.

You get **primary** and **secondary** amides depending on how many **carbon atoms** the nitrogen is bonded to.

$$R-C\overset{O}{\underset{N-H}{\big\langle}}$$
primary amide

$$R-C\overset{O}{\underset{N-H}{\big\langle}}$$
secondary amide

> one of the
> hydrogens is
> replaced with
> an alkyl group

Amines and Amides

Amino Acids have an Amino Group and a Carboxyl Group

1) An **amino acid** has a **basic amino group** (NH_2) and an **acidic carboxyl group** (COOH).

2) In an **α–amino acid**, both groups are attached to the **same** carbon atom — the 'α carbon'. The **general formula** of an α–amino acid is **RCH(NH₂)COOH**.

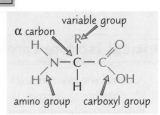

Amino Acids Can React with Acids and Alkalis

1) The **carboxylic acid group** in an amino acid can react with an **alkali** to form a **conjugate base** — RCH(NH₂)COO⁻. This can combine with a positive ion to form a **salt**. For example:

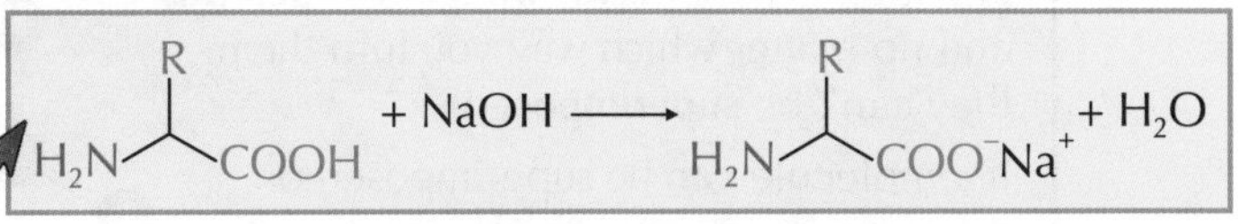

$$H_2N\text{—}\underset{R}{CH}\text{—}COOH + NaOH \longrightarrow H_2N\text{—}\underset{R}{CH}\text{—}COO^-Na^+ + H_2O$$

2) The **amino group** meanwhile can react with an **acid** to form a **salt** of the **conjugate acid**. For example:

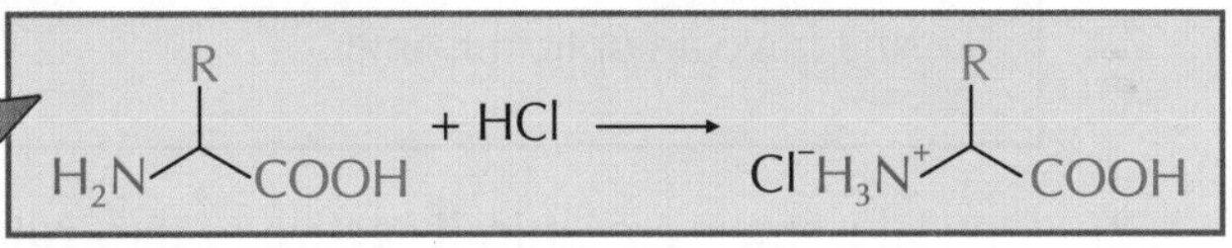

$$H_2N\text{—}\underset{R}{CH}\text{—}COOH + HCl \longrightarrow Cl^-H_3N^+\text{—}\underset{R}{CH}\text{—}COOH$$

Amino Acids React with Alcohols to Form Esters

Just like other carboxylic acids, the **carboxylic acid group** in an amino acid can react with an **alcohol** in the presence of a **strong acid catalyst** (normally sulfuric acid) to form an **ester**.

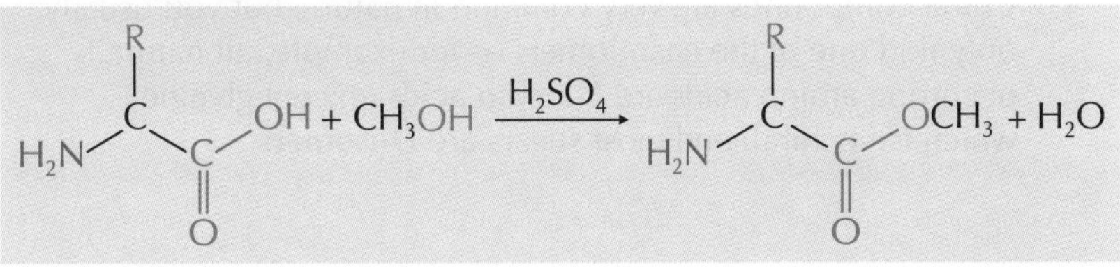

$$H_2N\text{—}\underset{O}{\overset{R}{C}}\text{—}C\text{—}OH + CH_3OH \xrightarrow{H_2SO_4} H_2N\text{—}\underset{O}{\overset{R}{C}}\text{—}C\text{—}OCH_3 + H_2O$$

Warm-Up Questions

Q1 Draw examples of a primary, secondary and tertiary amine, and a quaternary ammonium ion.

Q2 Why do amines act as bases?

Q3 Draw the general structure of a primary amide and a secondary amide.

Q4 What's the general formula of an α-amino acid?

Exam Questions

Q1 When 1-chloropropane is reacted with ammonia, a mixture of different amines are produced.

  a) Name two of the amines produced in the reaction. [2 marks]

  b) What technique could you use to separate the mixture? [1 mark]

  c) Outline the steps needed to reduce nitrobenzene to make phenylamine. [2 marks]

Q2 The organic compound shown on the right is leucine.
Which of the following statements is incorrect?

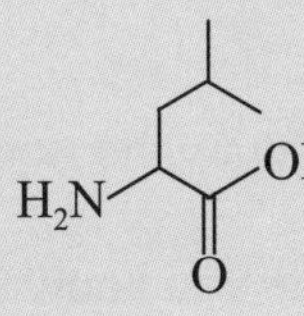

  A Leucine is an α-amino acid.

  B Leucine contains an amino group.

  C Leucine reacts with sodium hydroxide to form the salt of its conjugate acid.

  D Leucine reacts with alcohols to form esters. [1 mark]

This topic was quite amine one...

Amino acids don't just pop up in Chemistry. They're the building blocks of proteins in your body, so they're really quite important for life as well as for your exams. Make sure you understand the different ways they react — with acids, alkalis and alcohols. And while you're at it, you may as well go through the reactions for making amines as well.

Chirality

Stereoisomers have the same molecular formula and their atoms are arranged in the same way. The only difference is the orientation of their bonds in space. You met E/Z stereoisomerism in Year 1. Now it's time to find out about another type — optical isomerism. Something called chirality is the key here, as you're about to discover.

Optical Isomers are Mirror Images of Each Other

1) A **chiral** (or **asymmetric**) carbon atom is one which has **four different** groups attached to it. It's possible to arrange the groups in **two** different ways around the carbon atom so that two different molecules are made — these molecules are called **enantiomers** or **optical isomers**.

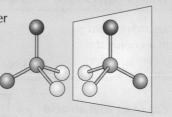

Enantiomers are **mirror images** of each other and no matter which way you turn them, they can't be **superimposed**.

If a molecule **can** be superimposed on its mirror image, it's **achiral** and it doesn't have an optical isomer.

You might use a molecular modelling kit in class to see for yourself how enantiomers are non-superimposable.

2) Optical isomers are **optically active** — they **rotate plane-polarised light**. One enantiomer rotates it in a **clockwise** direction, the other rotates it the **same amount** but in an **anticlockwise** direction.

Normal light vibrates in all directions, but plane-polarised light only vibrates in one direction.

3) The enantiomers are sometimes identified as the **D** isomer or the **L** isomer — luckily you don't have to worry about which is which.

4) Chiral compounds are very common in nature, but you usually only find **one** of the enantiomers — for example, all naturally occurring amino acids are **L-amino acids** (except glycine which isn't chiral) and most sugars are **D-isomers**.

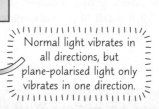

An anteateriomer.

Make Sure You Can Spot Chiral Centres

You have to be able to draw optical isomers. To do this you need to be able to identify the chiral centre...

Example: Draw the optical isomers for 2-hydroxypropanoic acid:

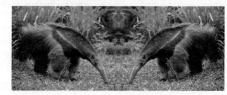

First locate the chiral centre:

Look for the carbon atom with **four** different groups attached. Here it's the carbon with the four groups H, OH, COOH and CH$_3$ attached.

chiral centre

Then draw the isomers:

Once you know the chiral carbon, **draw** one enantiomer in a **tetrahedral** shape. Don't try to draw the full structure of each group — it gets confusing. Then draw a **mirror image** beside it.

enantiomers of 2-hydroxypropanoic acid

Chirality

Some Molecules Have More Than One Chiral Centre

Some molecules have **more than one** chiral centre — you need to be able to spot them **all**.

Example: Label all the chiral centres in the following organic molecule:

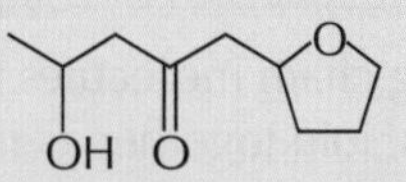

The structure shown is a **skeletal formula** — to find the carbon atoms that have **four different groups** attached, it can be helpful to show all the **hydrogen atoms** as well.

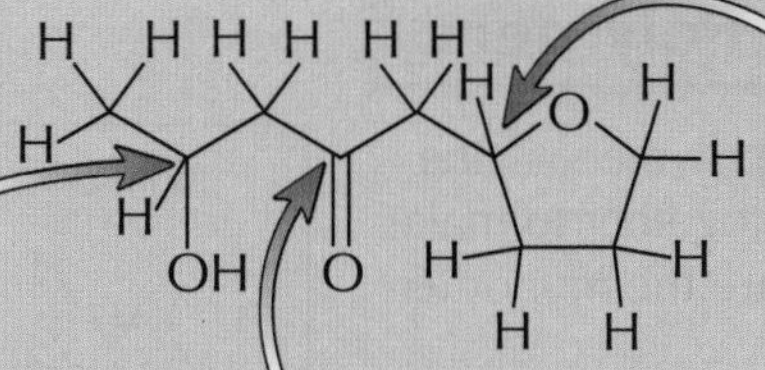

This carbon has four different groups attached, so it's chiral.

A carbon needs to have four different groups attached to be chiral, so this carbon is achiral, even though the three groups it's attached to are different.

Although this carbon is attached to the same ring twice, it's chiral because the order of the atoms in the ring is different depending on which way round you go. Going clockwise round the ring from the chiral carbon you get -O-CH₂-CH₂-CH₂-, whilst going anticlockwise you get -CH₂-CH₂-CH₂-O-. So they count as two **different** groups.

The chiral centres are:

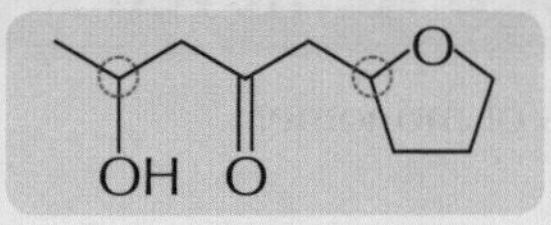

If a molecule has **more** than **one chiral centre**, it will have **more** than **two optical isomers**.

Example: The molecule 3-methylpentan-2-ol is shown on the right. It contains two chiral carbons, which are marked with asterisks. Draw all the optical isomers of the molecule.

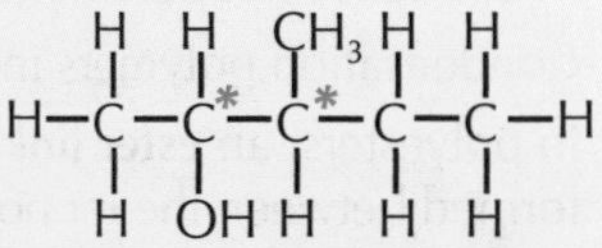

The molecule has two chiral centres, so there are four different optical isomers of this molecule:

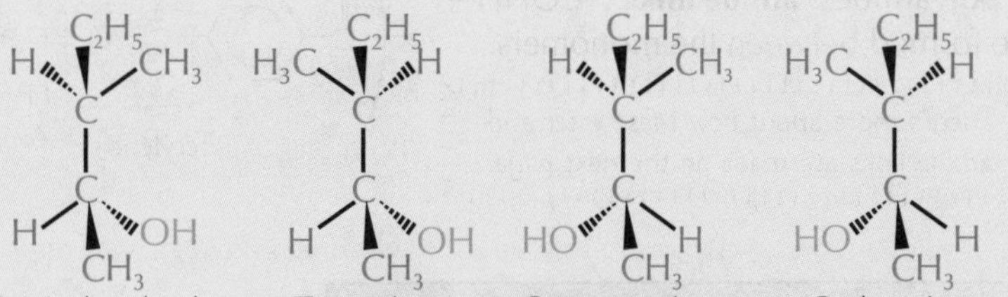

Original molecule. | Top carbon mirror-imaged. | Bottom carbon mirror-imaged. | Both carbons mirror-imaged.

Warm-Up Questions

Q1 What makes a carbon atom chiral?
Q2 What are enantiomers?
Q3 How do optical isomers affect plane polarised light?

Exam Question

Q1 The skeletal formula of 3-ethyl-4-phenylhexan-2-one is shown on the right.

a) Mark each chiral centre with an asterisk. [1 mark]

b) Draw all the optical isomers of the molecule. [4 marks]

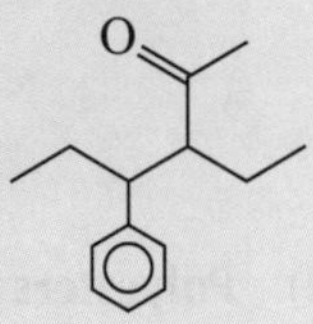

Mirror, mirror on the wall, who's the fairest molecule of them all...

This isomer stuff's not all bad — you get to draw little pretty pictures of molecules. If you're having difficulty picturing them as 3D shapes, you could always make models with Blu® Tack and those matchsticks that're propping your eyelids open. Blu® Tack's very therapeutic anyway and squishing it about'll help relieve all that revision stress. It's great stuff.

Polymers

You met polymers for the first time in Year 1, and I bet you thought you'd never have to see their ugly faces again.
You were wrong — they're back. Unlike those pesky polymers, I'll try not to be too long, or repeat myself too much.

There are **Two Types** of Polymerisation — **Addition** and **Condensation**

1) **Polymers** are long chain molecules formed when lots of small molecules,
called **monomers**, join together as if they're holding hands.

2) There are two ways of **making** polymers — by **addition polymerisation**, or **condensation polymerisation**.

Alkenes **Join Up** to form **Addition Polymers**

1) You saw in Module 4 that alkenes can form polymers — the
double bonds open up, and molecules join together to make
long chains. The individual, small alkenes are the monomers.

2) This is called **addition polymerisation**.

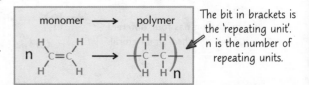

The bit in brackets is the 'repeating unit'. n is the number of repeating units.

Condensation Polymers are formed as **Water** is **Removed...**

1) Condensation polymers are normally formed from **two types** of monomer,
each of which has at least **two functional groups**.

2) The functional group on one monomer reacts with a group on the other
type of monomer to form a **link**, creating the polymer **chain**.

3) In condensation polymerisation, each time a link is formed, a small molecule is lost (often it's **water**).

4) Condensation polymers include **polyesters** and **polyamides**.

5) In polyesters, an **ester link** (–COO–) is
formed between the monomers.

6) In polyamides, **amide links** (–CONH–)
are formed between the monomers.

There's more about how these ester and
amide links are made on the next page.

ester link

Terylene®

amide link

nylon 6,6

...and **Broken Down** by Adding It

1) Condensation polymerisation can be reversed by **hydrolysis**
— water molecules are added back in and the links are broken.

2) In practice, hydrolysis with just water is far too **slow**, so the reaction is done with an **acid** or **base**.

3) **Polyamides** will hydrolyse more easily with an **acid** than a base:

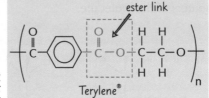

amide link

polyamide

$+ 2n\, H_2O \xrightarrow{H^+}$

$n\, HO-\overset{\overset{O}{\|}}{C}-R-\overset{\overset{O}{\|}}{C}-OH$

dicarboxylic acid

$+ n\, H-\overset{\underset{H}{|}}{N}-R'-\overset{\underset{H}{|}}{N}-H$

diamine

4) **Polyesters** will hydrolyse more easily with a **base**. A **metal salt** of the carboxylic acid is formed.

polyester

$+ 2n\, NaOH \longrightarrow$

$n\, Na^+O^--\overset{\overset{O}{\|}}{C}-R-\overset{\overset{O}{\|}}{C}-O^-Na^+$

dicarboxylic acid salt

$+ n\, H-O-R'-O-H$

diol

Polymers

Reactions Between **Dicarboxylic Acids** and **Diamines** Make **Polyamides**

1) **Carboxyl** (–COOH) groups react with **amino** (–NH$_2$) groups to form **amide** (–CONH–) links.
2) A water molecule is lost each time an amide link is formed — it's a **condensation** reaction.
3) The condensation polymer formed is a **polyamide**.

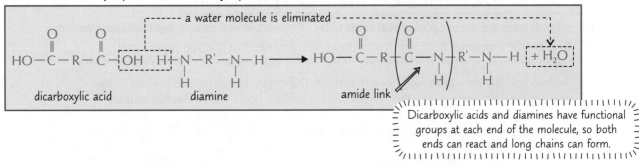

Dicarboxylic acids and diamines have functional groups at each end of the molecule, so both ends can react and long chains can form.

Reactions Between **Dicarboxylic Acids** and **Diols** Make **Polyesters**

Carboxyl groups (–COOH) react with **hydroxyl** (–OH) groups to form **ester links** (–COO–).
It's another **condensation** reaction, and the polymer formed is a **polyester**

Compounds where one of the carboxylic acid groups is changed to an acyl chloride will also react to form polyesters and polyamides. Instead of water, hydrochloric acid is eliminated in the condensation reaction.

Warm-Up Questions

Q1 Name the two types of polymerisation reaction.
Q2 What type of link forms between monomers in a polyester? And in a polyamide?
Q3 What is a polyamide made from?
Q4 What functional groups react together to form the link in a polyester?

Exam Question

Q1 Kevlar® is a polymer used in bulletproof vests. Its repeating unit is shown below.

a) What type of polymer is Kevlar® and what type of reaction is used to make it? [2 marks]

b) Kevlar® is made by reacting two different monomers together.
What type of compounds are these monomers? [1 mark]

c) How could you break up Kevlar® into its constituent monomers? [1 mark]

Conversation polymerisation — when someone just goes on and on and on...

Condensation polymers are like those friends who are in an on-off relationship. They get together, then they hydrolyse apart, only to get back together again. And you have to keep up with it — monomers, polymers, amides, esters and all.

More on Polymers

So, you know the basics of polymerisation, but you also need to be able to look at a polymer and work out what the monomers that made it are. Or look at some monomers and work out how they join together to form a polymer.

The Repeat Units of **Addition** Polymers are Based Around the **Double Bond**

You Can Work Out the **Monomer** From the **Polymer Chain**

1) All polymers are made up of **repeat units** (a bit of molecule that repeats over and over again).

2) To draw the **monomer** from a polymer chain, you first need to find the **repeat unit**.
For an addition polymer, the backbone of the repeat unit will always be **two** carbons long.

3) To then find the monomer, you need to remove the empty bonds (which join on to the
next repeat unit) and replace the central carbon-carbon bond with a **double bond**.

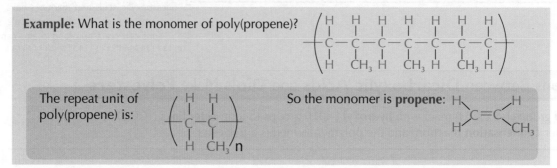

Example: What is the monomer of poly(propene)?

The repeat unit of poly(propene) is:

So the monomer is **propene**:

You Can Work Out the **Repeat Unit** From the **Monomer**

1) To draw the **repeat unit** of an addition polymer from its **monomer**, first draw the two alkene carbons, replace the double bond with a single bond and add a bond to each of the carbons. This forms the polymer backbone.

2) Then just fill in the rest of the groups in the same way they surrounded the double bond.

Example: Draw the repeat unit and a section of the polymer chain of the polymer formed from chloroethene, CH_2CHCl.

First draw the double bond opening up to form the polymer backbone.

Then fill in the groups as they surround the double bond.

chloroethene monomer

poly(chloroethene) repeat unit

Pretty Polymer.

'n' just means the number of repeating units in the polymer.

The polymer chain is made up of repeat units joined together, so this is what a section of the chain would look like:

section of poly(chloroethene) polymer

Break the **Amide** or **Ester** Link to Find the **Monomers** of a **Condensation** Polymer

You can find the formulas of the **monomers** used to make a condensation polymer by looking at its formula.

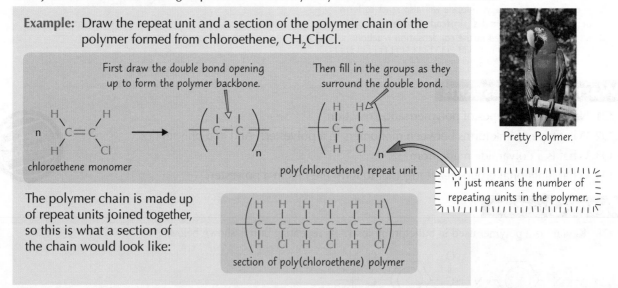

1) First find the amide (**HN–CO**) or ester (**CO–O**) link. Break it down the middle.

ester link

break here

2) Then add an **H** or an **OH** to **both ends** of **both molecules** to find the monomers.
(Always add Hs to O or N atoms, and OH groups to C atoms.)

More on Polymers

Join the **Monomer Functional Groups** to Find a **Condensation Polymer**

If you know the **formulas** of a pair of **monomers** that react together in a **condensation polymerisation** reaction, you can work out the **repeat unit** of the condensation polymer that they would form.

Example: A condensation polymer is made from 1,4-diaminobutane, $H_2N(CH_2)_4NH_2$, and decanedioic acid, $HOOC(CH_2)_8COOH$. Draw the repeat unit of the polymer that is formed.

1) Draw out the two **monomer** molecules next to each other.
2) Remove an **OH** from the **dicarboxylic acid**, and an **H** from the **diamine** — that gives you a water molecule.
3) Join the C and the N together to make an **amide link**.
4) Take another **H** and **OH** off the ends of your molecule. Draw brackets around it, and there's your **repeat unit**.

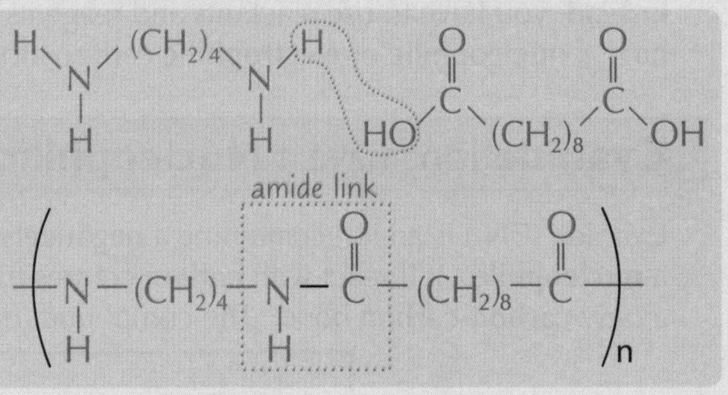

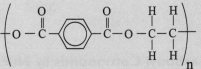

If the monomer molecules are a **dicarboxylic acid** and a **diol**, then you take an **H** atom from the **diol** and an **OH** group from the **dicarboxylic acid**, and form an **ester** link instead.

Watch Out for More **Complex** Condensation Polymers

1) Molecules that contain **both** an amine and an **alcohol** group can react with **dicarboxylic acids** in a condensation polymerisation reaction. The polymers they form contain both **amide** and **ester** links.

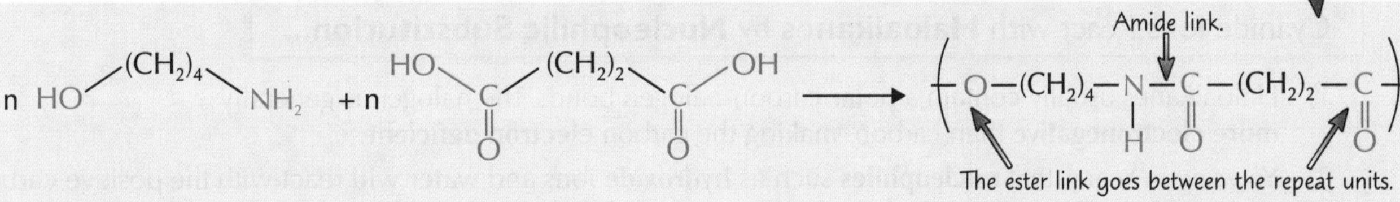

The ester link goes between the repeat units.

2) If a molecule contains a **carboxylic acid** group and either an **alcohol** or an **amine** group, it can polymerise with **itself** to from a condensation polymer with only **one monomer**.

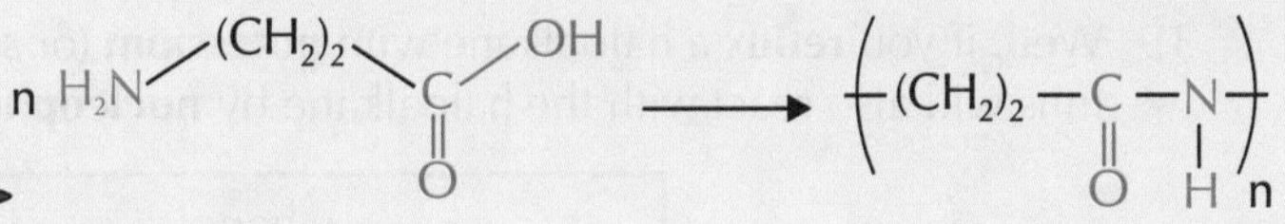

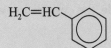

Warm-Up Questions

Q1 Draw the monomer of poly(propene), $(-CH_2CH(CH_3)-)_n$.

Q2 Name two functional groups a molecule could contain in order to form a condensation polymer with itself.

Exam Questions

Q1 PET is a polymer used in the making of plastic bottles. The repeat unit of the polymer is shown on the right.

a) Draw the monomers that make up this polymer. [1 mark]

b) Name the type of polymerisation reaction by which this polymer is formed. [1 mark]

Q2 Polystyrene is a polymer that is commonly used in packaging materials. Its monomer is shown on the right. $H_2C=HC$

a) Draw the repeat unit of polystyrene. [1 mark]

b) Draw a section of the polymer chain of polystyrene that is three repeat units long. [1 mark]

All this stuff on polymers is really quite repetitive...

Condensation polymers can look quite confusing when there are lots of groups in the repeating unit, but all you need to worry about is finding the amide or ester link. Once you've found that, split the repeating unit in two, play around with a few Hs and Os and hey presto — you've got your monomers. Have a practice with the example on page 82.

Carbon-Carbon Bond Synthesis

The whole of Organic Chemistry revolves around carbon compounds and how they react, but getting one carbon to react with another and form a new carbon-carbon bond is surprisingly hard. Here are some reactions that let you do it.

You Use Carbon-Carbon Bond Synthesis to **Extend** the **Carbon Chain**

In organic synthesis, it's useful to have ways of making a carbon chain **longer**.

You can't just put two carbon chains together and expect them to react though. Instead, you have to use reactants and reagents that have a **nucleophilic** or **electrophilic** carbon atom.

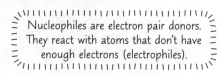
Nucleophiles are electron pair donors. They react with atoms that don't have enough electrons (electrophiles).

Cyanide Ions have a **Nucleophilic** Carbon

Cyanide (CN⁻) is an ion containing a **negatively charged** carbon atom, so it's a **nucleophile**. It'll react with carbon centres that have a **slight positive charge** to create a new **carbon-carbon** bond. The compound that's initially produced is a **nitrile**.

$$-\overset{|}{\underset{|}{C}}{}^{\delta+}-X^{\delta-} + {}^-C\equiv N \longrightarrow -\overset{|}{\underset{|}{C}}-C\equiv N$$

If the electron withdrawing group (X) is a carbonyl group (=O), then the double bond opens up and the product is:

$$-\overset{|}{\underset{OH}{C}}-C\equiv N$$

(See the reaction mechanism below.)

So you can **increase** the length of a carbon chain by reacting an organic compound that contains a **slightly positive carbon centre** with a **cyanide** reagent such as **potassium cyanide** (KCN), **sodium cyanide** (NaCN) or **hydrogen cyanide** (HCN).

Cyanide Ions React with **Haloalkanes** by **Nucleophilic Substitution...**

1) Haloalkanes usually contain a **polar** carbon-halogen bond. The halogen is generally **more electronegative** than carbon, making the carbon **electron deficient**.

2) You saw in Year 1 that **nucleophiles** such as **hydroxide** ions and **water** will react with the positive carbon centre in haloalkanes to **replace** the **halogen** atom. This is a **nucleophilic substitution reaction**.

3) Well, if you **reflux** a haloalkane with **potassium** (or sodium) **cyanide** in **ethanol**, then the cyanide ions will also react with the haloalkane by **nucleophilic substitution** to form a **nitrile**.

$$R\text{-}X + CN^- \xrightarrow[\text{reflux}]{\text{ethanol}} R\text{-}C\equiv N + X^-$$

4) The mechanism is:

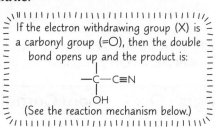

Naming nitriles is pretty simple. You just name the alkyl chain in the normal way (don't forget to include the carbon atom in the CN group when doing this), then add the suffix 'nitrile' on the end. So the product in the example on the left is propanenitrile.

...and with **Carbonyl Compounds** by **Nucleophilic Addition**

Aldehydes and **ketones** are both carbonyl compounds — they contain a **polar C=O** bond. If you mix them with **hydrogen cyanide**, the cyanide ion will react with the **positive carbon centre** to form a **hydroxynitrile**.

There's loads more about the reactions of carbonyls on p.70-71.

Carbon-Carbon Bond Synthesis

Nitriles Can React to Form **New** Functional Groups

1)   Once you've added another carbon atom onto the carbon chain and formed a **nitrile** (or a **hydroxynitrile**), it's easy to **convert** the nitrile into a new functional group. This is because nitrile groups are very **reactive**.

2)   This is really **useful** in **synthesis** — you can make a number of different compounds from the nitrile.

Nitriles Can Be **Reduced** to Form **Amines**

You can **reduce** a nitrile to a **primary amine** by a number of different methods.

1)   You can use **lithium aluminium hydride** (**LiAlH$_4$** — a strong reducing agent), followed by some **dilute acid**.
     E.g.

$$R-CH_2-C\equiv N + 4[H] \xrightarrow[\text{(2) dilute acid}]{\text{(1) LiAlH}_4} R-CH_2-CH_2N\begin{smallmatrix}H\\ \\H\end{smallmatrix}$$

nitrile   primary amine

You can also reduce **hydroxynitriles** using this method.
E.g.

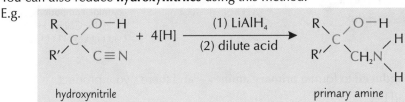

hydroxynitrile   primary amine

Knight Rile   Knight Rile reduction

2)   You can also reduce the nitrile (or hydroxynitrile) with **sodium** metal and **ethanol**.

3)   The two methods above are great in the lab, but LiAlH$_4$ and sodium are too **expensive** for industrial use. In industry, nitriles are reduced using **hydrogen gas** with a **metal catalyst** such as platinum or nickel at a high temperature and pressure — this is called **catalytic hydrogenation**.
     E.g.

$$R-CH_2-C\equiv N + 2H_2 \xrightarrow[\substack{\text{high temperature}\\\text{and pressure}}]{\text{nickel catalyst}} R-CH_2-CH_2N\begin{smallmatrix}H\\ \\H\end{smallmatrix}$$

nitrile   primary amine

This method also works for hydroxynitriles — the product is the same as above.

Nitriles Can Be **Hydrolysed** to Form **Carboxylic Acids**

If you reflux a nitrile in dilute hydrochloric acid, then the nitrile group will be **hydrolysed** to form a **carboxylic acid**. The **carbon** of the **nitrile** starting material becomes the carbon of the carboxyl group in the product.

$$R-CH_2-C\equiv N + 2H_2O + HCl \longrightarrow R-CH_2-C\begin{smallmatrix}O\\ \\OH\end{smallmatrix} + NH_4Cl$$

nitrile   carboxylic acid

Hydrolysis means using water to break up a compound. Here, the -C≡N bond reacts with water to break up and form -COO$^-$ and NH$_4^+$.

You can do the same with a hydroxynitrile:

hydroxynitrile   2-hydroxycarboxylic acid

Carbon-Carbon Bond Synthesis

Think About **Nitrile Reactions** When You're Planning **Synthetic Routes**

If the product of a synthesis reaction contains one more carbon in the chain than the starting compound had, then it's likely that the synthetic route will include formation of a **nitrile** or **hydroxynitrile**.

Example: Plan a two-step synthetic route to synthesise 3-methylbutamine from 1-chloro-2-methylpropane. You should include all reagents and conditions as well as showing any intermediate products.

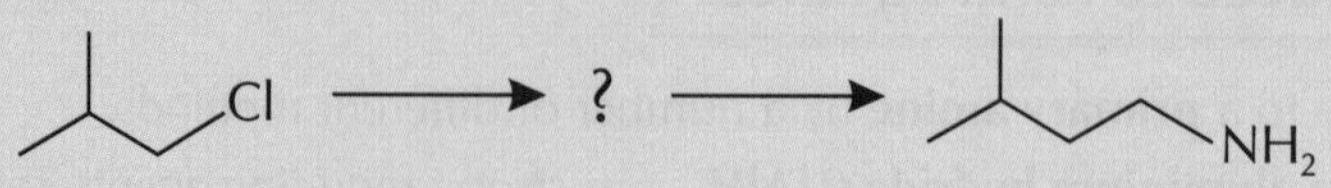

The **product** has **one more carbon** than the starting compound, so the synthetic route must include formation of a **new carbon-carbon bond**. The starting compound is a **chloroalkane** so it can react with a **cyanide ion** in a **nucleophilic substitution reaction** to form a **nitrile**. The first step of the synthetic route is:

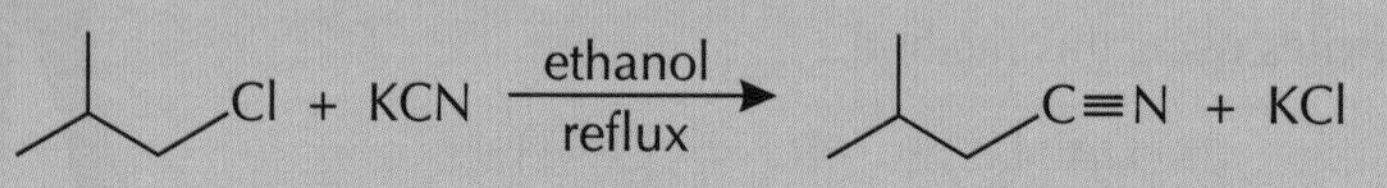

You could also use other cyanide compounds, such as NaCN or HCN.

The nitrile can then be **reduced** to form a **primary amine** — and there's your product. So the second step could be:

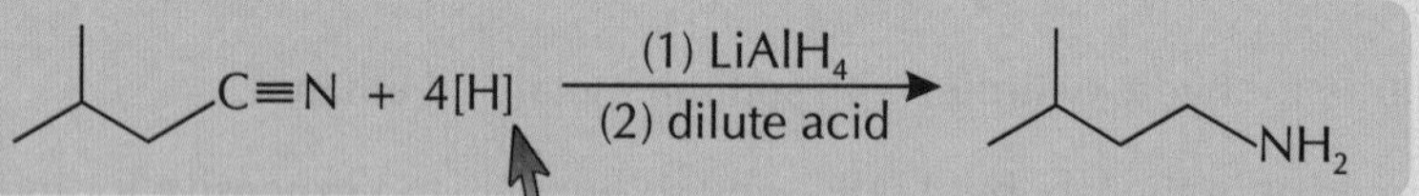

There are other ways to reduce a nitrile on page 85.

Remember to balance the reaction equation using [H].

Overall the synthetic route is:

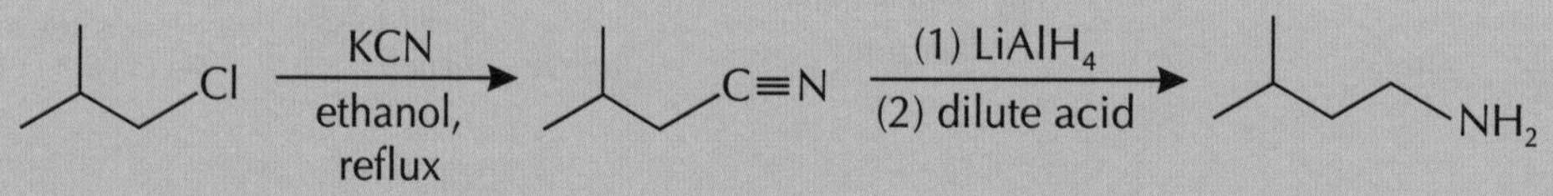

Friedel-Crafts Reactions Form Carbon-Carbon Bonds with **Benzene Rings**

1) If you reflux benzene with a **halogen carrier** (e.g. $AlCl_3$) and either a **haloalkane** or an **acyl chloride** then a new carbon-carbon bond will form between the **benzene ring** and the **halogenated carbon** in the organic reactant.

2) This is an **electrophilic substitution reaction**.

3) If you use a **haloalkane**, you get **alkylation**:

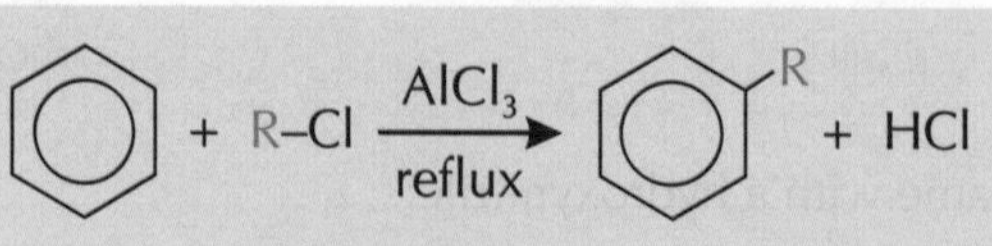

See page 67 for more on Friedel-Crafts reactions.

4) If you use an **acyl chloride**, you get **acylation**:

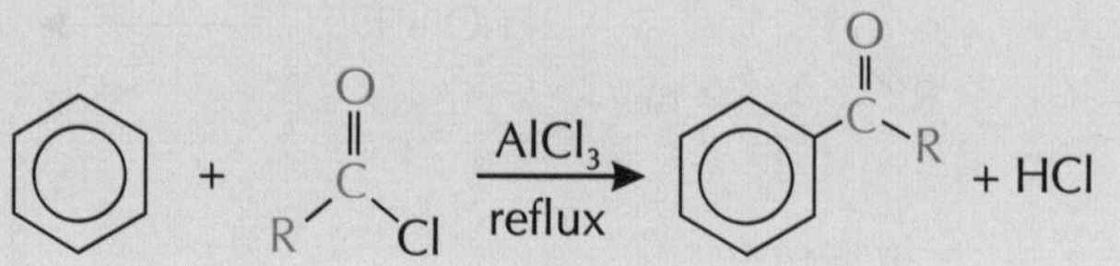

Carbon-Carbon Bond Synthesis

Friedel-Crafts Reactions May be Useful in Synthetic Routes

You may have to design a synthetic route that includes using a **Friedel-Crafts** reaction.

Example: Consider the following reaction scheme:

$$\text{benzene} \xrightarrow[\text{AlCl}_3 \text{ (catalyst)}]{\text{CH}_3\text{CH}_2\text{Cl}} \text{A} \xrightarrow[\text{AlCl}_3 \text{ (catalyst)}]{\text{B}} \text{product}$$

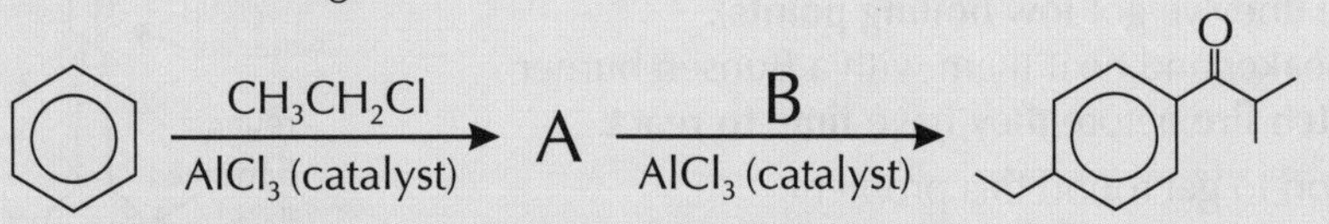

a) What is A, the organic product of the first step?

> In the first step, benzene is reacted with **chloroethane** and a halogen carrier. It's a **Friedel-Crafts alkylation** reaction, so the product is **ethylbenzene**:

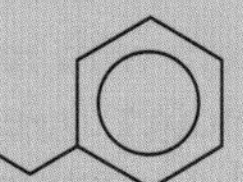

b) What is the reagent, B, in the second step?

> Ethylbenzene (the product from the first step) is **acylated** in the second step, so the reaction will be a **Friedel-Crafts acylation**.
> The reagent is **2-methylpropanoylchloride**:

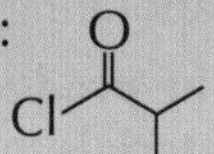

Warm-Up Questions

Q1 What type of reaction is the reaction between potassium cyanide and a haloalkane?

Q2 What is the organic product of the reaction between hydrogen cyanide and a carbonyl compound?

Q3 Give the reagents and conditions for two different methods of converting a nitrile to an amine.

Q4 What are the reagents and conditions needed to put an acyl group onto a benzene ring?

Exam Questions

Q1 Consider the following reaction scheme:

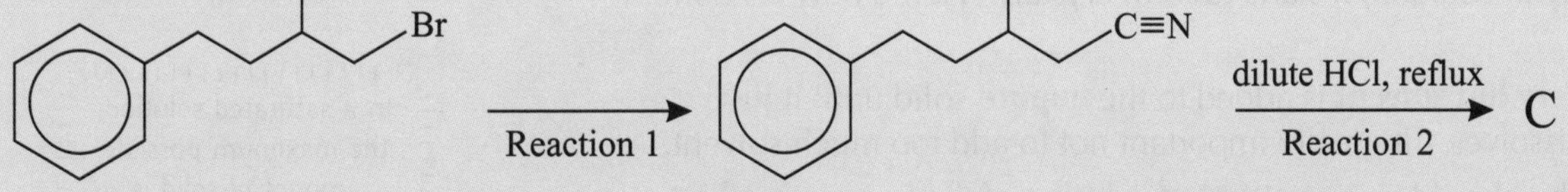

$$\text{A} \xrightarrow{\text{Reaction 1}} \text{B} \xrightarrow[\text{Reaction 2}]{\text{dilute HCl, reflux}} \text{C}$$

a) What are the reagents and conditions needed for Reaction 1? [2 marks]

b) Draw the skeletal formula of compound C, the organic product of Reaction 2. [1 mark]

c) Compound A can be made in one step from benzene.
What are the reagents and conditions needed for this reaction? [2 marks]

Q2 Draw the structure of the organic product that is formed
when butanone is reacted with hydrogen cyanide. [1 mark]

My friends are really creative — Aisling likes drawing and Friedel crafts...

Most of these reactions have come up before, but now we're using them for a specific purpose. Making new carbon-carbon bonds is really useful — new drug molecules are often based on compounds found in nature, which chemists then tweak so they work better. Often they'll need to extend a carbon chain, so they'll use reactions like these.

Organic Synthesis — Practical Techniques

You can't call yourself a chemist unless you know these practical techniques. Not unless your name's Boots.

Reactions Often Need to be Heated to Work

1) **Organic reactions** are **slow** and the substances are usually **flammable** and **volatile** (they've got **low boiling points**). If you stick them in a beaker and heat them with a Bunsen burner they'll **evaporate** or **catch fire** before they have **time to react**.

2) You can **reflux** a reaction to get round this problem.

3) The mixture's **heated in a flask** fitted with a **vertical Liebig condenser** — so when the mixture boils, the vapours are condensed and **recycled** back into the flask. This stops reagents being **lost** from the flask, and gives them **time to react**.

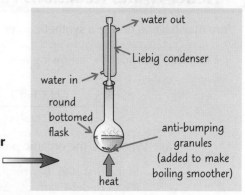

4) One problem with **refluxing** a reaction is that it can cause the desired product to **react further**. If this is the case you can carry out the reaction in a **distillation apparatus** instead.

5) The mixture is **gently heated** and substances **evaporate** out of the mixture in order of **increasing boiling point**.

6) If you know the boiling point of your **pure product**, you can use the thermometer to tell you when it's evaporating, and therefore when it's condensing.

7) If the **product** of a reaction has a **lower boiling point** than the **starting materials** then the reaction mixture can be **heated** so that the product **evaporates** from the reaction mixture as it forms. The **starting materials** will stay in the reaction mixture as long as the temperature is **controlled**.

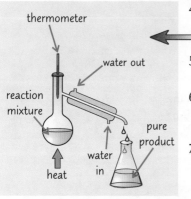

Have a look back at your Year 1 notes for more about distillation and reflux, as well as other organic techniques.

Organic Solids can be Purified by Recrystallisation

If the product of an organic reaction is a solid, then the simplest way of purifying it is a process called **recrystallisation**. First you dissolve your solid in a solvent to make a **saturated** solution. Then you let it cool. As the solution cools, the solubility of the product falls. When it reaches the point where it can't stay in solution, it starts to form crystals. Here's how it's done:

1) **Very hot solvent** is added to the **impure** solid until it **just** dissolves – it's really important not to add too much solvent.

2) This should give a **saturated solution** of the **impure product**.

3) This solution is left to **cool** down **slowly**. **Crystals** of the **product** form as it cools. The **impurities** stay in solution. They're present in much smaller amounts than the product, so they'd take much longer to crystallise out.

4) The crystals are removed by **filtration** under **reduced pressure** (see next page) and **washed** with ice-cold solvent. Then they are dried — leaving you with crystals of your product that are **much purer** than the original solid.

In a saturated solution, the maximum possible amount of solid is dissolved in the solvent.

The Choice of Solvent for Recrystallisation is Very Important

1) When you **recrystallise** a product, you must use an **appropriate solvent** for that particular substance. It will only work if the solid is **very soluble** in the **hot** solvent, but **nearly insoluble** when the solvent is **cold**.

2) If your product **isn't soluble enough** in the hot solvent you **won't** be able to dissolve it at all.

3) If your product **is too soluble** in the cold solvent, most of it will **stay in the solution** even after cooling. When you filter it, you'll **lose** most of your product, giving you a very low **yield**.

Organic Synthesis — Practical Techniques

You Can **Filter** an Organic Solid Under **Reduced Pressure**

1) If your **product** is a **solid**, you can separate it from any **liquid** imperitites by filtering it under **reduced pressure**.

2) The reaction mixture is poured into a **Büchner funnel** with a piece of **filter paper** in it. The Büchner funnel is on top of a sealed sidearm flask which is connected to a **vacuum line**, causing it to be under **reduced pressure**.

3) The reduced pressure causes **suction** through the funnel which causes the liquid to pass **quickly** into the flask, leaving behind **dry crystals** of your product.

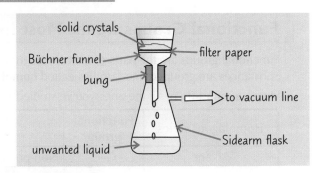

Melting and Boiling Points are Good Indicators of Purity

Most **pure substances** have a **specific melting** and **boiling point**. If they're **impure**, the **melting point's lowered** and the **boiling point is raised**. If they're **very impure**, melting and boiling will occur across a wide range of temperatures.

> To accurately measure the melting point:
>
> Put a small amount of the solid in a capillary tube and place it in a beaker of oil with a very sensitive thermometer. Slowly heat, with constant stirring, until the solid just melts and read the temperature on the thermometer.

Once you've measured the melting point of your sample, you can **compare** it to the **known** melting point of the substance to determine its purity. If the melting points are **similar** then your sample is quite pure, but if your value is much **lower** than the standard value, your sample contains impurities.

Warm-Up Questions

Q1 Why is refluxing needed in many organic reactions?

Q2 Give two factors you should consider when choosing a solvent for recrystallisation.

Q3 How could you separate a solid product from liquid impurities?

Q4 Why is the melting point of a substance helpful in deciding its purity?

Exam Questions

Q1 Two samples of impure stearic acid melt at 69 °C and 64 °C respectively.
Stearic acid dissolves in hot propanone but not in water.

    a) Explain which sample is purer. [1 mark]

    b) Write a method for how the impure sample could be purified. [3 marks]

    c) How could the sample from b) be tested for purity? [1 mark]

Q2 A student is carrying out an experiment using the apparatus shown on the right.
What type of experiment is she doing?

    A reflux   **B** filtration under reduced pressure

    C distillation   **D** recrystallisation [1 mark]

I hope that everything's now crystal clear...

You'll probably have a chance to use these techniques in practicals. The key to a good recrystallisation is patience. You have to add as little solvent as possible, so the solution is completely saturated. Then slowly cool the solution and leave it a while to make sure as much of your product as possible has crystallised. The longer you wait, the better your yield.

Functional Groups

It's been a bit of a hard slog of equations and reaction conditions and dubious puns to get this far. But with a bit of luck it should all be starting to come together now. If not, don't panic — there's always revision bunny.

Functional Groups are the Most Important Parts of a Molecule

Functional groups are the parts of a molecule that are responsible for the way the molecule reacts.
Substances are grouped into families called **homologous series** based on what functional groups they contain.
Here's a round-up of all the ones you've studied:

Homologous series	Functional group	Properties	Typical reactions
Alkane	C–C	Non-polar, unreactive.	Radical substitution
Alkene	C=C	Non-polar, electron-rich double bond.	Electrophilic addition
Aromatic compounds	C_6H_5-	Stable delocalised ring of electrons.	Electrophilic substitution
Alcohol	C–OH	Polar C–OH bond.	Nucleophilic substitution Dehydration/elimination
		Lone pair on oxygen can act as a nucleophile.	Esterification Nucleophilic substitution
Haloalkane	C–X	Polar C–X bond.	Nucleophilic substitution Elimination
Amine	$C–NR_2$	Lone pair on nitrogen is basic and can act as a nucleophile.	Neutralisation Nucleophilic substitution
Nitrile	C–C≡N	Electron deficient carbon centre.	Reduction Hydrolysis
Aldehyde/Ketone	C=O	Polar C=O bond.	Nucleophilic addition Reduction Aldehydes will oxidise.
Carboxylic acid	-COOH	Electron deficient carbon centre.	Neutralisation Esterification
Ester	RCOOR'	Electron deficient carbon centre.	Hydrolysis
Acyl chloride	-COCl	Electron deficient carbon centre.	Nucleophilic addition-elimination Condensation (lose HCl) Friedel-Crafts acylation
Acid anhydride	RCOOCOR'	Electron deficient carbon centre.	Esterification

The functional groups in a molecule give you clues about its **properties** and **reactions**.
For example, a **–COOH group** will (usually) make the molecule **acidic** and mean it will
form esters with alcohols. Molecules containing **ester groups** will have **distinctive smells**.

You May Have to Identify Functional Groups

You need to be able to **recognise** functional groups.

Example: Look at compounds A, B and C, shown below.
For each compound, circle and name the functional groups.

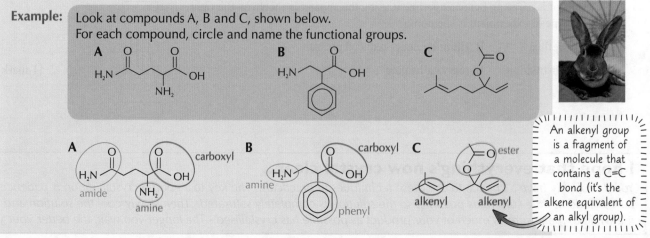

An alkenyl group is a fragment of a molecule that contains a C=C bond (it's the alkene equivalent of an alkyl group).

Functional Groups

Organic Chemistry **Reactions** can be Classified into **Seven Types**

In organic chemistry you can **classify** all the different reactions based on what happens to the molecules involved. All of the reactions you've met will fit into one of these seven types.

Reaction Type	Description	Functional groups that undergo this type of reaction
Addition	Two molecules join together to form a single product. Involves breaking a double bond.	$\diagdown C{=}C\diagup$ $-C\diagup^{O}_{\diagdown H}$ $\diagdown C{=}O$
Elimination / Dehydration	Involves removing a functional group which is released as part of a small molecule. Often a double bond is formed.	$-X$ (H–X eliminated) $-OH$ (H_2O eliminated) X = halogen
Substitution	A functional group on a molecule is swapped for a new one.	$-X$ $-OH$ ⬡ (H replaced)
Condensation	Two molecules get joined together with the loss of a small molecule, e.g. water or HCl.	$-C\diagup^{O}_{\diagdown OH}$ $-C\diagup^{O}_{\diagdown Cl}$ $-C\diagup^{O}_{\diagdown NH_2}{-}OH$
Hydrolysis	Water is used to split apart a molecule, creating two smaller ones. Opposite of condensation.	$-\overset{O}{\underset{}{C}}-O-$ $-C-O-C-$ (with =O) polyamides and polyesters
Oxidation	Oxidation is loss of electrons. In organic chemistry, it usually means gaining an oxygen atom or losing a hydrogen atom.	$-\overset{H}{\underset{H}{C}}-OH \rightarrow -C\diagup^{O}_{\diagdown H} \rightarrow -C\diagup^{O}_{\diagdown OH}$ $-\overset{}{\underset{}{C}}-OH \rightarrow \diagdown C{=}O$
Reduction	Reduction is gain of electrons. In organic chemistry, it usually means gaining a hydrogen atom or losing an oxygen atom.	$-C\diagup^{O}_{\diagdown OH} \rightarrow -C\diagup^{O}_{\diagdown H} \rightarrow -\overset{H}{\underset{H}{C}}-OH$ $\diagdown C{=}O \rightarrow -\overset{}{\underset{}{C}}-OH$

Warm-Up Questions

Q1 Name these functional groups:
  a) –COCl,   b) –COOCO–,   c) –COO–.

Q2 Draw the functional group of each of these families of compounds:
  a) amines,   b) aromatic compounds,   c) nitriles.

Exam Question

Q1 a) Name the reactive functional groups in molecules A–C.   [3 marks]

  b) Which molecule(s) are aromatic?   [1 mark]

  c) Which molecule(s) can be oxidised to an aldehyde?   [1 mark]

  d) Which molecule(s) take part in addition reactions?   [1 mark]

A $CH_3CH_2CH_2OH$

B $CH_3{-}\underset{OH}{\overset{|}{C}}{=}CH{-}CH_3$

C OH ⬡

The Alcohols have lots of properties — a flat in London, a house in France...

There's lots of information on these pages, but you've seen it all before. If some of it's been eliminated from your brain, or substituted by more interesting things (like what's for tea) you can find more detail in this Module and in Module 4. Have another look at those functional groups — being able to identify them quickly will make life a whole lot easier.

Synthetic Routes

In your exam you may be asked to suggest a pathway for the synthesis of a particular molecule. These pages contain a summary of some of the reactions you should know.

Chemists use **Synthesis Routes** to Get from One Compound to Another

Chemists have got to be able to make one compound from another. It's vital for things like **designing medicines**. It's also good for making imitations of **useful natural substances** when the real things are hard to extract.

If you're asked how to make one compound from another in the exam, make sure you include:

1) Any special procedures, such as refluxing.
2) The conditions needed, e.g. high temperature or pressure, or the presence of a catalyst.
3) Any safety precautions, e.g. do it in a fume cupboard.

Here's a round-up of the reactions you've covered in this Module and also in Year 1:

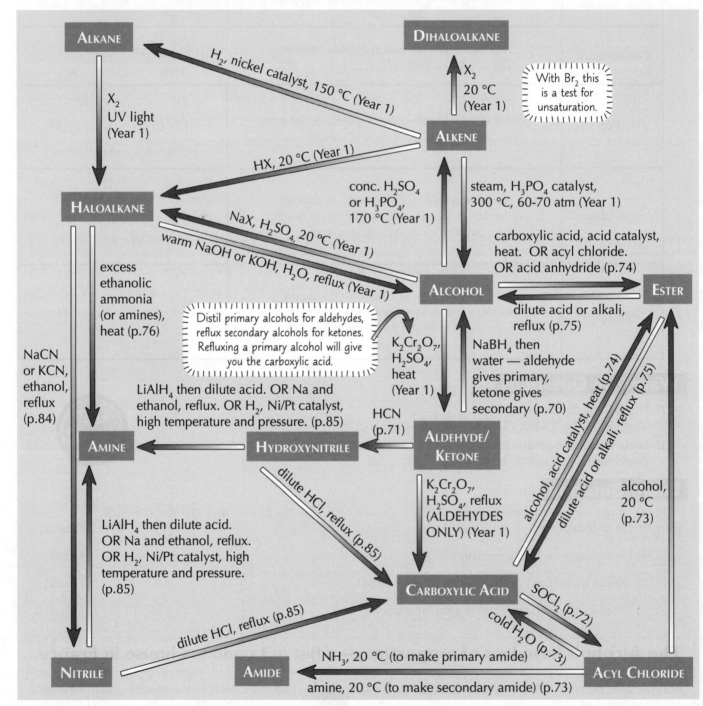

Synthetic Routes

Synthesis Route for Making **Aromatic Compounds**

There aren't so many of these reactions to learn — so make sure you know all the itty-bitty details.
If you can't remember any of the reactions, look back to the relevant pages and take a quick peek over them.

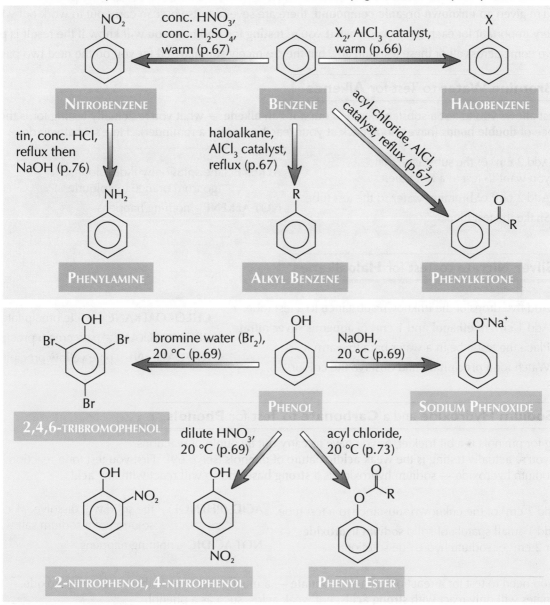

Warm-Up Questions

Q1 How do you make an alkene from an aldehyde?

Q2 How do you make phenylamine from benzene?

PRACTICE QUESTIONS

Exam Questions

Q1 Ethyl methanoate is one of the compounds responsible for the smell of raspberries.
Outline, with reaction conditions, how it could be synthesised in the laboratory from methanol. [2 marks]

Q2 How would you synthesise propanol starting with propane?
State the reaction conditions and reagents needed for each step. [2 marks]

Big red buses are great at Organic Synthesis — they're Route Masters...

There's loads of information here. Tons and tons of it. But you've covered pretty much all of it before, so it shouldn't be too hard to make sure it's firmly embedded in your head. If it's not, you know what to do — go back over it again. Then cover the diagrams up and try to draw them out from memory. Keep going until you can do it perfectly.

Tests for Organic Functional Groups

Now it's time for a spot of qualitative analysis. Don't be put off by those posh words though — all it really means is testing to see whether a particular substance is present in a sample. Couldn't be easier...

You Can Carry Out **Tests** to **Identify** Unknown **Organic Compounds**

1) If you're given an **unknown organic compound**, there are several tests you can carry out to work out what it is.

2) It's very important for each test to know **what** you're **testing** for, and how you will know if the result is **positive**.

3) You've come across all of these tests already, but they're nicely **summarised** for you on the next two pages.

Use **Bromine Water** to Test for **Alkenes**

This test allows you to test a substance to find out if it's an **alkene** — what you're actually testing for is the presence of **double bonds** (have a look back at your Year 1 notes for a reminder). Here's what you do:

1) Add 2 cm³ of the substance that you want to test to a test tube.

2) Add 2 cm³ of **bromine water** to the test tube.

3) **Shake** the test tube.

> **ALKENE** – the solution will decolourise (go from orange to colourless).
> **NOT ALKENE** – nothing happens.

Use **Silver Nitrate** to Test for **Haloalkanes**

1) Add five drops of the unknown substance to a test tube.

2) Add 1 cm³ of **ethanol** and 1 cm³ of **aqueous silver nitrate**.

3) Place the test tube in a water bath to warm it.

4) Watch for a **precipitate** and observe the colour.

> **CHLOROALKANE** – white precipitate.
> **BROMOALKANE** – pale cream precipitate.
> **IODOALKANE** – pale yellow precipitate.

Use **Sodium Hydroxide** and a **Carbonate** to Test for **Phenols**

Testing for phenols is a bit trickier, as you have to carry out a couple of reactions. What you're actually testing is the **weak acidic** nature of phenols (see p.69). First you test for a reaction with sodium hydroxide — sodium hydroxide is a **strong base** and so will react with any **acid**.

1) Add 2 cm³ of the unknown substance to a test tube.

2) Add 1 small spatula of solid **sodium hydroxide** (or 2 cm³ of sodium hydroxide solution).

> **ACID (PHENOL)** – the solid will dissolve. A colourless solution of a sodium salt will form.
> **NOT ACIDIC** – nothing happens.

Next you need to test for a reaction with a **carbonate** — a much weaker base than sodium hydroxide. Carbonates will only react with **strong acids**, not weak acids, such as a phenol.

1) Add 2 cm³ of the unknown substance to a test tube.

2) Add 1 small spatula of a solid **carbonate** or 2 cm³ of a carbonate solution (**sodium carbonate** will work nicely).

> **PHENOL/BASE** – nothing happens.
> **STRONG ACID** – effervescence.

Effervescence is just another way to describe fizzing and bubbling.

Use **Sodium Carbonate** to Test for **Carboxylic Acids**

Unlike phenols, **carboxylic acids** do react with carbonates to form a salt, **carbon dioxide** and water (see page 72). You can use this reaction to test whether a substance is a carboxylic acid.

1) Add 2 cm³ of the substance that you want to test to a test tube.

2) Add 1 small spatula of a solid **carbonate** (or 2 cm³ of a carbonate solution) e.g. **sodium carbonate**.

3) If the solution begins to **fizz**, bubble the gas that it produces through some **limewater** in a second test tube.

> **CARBOXYLIC ACID** – the solution will fizz. The carbon dioxide gas that is produced will turn limewater cloudy.
> **NOT CARBOXYLIC ACID** – nothing happens.

Tests for Organic Functional Groups

Use 2,4-DNP to Test for a Carbonyl Group

With this test, you need to use the reagent **2,4-dinitrophenylhydrazine** (2,4-DNP).
It may be a bit of a mouthful to say, but it's great for testing for **aldehydes** and **ketones** (see page 71).

1) Dissolve 0.2 g of 2,4-DNP in 1 cm³ of sulfuric acid, 2 cm³ of water and 5 cm³ of methanol.
2) In a different test tube, add 5 drops of the unknown substance to 2 cm³ of your solution from 1).
3) Shake the test tube and watch for a precipitate.

ALDEHYDE/KETONE – bright orange precipitate.

NOT ALDEHYDE/KETONE – nothing happens.

The solution you've made at the end of step 1) is known as Brady's reagent.

Use Tollens' Reagent to Test for Aldehydes

This is another test for **aldehydes** (see page 71) but this time it allows you to tell aldehydes and ketones apart. Unfortunately you have to prepare the reagent yourself. Mean.

1) Put 2 cm³ of 0.10 mol dm⁻³ **silver nitrate solution** in a test tube.
2) Add 5 drops of 0.80 mol dm⁻³ sodium hydroxide solution. A **light brown precipitate** should form.
3) Add drops of dilute ammonia solution until the brown precipitate **dissolves** completely.
4) Place the test tube in a hot water bath and add 10 drops of **aldehyde** or **ketone**. Wait for a few minutes.

ALDEHYDE – a silver mirror (a thin coating of silver) forms on the walls of the test tube.

KETONE/NOT ALDEHYDE – nothing happens.

The solution you've made at the end of step 3) is Tollens' reagent.

Use Acidified Dichromate to Test for Primary and Secondary Alcohols

1) Add 10 drops of the alcohol to 2 cm³ of **acidified potassium dichromate** solution in a test tube.
2) Warm the mixture gently in a hot water bath.
3) Then watch for a **colour change**:

The colour change is the orange dichromate(VI) ion ($Cr_2O_7^{2-}$) being reduced to the green chromium(III) ion (Cr^{3+}).

PRIMARY – the orange solution slowly turns green as an aldehyde forms. (If you carry on heating, the aldehyde will be oxidised further to give a carboxylic acid.)

SECONDARY – the orange solution slowly turns green as a ketone forms.

TERTIARY – nothing happens — boring, but easy to remember.

Warm-Up Questions

Q1 Describe how you would test a sample of a compound to find out if it contained a haloalkene.
Q2 What reagent would you use to test if a solution contained either a primary or secondary alcohol?

Exam Questions

Q1 Which one of these statements about cyclohexene is correct?
  A It produces a bright orange precipitate with 2,4-DNP solution.
  B It decolourises bromine water.
  C It turns limewater cloudy.
  D It forms a silver mirror with Tollens' reagent. [1 mark]

Q2 Describe a chemical test you could use to show that a solution is a carboxylic acid.
  Include any reagents, conditions and expected observations in your answer. [3 marks]

It's not the winning that counts, but the precipitation...

There are a fair few precipitates on this page — they can give a clear indication of what mystery compound you've got. But remember — when testing something, you might need to work through several tests before you can identify it.

Chromatography

You've probably tried chromatography with a spot of ink on a piece of filter paper — it's a classic experiment.

Chromatography is Good for **Separating** and **Identifying** Things

1) Chromatography is used to **separate** stuff in a mixture — once the mixture's separated out, you can often **identify** the different components, for example, different organic compounds.

2) There are quite a few different types of chromatography — you might have tried paper chromatography before — but the ones you need to know about are **thin-layer chromatography** (TLC) and **gas chromatography** (GC).

Thin-Layer Chromatography Separates Components by **Adsorption**

In **thin-layer chromatography** (TLC) a **solvent**, such as ethanol, moves over a **glass or plastic plate** which is covered in a **thin layer of solid** (e.g. silica gel or aluminium powder).

Here's the method for setting it up:

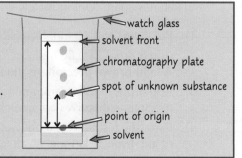

1) Draw a **pencil line** near the bottom of the plate and put a **spot** of the mixture to be separated on the line.

2) Dip the bottom of the plate (not the spot) into a **solvent**.

3) As the solvent spreads up the plate, the different substances in the mixture move with it, but **different distances** — so they separate out.

4) When the solvent's **nearly** reached the top of the plate, take the plate out and **mark** the distance that the solvent has moved (**solvent front**) in pencil.

watch glass
solvent front
chromatography plate
spot of unknown substance
point of origin
solvent

R$_f$ Values Help to **Identify** Organic Molecules

You can work out what was in the mixture by calculating an **R$_f$ value** for each spot on the TLC plate and looking them up in a **table of known values**.

$$R_f \text{ value} = \frac{\text{distance travelled by spot}}{\text{distance travelled by solvent}}$$

1) **How far** an organic molecule travels up the plate depends on **how strongly** it's **attracted** to the **layer of solid** on the surface of the plate.

2) The **attraction** between a substance and the surface of the plate is called **adsorption**.

3) A substance that is **strongly adsorbed** will move **slowly**, so it **won't travel as far** as one that's only **weakly adsorbed**. This means it will have a **different R$_f$ value**.

4) Chemical properties, such as **polarity**, affect how strongly adsorbed a particular substance is to the plate.

5) The distance a particular substance moves up the plate also depends on the **solid coating** on the plate, the **solvent** used, and external variables such as **temperature**. This means small changes in the TLC set-up can cause changes in the R$_f$ value. So once you've identified what you think an unknown compound is, it's best to check you're right by **running a pure sample** of the **known substance alongside** your **unknown compound** on a TLC plate. Identical substances should travel the same distance up the plate, i.e. have the **same R$_f$ value**.

Gas Chromatography is a Bit More **High-Tech**

1) In **gas chromatography** (GC) the **sample** to be analysed is **injected** into a stream of **gas**, which carries it through a coiled **tube** coated with a **viscous liquid** (such as an oil) or a **solid**.

2) The components of the mixture constantly **dissolve in the oil** or **onto the solid**, **evaporate back** into the gas and then **redissolve** as they travel through the tube.

3) The time taken for the substances to pass through the coiled tube and reach the detector is called the **retention time**. It can be used to help **identify** the substances.

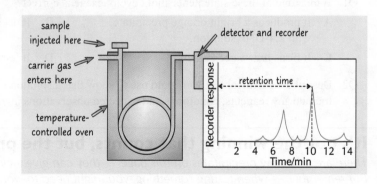

sample injected here
carrier gas enters here
temperature-controlled oven
detector and recorder
retention time
Recorder response
2 4 6 8 10 12 14
Time/min

Chromatography

GC Chromatograms Show the Proportions of the Components in a Mixture

A **gas chromatogram** shows a **series of peaks** at the times when the **detector** senses something other than the carrier gas **leaving the tube**. They can be used to **identify the substances** within a sample and their **relative proportions**.

1) Each **peak** on a chromatogram corresponds to a substance with a particular **retention time**.

2) **Retention times** are measured from **zero** to the **centre** of each peak, and can be looked up in a **reference table** to **identify** the **substances** present.

3) The **area** under each peak is proportional to the relative **amount of each substance** in the original mixture. Remember, it's **area**, not height, that's important — the **tallest** peak on the chromatogram **won't always** represent the **most abundant substance**.

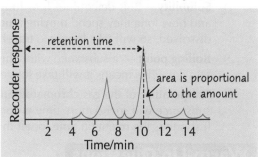

External Calibration Curves Help Find Concentration

The **area** under the peak of a GC chromatogram gives you the **relative amount** of a substance, but finding the exact concentration is a bit trickier. To work out the **concentration** of a particular substance in a sample you need create an **external calibration curve**. Here's how:

1) Create a series of **standard solutions** of **different concentrations** of analyte — this is just the substance you've chosen to detect for your calibration.

2) One by one, inject your standard solutions into a gas chromatography instrument and **record** the **result**.

3) Calculate the **area** under the peak of each response for each standard solution.

4) Plot these values on a graph of **area vs concentration**.

5) **Join your points** up to create an external calibration curve.

Your calibration curve can be a straight line or a curve.

It's a good idea to run a **blank** when you're making a calibration curve. A **blank** is just a solution containing all the solvents and reagents used when making the standard solutions, but **no analyte**. By **subtracting** the response of the blank from each of the responses of your standard solutions, you can find a **corrected peak value** — one that takes into account the effect of reagents and solvents on the peak areas.

Example: On a chromatogram, the area under the peak for substance X is 360 units. Estimate the concentration of substance X in the sample by drawing an external calibration curve, using the data in the table below. The areas have been corrected using a blank.

Concentration (mol dm⁻³)	0.00	0.25	0.50	0.75
Area (units)	0	190	410	625

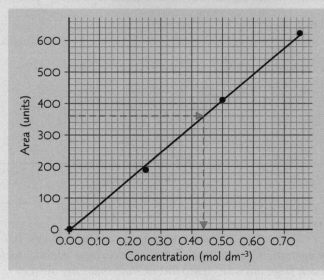

1) First, plot the points from the table on a graph. Concentration is always plotted on the x-axis and area on the y-axis.

2) Draw a line (or curve) of best fit.

3) Now work out what concentration corresponds to an area of **360 units** by drawing a line from 360 on the y-axis to where it meets the line of best fit, and then drawing a line from this point, down to the x-axis.

4) Read off the result on the x-axis.

5) So the concentration of substance X is **0.44 mol dm⁻³**.

Your answer is only an estimate — you don't know exactly what the concentration is.

Chromatography

Retention Time Helps Identify Different Molecules

You saw on the last page that retention times can be used to identify the presence of different substances in a mixture. There are several factors that affect retention times:

1) **Solubility** — this determines **how long** each component of the mixture spends **dissolved in the oil** or **on the solid** and how long they spend **moving along** the tube in the **gas**. A highly soluble substance will spend more time dissolved, so will take longer to travel through the tube to the detector than one with a lower solubility.

2) **Boiling point** — a substance with a **high boiling point** will spend more time **condensed** as a liquid in the tube than as a gas. This means it will take longer to travel through the tube than one with a lower boiling point.

3) **Temperature of the gas chromatography instrument** — a **high temperature** means the substance will spend more time **evaporated** in the gas and so will move along the tube quickly. It shortens the retention time for **all** the substances in the tube.

Warm-Up Questions

Q1 Describe how you would calculate the R_f value of a substance on a TLC plate.

Q2 Give three factors that affect the retention time in gas chromatography.

PRACTICE QUESTIONS

Exam Questions

Q1 Look at this diagram of a chromatogram produced using TLC on a mixture of substances A and B.

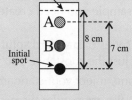

a) Calculate the R_f value of spot A. [2 marks]

b) Explain why substance A has moved further up the plate than substance B. [1 mark]

Q2 A scientist has a mixture of several organic chemicals. He wants to know if it contains any hexene. He runs a sample of pure hexene through a GC machine and finds that its retention time is 5 minutes. Then he runs a sample of his mixture through the same machine, under the same conditions,and produces the chromatogram shown on the right.

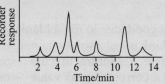

a) What feature of the chromatogram suggests that the sample contains hexene? [1 mark]

b) The mixture is also found to contain small amounts of ethene. How would you expect the retention time of ethene to compare with that of hexene? Explain your answer. [2 marks]

Q3 A mixture of 25% ethanol and 75% benzene is run through a GC apparatus.

a) Describe what happens to the mixture in the apparatus. [4 marks]

b) Given that ethanol and benzene have very similar boiling points, explain why the substances separate. [2 marks]

c) How will the resulting chromatogram show the proportions of ethanol and benzene present in the mixture? [1 mark]

Q4 The graph on the right is an external calibration curve for substance A. On a chromatogram for a sample containing substance A, the area under the peak for substance A is 16 units. Estimate the concentration of substance A in the sample?

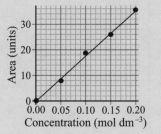

A 0.06 mol dm⁻³   B 0.28 mol dm⁻³

C 0.09 mol dm⁻³   D 0.16 mol dm⁻³   [1 mark]

A little bit of TLC is what you need...

If you only remember one thing about chromatography, remember that it's really good at separating mixtures, but not so reliable at identifying the substances that make up the mixture. Or does that count as two things? Hmm... well it's probably not the best idea to only learn one thing from each page anyway. Learn lots of stuff, that's my advice.

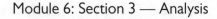

NMR Spectroscopy

NMR isn't the easiest of things, so ingest this information one piece at a time — a bit like eating a bar of chocolate.

NMR Gives You Information about the Structure of Molecules

Nuclear magnetic resonance (**NMR**) **spectroscopy** is an analytical technique that you can use to work out the **structure** of an organic molecule. The way that NMR works is pretty **complicated**, but here are the **basics**:

1) A sample of a compound is placed in a **strong magnetic field** and exposed to a range of different **frequencies** of **radio waves**.

2) The **nuclei** of certain atoms within the molecule **absorb energy** from the radio waves.

3) The amount of energy that a nucleus absorbs at each frequency will depend on the **environment** that it's in — there's more about this further down the page.

4) The **pattern** of these absorptions gives you information about the **positions** of certain atoms within the molecule, and about **how many** atoms of that type the molecule contains.

5) You can piece these bits of information together to work out the **structure of the molecule**.

The two types of NMR spectroscopy you need to know about are **carbon-13 NMR** and **high resolution proton NMR**.

> **Carbon-13** (or ^{13}C) **NMR** gives you information about the **number of carbon atoms** that are in a molecule, and the **environments** that they are in.

> **High resolution proton NMR** gives you information about the **number of hydrogen atoms** that are in a molecule, and the **environments** that they're in.

Nuclei in Different Environments Absorb Different Amounts of Energy

1) A nucleus is partly **shielded** from the effects of external magnetic fields by its **surrounding electrons**.

2) Any **other atoms** and **groups of atoms** that are around a nucleus will also affect its amount of electron shielding.
E.g. If a carbon atom bonds to a more electronegative atom (like oxygen) the amount of electron shielding around its nucleus will decrease.

3) This means that the nuclei in a molecule feel different magnetic fields depending on their **environments**. Nuclei in different environments will absorb **different amounts** of energy at **different frequencies**.

4) It's these **differences in absorption** of energy between environments that you're looking for in **NMR spectroscopy**.

5) An atom's **environment** depends on **all** the groups that it's connected to going **along the molecule** — not just the atoms it's actually bonded to. To be in the **same environment**, two atoms must be joined to **exactly the same things**.

H H | | H–C–C–Cl | | H H	H Cl H | | | H–C–C–C–H | | | H H H	H H H H | | | | H–C–C–C–C–Cl | | | | H H H H
Chloroethane has 2 carbon environments — its carbons are bonded to different atoms.	*2-chloropropane has 2 carbon environments:* *• 1 C in a CHCl group, bonded to (CH₃)₂* *• 2 Cs in CH₃ groups, bonded to CHCl(CH₃)*	*1-chlorobutane has 4 carbon environments. (The two carbons in CH₂ groups are **different** distances from the electronegative Cl atom — so their **environments** are different.)*

Tetramethylsilane is Used as a Standard

The diagram below shows a typical **carbon-13 NMR spectrum**. The **peaks** show the **frequencies** at which **energy was absorbed** by the carbon nuclei. **Each peak** represents one **carbon environment** — so this molecule has two.

1) The **differences in absorption** are measured relative to a **standard substance** — **tetramethylsilane** (**TMS**).

2) TMS produces a **single absorption peak** in both types of NMR because all its carbon and hydrogen nuclei are in the **same environment**.

3) It's chosen as a standard because the **absorption peak** is at a **lower frequency** than just about everything else.

4) This peak is given a value of **0** and all the peaks in other substances are measured as **chemical shifts** relative to this.

Carbon-13 NMR Spectrum

absorption

TMS

200   150   100   50   0
Chemical shift, δ (ppm)

Chemical shift is the **difference in the radio frequency** absorbed by the nuclei (hydrogen or carbon) in the molecule being analysed and that absorbed by the same nuclei in **TMS**. They're given the symbol δ and are measured in **parts per million**, or **ppm**. A small amount of TMS is often added to samples to give a **reference peak** on the spectrum.

The chemical formula for TMS is Si(CH₃)₄.

NMR Spectroscopy

^{13}C NMR Spectra Tell You About Carbon Environments

It's very likely that you'll be given an **NMR spectrum** to **interpret** in your exam. It might be a **carbon-13 NMR spectrum** or a **proton NMR spectrum** (you might even see both if you're really lucky), so you need to have both kinds sussed. First, here's a **step-by-step guide** to interpreting carbon-13 spectra.

1) Count the Number of Carbon Environments

First, count the **number of peaks** in the spectrum — this is the **number of carbon environments** in the molecule. If there's a peak at δ = 0, **don't count it** — it's the reference peak from **TMS**.

The spectrum on the right has **three peaks** — so the molecule must have **three different carbon environments**. This **doesn't** necessarily mean it only has **three carbons**, as it could have **more than one** in the **same environment**. In fact the molecular formula of this molecule is $C_5H_{10}O$, so it must have **several carbons** in the **same environment**.

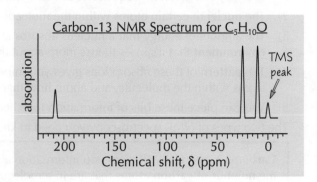

Carbon-13 NMR Spectrum for $C_5H_{10}O$

absorption

TMS peak

200   150   100   50   0
Chemical shift, δ (ppm)

2) Look Up the Chemical Shifts in a Shift Diagram

In your exam you'll get a **data sheet** that will include a **diagram** like the one below. The diagram shows the **chemical shifts** experienced by **carbon nuclei** in **different environments**. The boxes show the range of shift values a carbon in that environment could have, e.g. **C=O** could have a shift value anywhere between 160 – 220 ppm.

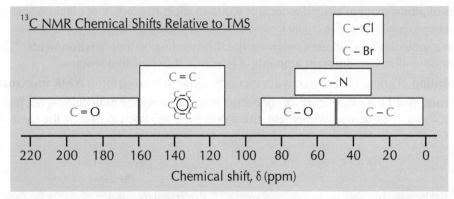

^{13}C NMR Chemical Shifts Relative to TMS

C – Cl
C – Br
C = C
C – N
C = O
C – O
C – C

220 200 180 160 140 120 100 80 60 40 20 0
Chemical shift, δ (ppm)

> Matching peaks to the groups that cause them isn't always straightforward, because the chemical shifts can overlap. For example, a peak at δ ≈ 40 might be caused by C–C, C–Cl, C–N or C–Br.

You need to **match up** the **peaks** in the spectrum with the **chemical shifts** in the diagram to work out which **carbon environments** they could represent. For example, the peak at δ ≈ **10** in the spectrum above represents a **C–C** bond. The peak at δ ≈ **25** is also due to a **C–C** bond. The carbons causing this peak have a different chemical shift to those causing the first peak — so they must be in a slightly different environment. The peak at δ ≈ **210**, is due to a **C=O** group, but you don't know whether it could be an aldehyde or a ketone (you know it can't be a carboxylic acid as the molecular formula only contains one **O**).

3) Try Out Possible Structures

An **aldehyde** with 5 carbons:

H   H   H   H
| | | | O
H–C–C–C–C–C
| | | | H
H   H   H   H

This doesn't work — it does have the right **molecular formula** ($C_5H_{10}O$), but it also has **five carbon environments**.

A **ketone** with five carbons:

H   H   O   H   H
| | ‖ | |
H–C–C–C–C–C–H
| | | |
H   H   H   H

This works. **Pentan-3-one** has **three** carbon environments — two CH_3 carbons, each bonded to $CH_2COCH_2CH_3$, two CH_2 carbons, each bonded to CH_3 and $COCH_2CH_3$, and one **CO** carbon bonded to $(CH_2CH_3)_2$. It has the right **molecular formula** ($C_5H_{10}O$) too.

> It can't be pentan-2-one — that has 5 carbon environments.

So, the molecule analysed was **pentan-3-one**.

NMR Spectroscopy

Interpreting NMR Spectra Gets Easier with Practice

Example: The diagram shows the carbon-13 NMR spectrum of an alcohol with the molecular formula $C_4H_{10}O$. Analyse and interpret the spectrum to identify the structure of the alcohol.

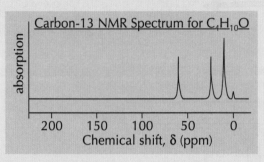

Carbon-13 NMR Spectrum for $C_4H_{10}O$

absorption

200   150   100   50   0
Chemical shift, δ (ppm)

1) Looking at the **diagram** on the **previous page**, the peak with a **chemical shift** of $\delta \approx 65$ is likely to be due to a **C–O** bond.

2) The two peaks around $\delta \approx 20$ probably both represent carbons in **C–C** bonds, but with slightly different environments. Remember the alcohol doesn't contain any **chlorine**, **bromine** or **nitrogen** so you know the peak can't be caused by C–Cl, C–Br or C–N bonds.

3) The spectrum has **three peaks**, so the alcohol must have three **carbon environments**. There are **four carbons** in the alcohol, so two of the carbons must be in the **same environment**.

4) Put together all the **information** you've got so far, and try out some **structures**:

H H H H
   | | | |
H–C–C–C–C–OH
   | | | |
H H H H
 	
This has a C–O bond, and some C–C bonds, which is right. But all four carbons are in different environments.
	H H H H
	   | | | |
	H–C–C–C–C–H
	   | | | |
	H H OH H
	
	Again, this has a C–O bond, and some C–C bonds. But the carbons are still all in different environments.
		OH
		|
		H–C–H
		H | H
		| | |
		H–C–C–C–H
		| | |
		H H H
		
		This molecule has a C–O bond and C–C bonds and two of the carbons are in the same environment. So this must be the correct structure.

You'll also need to be able to predict what the carbon-13 NMR spectrum of a molecule may look like. This isn't as hard as it sounds — just identify the number of unique carbon environments, then use your data sheet to work out where the peaks of each carbon environment would appear.

Warm-Up Questions

Q1 What part of the electromagnetic spectrum does NMR spectroscopy use?

Q2 What is meant by chemical shift? What compound is used as a reference for chemical shifts?

Q3 How can you tell from a carbon-13 NMR spectrum how many carbon environments a molecule contains?

Q4 Which types of bond could a shift of $\delta \approx 150$ correspond to?

For these questions, use the shift values from the diagram on p.100.

Exam Questions

Q1 The carbon-13 NMR spectrum shown on the right was produced by a compound with the molecular formula C_3H_9N.

Carbon-13 NMR Spectrum

absorption

200   150   100   50   0
Chemical shift, δ (ppm)

a) Explain why there is a peak at $\delta = 0$. [1 mark]

b) The compound does not have the formula $CH_3CH_2CH_2NH_2$. Explain how the spectrum shows this. [2 marks]

c) Suggest and explain a possible structure for the compound. [4 marks]

Q2 Look at the molecule X, on the right. Which of the following statements is/are true?

1. The carbon-13 NMR spectrum of X has a peak in the region of 160 - 220.
2. Molecule X has three different carbon environments.
3. The carbon-13 NMR spectrum of X shows four peaks.

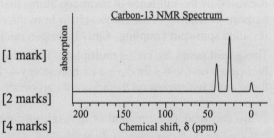

A 1, 2 and 3	**B** Only 1 and 2	**C** Only 1 and 3	**D** Only 3 [1 mark]

Why did the carbon peak? Because it saw the radio wave...

The ideas behind NMR are difficult, but don't worry too much if you don't really understand them. The important thing is to know how to interpret a spectrum — that's what will get you marks in the exam. If you're having trouble, go over the examples and practice questions a few more times. You should have the "ahh... I get it" moment sooner or later.

Proton NMR

So, you know how to interpret carbon-13 NMR spectra — now it's time to get your teeth into some proton NMR spectra.

¹H NMR Spectra Tell You About Hydrogen Environments

Interpreting **proton NMR spectra** is similar to interpreting carbon-13 NMR spectra:

1) Each peak represents one **hydrogen environment**.

2) Look up the **chemical shifts** on a **data diagram** to identify possible environments. They're different from ¹³C NMR, so make sure you're looking at the **correct data diagram**.

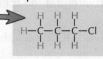

For example, 1-chloropropane has 3 hydrogen environments.

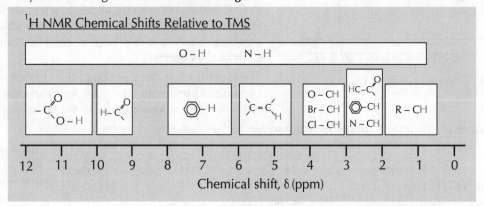

3) In ¹H NMR, the **relative area** under each peak tells you the relative number of H atoms in each environment. For example, if the area under two peaks is in the **ratio** 2:1, there will be **two** H atoms in the first environment for every **one** in the second environment.

4) Areas can be shown using **numbers** above the peaks or with an **integration trace**.

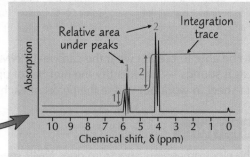

The **integration trace** is the red line.

The **height increases** are proportional to the area under each peak.

The big difference between carbon-13 NMR and proton NMR spectra is that the peaks in a spectrum **split** according to how the **hydrogen environments are arranged**. Putting all this info together should let you work out the structure.

Spin-Spin Coupling Splits the Peaks in a Proton NMR Spectrum

In a proton NMR spectrum, a peak that represents a hydrogen environment can be **split**. The splitting is caused by the influence of hydrogen atoms that are bonded to **neighbouring carbons** — these are carbons one along in the carbon chain from the carbon the hydrogen's attached to. This effect is called **spin-spin coupling**. Only hydrogen nuclei on **adjacent** carbon atoms affect each other.

The **splitting** of the peak for this H... ...tells you about the hydrogens on this adjacent carbon.

These **split peaks** are called **multiplets**. They always split into one more than the number of hydrogens on the neighbouring carbon atoms — it's called the **n + 1 rule**. For example, if there are **2 hydrogens** on the adjacent carbon atoms, the peak will be split into 2 + 1 = 3.

You can work out the **number** of **neighbouring hydrogens** by looking at how many the peak splits into:

If a peak's split into *two* (a *doublet*) then there's *one hydrogen* on the neighbouring carbon atoms.

If a peak's split into *three* (a *triplet*) then there are *two hydrogens* on the neighbouring carbon atoms.

If a peak's split into *four* (a *quartet*) then there are *three hydrogens* on the neighbouring carbon atoms.

Example: Look at the ¹H NMR spectrum of *1,1,2-trichloroethane*:

The peak due to the blue hydrogens is split into *two* because there's *one hydrogen* on the adjacent carbon atom.

The peak due to the red hydrogen is split into *three* because there are *two hydrogens* on the adjacent carbon atom.

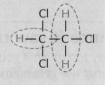

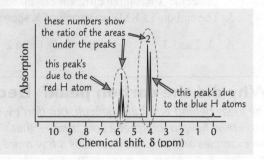

these numbers show the ratio of the areas under the peaks

this peak's due to the red H atom

this peak's due to the blue H atoms

Proton NMR

Deuterated Solvents are used in Proton NMR Spectroscopy

NMR spectra are recorded with the molecule that is being analysed in **solution**. But if you used a ordinary solvent like water or ethanol, the **hydrogen nuclei** in the solvent would **add peaks** to the spectrum and confuse things. To overcome this, the **hydrogen nuclei** in the solvent are **replaced** with **deuterium** (D) — an **isotope** of hydrogen with **one proton** and **one neutron**. Deuterium nuclei don't absorb the radio wave energy, so they don't add peaks to the spectrum. A commonly used example of a '**deuterated solvent**' is **deuterated chloroform**, $CDCl_3$.

OH and NH Protons can be Identified by Proton Exchange Using D_2O

The **chemical shift** due to protons attached to oxygen (OH) or nitrogen (NH) is very **variable** — check out the huge **ranges** given in the **table** on the previous page. They make quite a **broad** peak that isn't usually split. Don't panic, though, as there's a clever little trick chemists use to identify OH and NH protons:

1) Run **two** spectra of the molecule — one with a little **deuterium oxide**, D_2O, added.

2) If an OH or NH proton is present it'll swap with deuterium and, hey presto, the peak will **disappear**. (This is because deuterium doesn't absorb the radio wave energy). This can help you to identify the presence of hydroxyl or N–H groups.

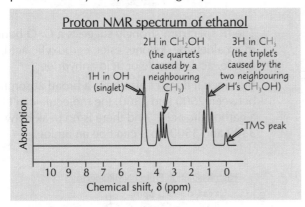

Proton NMR spectrum of ethanol

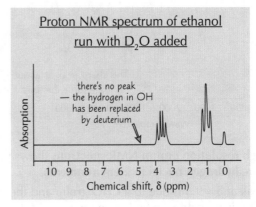

Proton NMR spectrum of ethanol run with D_2O added

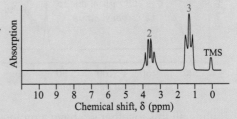

You might also be asked to predict the proton NMR spectrum for a molecule.

Warm-Up Questions

Q1 What causes the peaks on a high resolution proton NMR spectrum to split?

Q2 What causes a triplet of peaks on a high resolution proton NMR spectrum?

Q3 What are deuterated solvents? Why are they needed?

Q4 How can you get rid of a peak caused by an OH group?

PRACTICE QUESTIONS

Exam Question

Q1 The proton NMR spectrum on the right is for an alkyl halide. Use the diagram of chemical shifts on page 102 to answer this question.

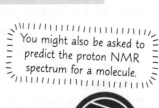

a) What is the likely environment of the two protons with a shift of 3.6 ppm? [1 mark]

b) What is the likely environment of the three protons with a shift of 1.3 ppm? [1 mark]

c) The molecular mass of the molecule is 64.5. Suggest a possible structure and explain your suggestion. [2 marks]

d) Explain the splitting patterns of the two peaks. [2 marks]

Never mind splitting peaks — this stuff's likely to cause splitting headaches...

Is your head spinning yet? I know mine is. Round and round like a merry-go-round. It's a hard life when you're tied to a desk trying to get NMR spectroscopy firmly fixed in your head. You must be looking quite peaky by now... so go on, learn this stuff, take the dog around the block, then come back and see if you can still remember it all.

More on Spectra

Yes, I know, it's yet another page on spectra — but it's the last one (alright, two) I promise.

You Can Use **Data From Several Spectra** to **Work Out a Structure**

All the **spectroscopy techniques** in this section will **give clues** to the **identity of a mystery molecule**, but you can be more **certain** about a structure (and avoid jumping to wrong conclusions) if you look at **data from several different types of spectrum**. Look back at your Year 1 notes for a reminder about mass spectroscopy and IR spectra.

Example: The following spectra are all of the same molecule. Deduce the molecule's structure.

The **mass spectrum** tells you the molecule's got a **mass of 44** and it's likely to contain a **CH₃ group**.

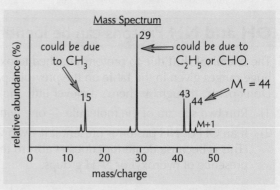

The **IR spectrum** strongly suggests a **C=O bond** in an aldehyde, ketone, ester, carboxylic acid, amide, acyl chloride or acid anhydride.

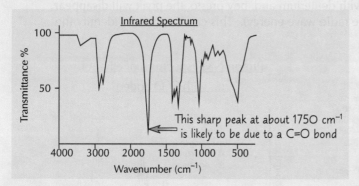

But since it **doesn't** also have a broad absorption between 2500 and 3300, the molecule **can't** be a carboxylic acid. And there is no peak between 3300 and 3500, so it can't be an amide.

The **high resolution proton NMR spectrum** shows that there are **hydrogen nuclei in 2 environments**.

The peak at $\delta \approx 9.5$ is due to a **CHO group** and the one at $\delta \approx 2.5$ is probably the hydrogen atoms in **COCH₃**.

(You know that these can't be any other groups with similar chemical shifts thanks to the mass spectrum and IR spectrum.)

The **area** under the peaks is in the ratio **1 : 3**, which makes sense as there's **1 hydrogen in CHO** and **3 in COCH₃**.

The **splitting pattern** shows that the protons are on **adjacent carbon atoms**, so the group must be **HCOCH₃**.

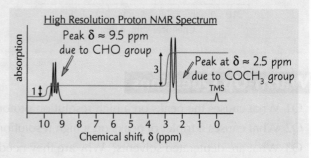

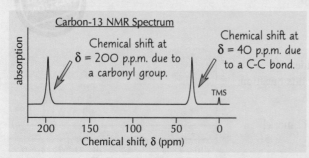

The **carbon-13 NMR spectrum** shows that the molecule has carbon nuclei in **2 different environments**.

The peak at $\delta = 200$ corresponds to a carbon in a **carbonyl group** and the other peak is due to a **C–C bond**.

Putting all this together we have a molecule with a **mass of 44**, which contains a **CH₃ group**, a **C=O bond**, and an **HCOCH₃ group**.

So, the structure of the molecule must be:

$$H_3C - C {\overset{O}{\underset{H}{\diagdown}}}$$

which is the aldehyde **ethanal**.

You probably could have worked the molecule's structure out **without** using all the spectra, but in more **complex examples** you might well need all of them, so it's good practice. And while we're on the subject, there are a couple **more examples** for you to practise on the next page — enjoy.

More on Spectra

Elemental Analysis also Helps to Work Out a Structure

1) In elemental analysis, experiments determine the **masses** or percentage compositions of different elements in a compound.

2) This data can help you to work out the **empirical** and **molecular formulae** of a compound. See your Year 1 notes to remind yourself how to do this.

3) Knowing the molecular formula is useful in working out the **structure** of the compound from different spectra.

Warm-Up Questions

Q1 Which type of spectrum gives you the mass of a molecule?

Q2 Which spectrum can tell you how many carbon environments are in a molecule?

Q3 Which spectrum can tell you how many different hydrogen environments there are in a molecule?

Q4 Which spectrum involves radio wave radiation?

PRACTICE QUESTIONS

Exam Questions

Q1 The four spectra shown were produced by running different tests on samples of the same pure organic compound.
Use them to work out:

a) The molecular mass of the compound. [1 mark]

b) The probable structure of the molecule. Explain your reasoning. [6 marks]

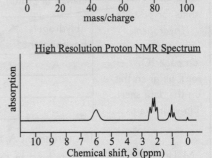

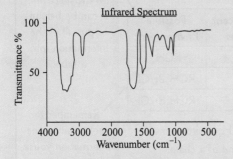

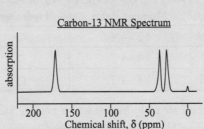

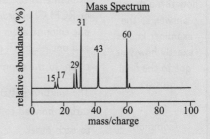

Q2 The four spectra shown were produced by running different tests on samples of the same pure organic compound.
Use them to work out:

a) The molecular mass of the compound. [1 mark]

b) The probable structure of the molecule. Explain your reasoning. [6 marks]

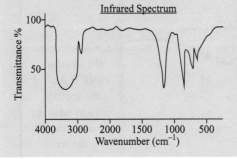

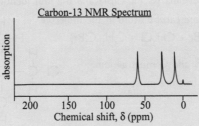

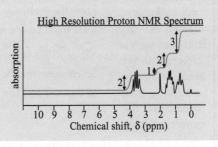

Spectral analysis — psychology for ghosts...

So that's analysis done and dusted, you'll be pleased to hear. But before you rush off to switch the kettle on, take a moment to check that you really know how to interpret all the different spectra. You might want to go back and have a look at page 90 too if you're having trouble remembering what all the different functional groups look like.

Extra Exam Practice

That's a wrap on Module 6. To see how well you know it all, try these questions based on the last three sections. Later on there'll be questions covering a range of topics, just like in your exams.

- Have a look at this example of how to answer a tricky exam question.
- Then check how much you've understood from Module 6 by having a go at the questions on the next page.

---

1 A compound was analysed by proton NMR and carbon-13 NMR.
The results are shown in **Figure 1**. The molecular formula of the compound is $C_5H_{10}ClBr$.
Deduce the structure of the compound, showing all of your working.

Figure 1

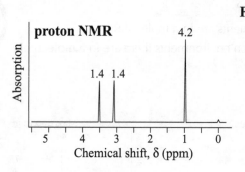

(5 marks)

The diagram showing the range of chemical shifts for possible hydrogen environments is on page 102 — you'll be given this on the data sheet in your exams.

1

The carbon-13 NMR spectrum has four peaks, so there are four C environments.
Analysis of proton NMR spectrum:

When analysing the proton NMR spectrum, it can be helpful to put all of the information into a table.

Hydrogen Environment	δ	Area Ratio → Whole Number Ratio	No. of Adjacent Hydrogens	Possible Environment
A	0.9	4.2 → 6	0	RCH_3
B	3.1	1.4 → 2	0	RCH_2Br/Cl
C	3.5	1.4 → 2	0	RCH_2Br/Cl

In environment A, there are six hydrogens with a possible RCH_3 environment, so there must be two $-CH_3$ groups, each positioned on the end of a chain.

Remember to look at all of the information you're given — you can use the carbon-13 NMR data and the molecular formula to help rule out other possible hydrogen environments.

Make sure you show a logical flow through your answer, so the examiner knows exactly how you got to the final answer.

In both environments B and C, there are two hydrogens with a possible RCH_2Br or RCH_2Cl environment. The molecular formula shows that the compound has one chlorine atom and one bromine atom, so there will be one $-CH_2Br$ group and one $-CH_2Cl$ group. Both of these groups will be positioned on the end of a chain, so the compound must be branched.

The splitting pattern shows that environments A, B and C are not adjacent to a carbon bonded to hydrogen. So these hydrogen environments cannot be adjacent to each other.

Common mistakes to look out for include drawing incorrect structures, such as carbons with five bonds, or drawing a structure that doesn't have the correct molecular formula.

From the molecular formula ($C_5H_{10}ClBr$) and the four identified groups, there must be one more carbon atom in the molecule ($CH_3 + CH_3 + CH_2Br + CH_2Cl = C_4H_{10}ClBr$).

So environments A, B and C must all join to this carbon. The structure must be:

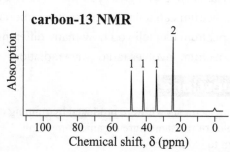

Once you've got the structure, check it against the splitting pattern again to make sure it's correct.

You'd get 1 mark for identifying four C environments, 1 mark for identifying the number of H's in each environment, 1 mark for identifying what type of environments the hydrogens are in and 1 mark for analysing the splitting pattern of the environments. Then you'd get 1 mark for the correct structure.

Extra Exam Practice

2   (6)-gingerol is one of the compounds in fresh ginger that gives the root its pungency.
When heated, (6)-gingerol reacts to form zingerone. This gives gingerbread its spicy-sweet flavour.
The structures of (6)-gingerol and zingerone are shown in **Figure 2**.

Figure 2

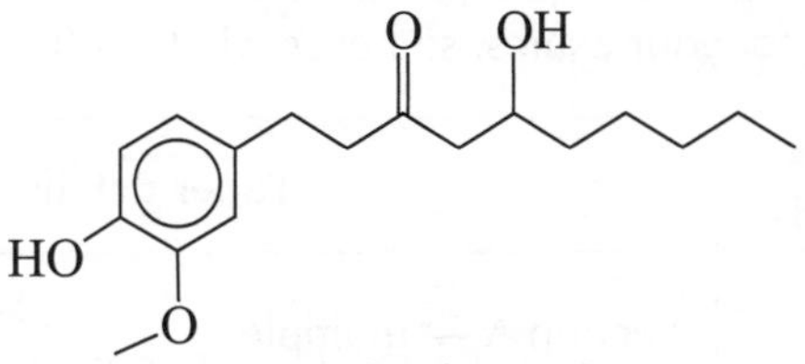

(6)-gingerol 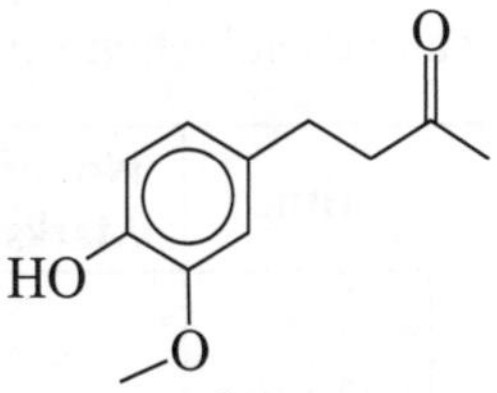   **zingerone**

(a)   (6)-gingerol is a chiral molecule.
Explain what this means and circle the chiral centre in (6)-gingerol.

(3 marks)

(b)   2-methoxyphenol, shown in **Figure 3**, reacts with 4-chlorobutan-2-one to form zingerone.
Draw the mechanism of this reaction, including the formation of the catalytic intermediate.

Figure 3

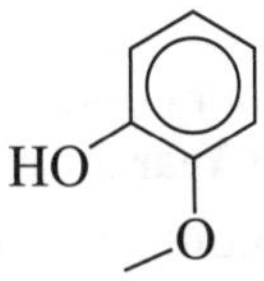

(6 marks)

(c)   Describe the key steps in purifying impure solid zingerone by recrystallisation.

(5 marks)

3   Threonine and cysteine, shown in **Figure 4**, are amino acids commonly found in proteins.

Figure 4

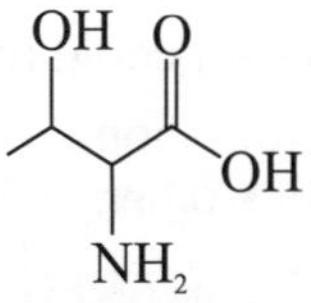

threonine 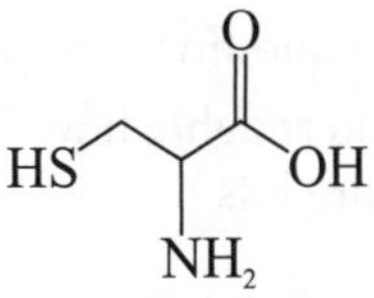   **cysteine**

(a)   Threonine reacts with ethanol in the presence of sulfuric acid.
Draw the structure of the product which is formed.

(1 mark)

(b)   Threonine can be polymerised to make the polyamide poly(threonine).
Draw the displayed formula of the repeating unit.

(1 mark)

(c)   A sample of cysteine reacts with hydrochloric acid.
Draw the structure of the salt that is formed.

(1 mark)

Do Well In Your Exams

Passing exams isn't all about revision — it really helps if you know how the exam is structured and have got your exam technique nailed so that you pick up every mark you can.

Make Sure You Know the Structure of Your Exams

For **A-Level Chemistry**, you'll be sitting **three papers**. Knowing what's going to come up in each paper and how much time you'll have will be really useful when you're preparing for your exams, so here's what you'll be up against:

Paper		Time	No. of Marks	Modules assessed	Paper details	
1	Periodic table, elements and physical chemistry	2 hrs 15 mins	100	1, 2, 3 and 5	Section A — multiple choice questions (15 marks)	Section B — short answer and extended response questions (85 marks)
2	Synthesis and analytical techniques	2 hrs 15 mins	100	1, 2, 4 and 6	Section A — multiple choice questions (15 marks)	Section B — short answer and extended response questions (85 marks)
3	Unified chemistry	1 hr 30 mins	70	All modules	Short answer and extended response questions.	

As you can see in the table...

1) All three papers cover theory from **both years** of your course — this means you need to make sure you revise your **Year 1 modules** (modules 1-4) as well as your **Year 2 modules** (modules 5-6) for these exams.

2) In **Section A** of papers **1** and **2**, you'll have some **multiple choice questions**. Never, ever leave these blank. Even if you don't know the answer, you can always have a **guess**.

3) All three papers will include **extended response questions**. Two of these questions in each paper will be marked with an asterisk (*), which means that there are **marks** available for the quality of your response.

   For these questions, as well as having all the right **scientific content**, your answer needs to:
   - Have a clear and logical structure.
   - Include the right scientific terms, spelt correctly.
   - Include detailed information that's relevant to the question.

Manage Your Time Sensibly

1) How **long** you spend on each question is important in an exam — it could make all the difference to your grade.

2) The **number of marks** tells you **roughly** how long to spend on a question.
   But some questions will require lots of work for a few marks while others will be quicker.

> **Example:**
> 1) Define the term 'enthalpy change of neutralisation'.   (2 marks)
> 2) Compounds A and B are hydrocarbons with relative molecular masses of 78 and 58 respectively. In their ^1H NMR spectra, A has only one peak and B has two peaks. Draw a possible structure for each compound.   (2 marks)

Question 1 only requires you to write down a **definition** — if you can remember it this shouldn't take too long.

Question 2 requires you to **apply your knowledge** of NMR spectra and **draw the structure** of two compounds — this may take you a lot longer, especially if you have to draw out a few structures before getting it right.

So if **time's running out**, it makes sense to do questions like Q1 **first** and **come back** to Q2 if there's time at the end.

3) If you get stuck on a question for too long, it may be best to **move on** and come back to it later.

4) You **don't** have to work through the paper **in order** — for example, you might decide **not** to do the multiple choice questions first, or leave questions on the topics you find hard till the end.

5) But if you **skip** any questions the first time round, don't forget to **go back** to do them.

Do Well In Your Exams

Make Sure You **Read the Question**

1) It sounds obvious, but it's really important you read each question **carefully**, and give an answer that fits.

2) **Command words** in the question give you an idea of the kind of answer you should write. You'll find answering exam questions much easier if you understand exactly what they mean. Here's a summary of the common ones:

Command word:	What to do:
Give / Name / State	Give a brief one or two word answer, or a short sentence.
Identify	Say what something is.
Describe (an observation)	Write about what you would expect to happen in a reaction, e.g. a colour change or the formation of a precipitate.
Explain	Give reasons for something.
Suggest / Predict	Use your scientific knowledge to work out what the answer might be.
Outline / Describe (an experiment)	Write about each step you would take in an experiment — including any equipment you would use, the reagents required and any reaction conditions (e.g. temperature, presence of a catalyst). If you are identifying a substance, you should also include any physical changes you would expect to see, such as a precipitate being formed.
Calculate	Work out the solution to a mathematical problem.
Deduce / Determine	Use the information given in the question to work something out.

From the looks on his classmates' faces, Ivor deduced that he had gone a bit overboard when decorating his lucky exam hat.

Some Questions Will Test Your Knowledge of **Practical Skills**

Some of the marks in your A-Level Chemistry exams will focus on **practical skills**. This means you will be given questions where you're asked to do things like comment on the **design** of **experiments**, make **predictions**, **draw graphs**, **calculate** percentage **errors** — basically, anything related to planning experiments or analysing results.

Remember to Use the **Exam Data Sheet**

When you sit your exams, you'll be given a **data sheet**. It will contain lots of useful information, including: the **characteristic infrared absorptions**, ^{13}C **NMR shifts** and ^1H **NMR shifts** of some common functional groups, some useful **constants** and **equations** and a copy of the **periodic table**.

Be **Careful** With **Calculations**

20% of the marks up for grabs in A-Level Chemistry will require maths skills, so make sure you know your stuff.

1) In calculation questions you should always **show your working** — you may get some marks for your **method** even if you get the answer wrong.

2) Don't **round** your answer until the **very end**. Some of the calculations in A-Level chemistry can be quite **long**, and if you round too early you could introduce errors to your final answer.

3) Be careful with **units**. Lots of formulas require quantities to be in specific units (e.g. temperature in Kelvin), so it's best to **convert** any numbers you're given into these before you start. And obviously, if the question **tells** you which units to give your **answer** in, don't throw away marks by giving it in different ones.

4) You should give your final answer to the correct number of **significant figures**. This is usually the same as the data with the **lowest number** of significant figures in the question.

5) It can be easy to mis-type numbers into your calculator when you're under pressure in an exam, so always **double-check** your calculations and make sure that your answer looks **sensible**.

I'd tell you another Chemistry joke, but I'm not sure it'd get a good reaction...

The key to preparing for your exams is to practise, practise, practise. If you haven't already, have a go at the synoptic questions on pages 110-116. You could also get your hands on some practice papers and try to do each of them in the time allowed. This'll flag up any topics that you're a bit shaky on, so you can go back and revise.

Synoptic Practice

You made it — so many pages read, so many facts absorbed. You're ready, almost...
In your exams, you're likely to get a few synoptic questions thrown your way.
These questions can be based on chemistry from any part of the course, so you'll
have to really know your stuff. What's more, they can use contexts that you
may have never seen before, just to make things extra tricky. But don't worry,
you've got pages and pages of practice right here — how exciting... get stuck in.

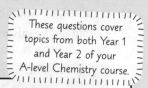
These questions cover
topics from both Year 1
and Year 2 of your
A-level Chemistry course.

1 Electrochemical cells can be produced by joining two half-cells together. The standard
electrode potential of a half-cell is measured relative to a standard hydrogen electrode.
Table 1 shows a range of standard electrode potentials of different half-cells.

Table 1

Half-reaction	$E^{\ominus}$/V
$Li^+_{(aq)} + e^- \rightarrow Li_{(s)}$	−3.04
$Mg^{2+}_{(aq)} + 2e^- \rightarrow Mg_{(s)}$	−2.37
$Zn^{2+}_{(aq)} + 2e^- \rightarrow Zn_{(s)}$	−0.76
$Fe^{2+}_{(aq)} + 2e^- \rightarrow Fe_{(s)}$	−0.44
$Fe^{3+}_{(aq)} + e^- \rightarrow Fe^{2+}_{(aq)}$	+0.77
$Ag^+_{(aq)} + e^- \rightarrow Ag_{(s)}$	+0.80
$Cr_2O_7^{2-}_{(aq)} + 14H^+_{(aq)} + 6e^- \rightarrow 2Cr^{3+}_{(aq)} + 7H_2O_{(l)}$	+1.33

(a) Using the data in **Table 1**, describe how you would set up an electrochemical cell with
an EMF of 1.61 V, including any conditions required. Give the redox reaction for the cell.

(4 marks)

(b) A student wants to produce solid silver from a solution of silver nitrate
using an electrochemical cell. Justify her decision to use a piece of iron.

(2 marks)

(c) A student is making an iron(II)/iron(III) half-cell using 1.00 mol dm^{-3} concentrations.

(i) Calculate the mass of hydrated iron(II) sulfate ($FeSO_4.7H_2O$) and hydrated iron(III) nitrate(V)
($Fe(NO_3)_3.9H_2O$) required to make 250.0 cm^3 of the appropriate solution for the half-cell.

(3 marks)

(ii) Iron(II) sulphate is an irritant. Given this information, suggest a safety precaution
that the student should take when setting up the half-cell.

(1 mark)

(iii) Give the balanced redox equation for the reaction that would occur if the student set up
an electrochemical cell with the iron(II)/iron(III) half-cell and a chromate(VI) half-cell.

(1 mark)

2 A student analysed a sample of an insoluble metal carbonate, MCO_3, to deduce the identity of M.
0.300 g of the MCO_3 was added to 50.0 cm^3 of 0.200 mol dm^{-3} hydrochloric acid and a gas syringe
was immediately fitted to the reaction vessel. The reaction was allowed to go to completion.
The reaction was carried out at a temperature of 50 °C and a pressure of 101 kPa.

(a) Write an ionic equation for the reaction between the metal carbonate and hydrochloric acid,
including state symbols.

(1 mark)

Synoptic Practice

(b) (i) 3.56×10^{-3} moles of the metal carbonate were used up in this reaction.
Calculate the volume of gas that was collected during the reaction. $R = 8.314$ J K^{-1} mol^{-1}

(3 marks)

(ii) Deduce the identity of M. Show your working.

(3 marks)

(c) The student wanted to check that the MCO$_3$ had fully reacted. To do this, he planned to determine the amount of hydrochloric acid left in the reaction vessel using a titration.

First he made up a standard solution of sodium carbonate using the following method:

1. Approximately 2 g of anhydrous sodium carbonate was weighed into a small beaker.

2. The beaker was weighed using a ±0.01 g balance.

3. The sodium carbonate was transferred to a large beaker, and the empty small beaker was weighed.

4. 150 cm^3 of deionised water was carefully added to the large beaker.

5. The solution was transferred to a 250 cm^3 volumetric flask using a funnel.

6. The solution was made up to the volumetric mark.

Identify three steps in the method that should be modified to improve the accuracy of the concentration of the standard solution. Explain in each case how it could be improved.

(3 marks)

(d) The student decided to use a standard solution of 0.0800 mol dm^{-3} sodium hydroxide for the titration. While carrying out the titration, the student continually measured the pH of the solution with a pH probe, adding sodium hydroxide 2.0 cm^3 at a time. **Figure 1** shows his results.

Figure 1

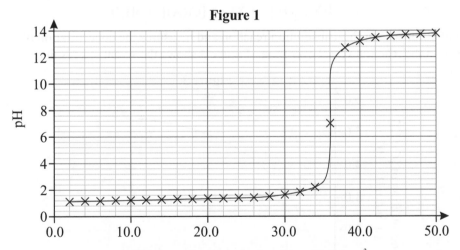

Use the data shown in **Figure 1** to determine whether the metal carbonate has fully reacted. Show your working.

(8 marks)

3 Methylbenzene is the starting reagent for the synthesis of nitromethylbenzene. Nitration is carried out with a mixture of concentrated nitric and sulfuric acid.

The structure of methylbenzene is shown in **Figure 2**.

Figure 2

Synoptic Practice

(a) For nitration to occur, an NO_2^+ electrophile is formed.
Show that the formation of the NO_2^+ electrophile is not a redox reaction.

(2 marks)

(b) Explain why benzene usually undergoes electrophilic substitution reactions rather than electrophilic addition reactions.

(3 marks)

(c) A scientist carries out the nitration of methylbenzene below 30 °C, which leads to the formation of two mono-nitrated compounds: 2-nitromethylbenzene and 4-nitromethylbenzene.
Explain how the spectra of these products can be distinguished by ^{13}C NMR spectroscopy.

(3 marks)

(d) Nitration of methylbenzene above 30 °C can lead to the formation of the explosive 2,4,6-trinitromethylbenzene (TNT). When detonated, two moles of TNT decompose to form an equal number of moles of carbon monoxide and carbon, along with water and nitrogen. Using the enthalpies of formation below, calculate the total enthalpy change of the reaction. Give your answer to 3 significant figures.

$$\Delta_f H[\text{TNT}] = -63.2 \text{ kJ mol}^{-1} \qquad \Delta_f H[\text{carbon monoxide}] = -110.5 \text{ kJ mol}^{-1}$$
$$\Delta_f H[\text{water}] = -241.8 \text{ kJ mol}^{-1}$$

(4 marks)

4 Chromium is a transition metal.
In aqueous solution it forms the hexaaquachromium(III) ion, $[Cr(H_2O)_6]^{3+}$.

(a) Hexaaquachromium(III) undergoes a ligand substitution reaction with a multidentate ligand, X. The overall equation for the reaction is:

$$[Cr(H_2O)_6]^{3+} + X^{4-} \rightarrow [Cr(X)]^- + 6H_2O$$

A scientist carries out this substitution reaction and measures the concentration of $[Cr(X)]^-$ in the reaction vessel over time. **Figure 3** shows the scientist's results.

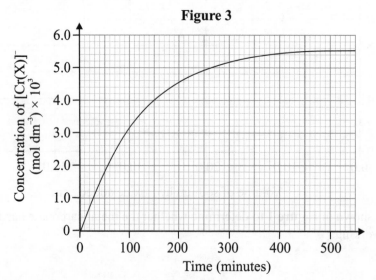

Figure 3

Calculate the initial rate of this reaction in mol dm^{-3} min^{-1}.

(2 marks)

(b) Give the full electron configuration of Cr^{3+} using subshell notation.

(1 mark)

Synoptic Practice

(c) When hexaaquachromium(III) reacts with excess ammonia, a colour change is observed.
Describe the colour change that occurs and write the equation for this reaction.

(2 marks)

(d) Describe a simple reaction that could be used to identify chromium(III) ions in a solution,
including what you would expect to observe for a positive result.

(2 marks)

5 A student is investigating the properties of several substances containing bromine.

(a) Sodium bromide is an ionic solid. **Table 2** shows enthalpy change data that can be used to
calculate the enthalpy of solution of $NaBr_{(s)}$.

Table 2

Enthalpy change	ΔH / kJ mol^{-1}
Enthalpy of formation of sodium bromide	−361
Enthalpy of atomisation of sodium	+107
Enthalpy of atomisation of bromine	+112
First ionisation energy of sodium	+496
First electron affinity of bromine	−325
Enthalpy of hydration of sodium ion	−406
Enthalpy of hydration of bromide ion	−348

(i) Using Born-Haber cycles and the values in **Table 2**,
calculate the enthalpy of solution of $NaBr_{(s)}$.

(6 marks)

(ii) State how the value for the first ionisation energy of lithium would compare
to the first ionisation energy of sodium. Explain your answer.

(3 marks)

(b) Hydrobromic acid is a strong acid. Calculate the pH of the solution formed
when 0.0400 g of HBr is fully dissolved in 50.0 cm^3 of deionised water.

(3 marks)

(c) Bromoethanoic acid has a pK_a of 2.90. Calculate the concentration of a solution of
bromoethanoic acid with a pH of 1.50. State any assumptions you have made.

(4 marks)

(d) The student adds bromine water to phenol and a reaction takes place.
Draw the organic product of this reaction.

(1 mark)

6 Alkanes and alkenes react with halogens, such as bromine, in different ways.

(a) Propane and bromine will react together in the gas phase in the presence of UV light.
Use this information to propose a mechanism for the reaction, giving four equations
to show each of the important steps. Name this type of mechanism.

(5 marks)

(b) Draw the mechanism for the reaction between propene and bromine. Name the mechanism.

(5 marks)

Synoptic Practice

(c) The initial rate of reaction between the haloalkane 2-bromo-2-methylbutane and sodium hydroxide was investigated. **Table 3** shows the results for the reaction. The experiments were carried out at a constant temperature.

Table 3

Experiment	[NaOH] / mol dm^{-3}	[C$_2$H$_5$CBr(CH$_3$)CH$_3$] / mol dm^{-3}	Rate / mol dm^{-3} s^{-1}
1	0.14	0.30	4.50×10^{-5}
2	0.14	0.60	9.00×10^{-5}
3	0.28	0.45	6.75×10^{-5}

Use the results to suggest the rate determining step of the mechanism of this reaction. Draw this step in the mechanism and explain your reasoning.

(4 marks)

(d) When hydrogen bromide reacts with propene, a mixture of organic products is formed. Name the major product of the reaction and explain why this is the main product formed.

(4 marks)

(e) The reaction of propene with bromine in sodium chloride solution leads to the formation of chiral products. Suggest the reason for the formation of these products and draw the three-dimensional structures of each possible product, indicating which are stereoisomers.

(3 marks)

7　Transition metals can exist in different complexes and in different oxidation states.

When nickel chloride solution is mixed with excess ammonia solution, the following reaction occurs:

$$NiCl_2 + 6NH_3 \rightarrow [Ni(NH_3)_6]Cl_2 \qquad \Delta H = -102 \text{ kJ mol}^{-1}$$

(a) (i) The free energy change of the reaction is –49.0 kJ mol^{-1}.
Calculate the entropy change of the reaction at 25.0 °C. Give your answer in J K^{-1} mol^{-1}.

(3 marks)

(ii) Calculate the lowest temperature at which the reaction occurs spontaneously.

(2 marks)

Other nitrogen containing compounds, such as ethane-1,2-diamine (en), also form complexes with nickel. The structure of en is shown in **Figure 4**.

Figure 4

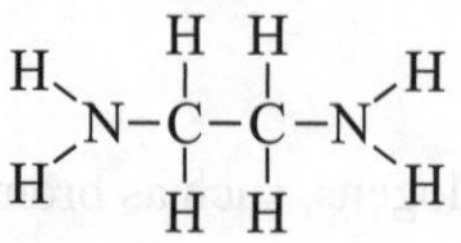

(b) (i) The ammonia-nickel complex [Ni(NH$_3$)$_4$(H$_2$O)$_2$]$^{2+}$ and [Ni(en)$_3$]$^{2+}$ complex can both show stereoisomerism. Draw the three-dimensional structure of each pair of isomers.

(4 marks)

(ii) Name the type of stereoisomerism shown by each complex.

(2 marks)

Synoptic Practice

(c) Pale yellow hexaaqua iron(III) ions reacts with thiocyanate ions
to form a red complex in an exothermic reaction.

$$[Fe(H_2O)_6]^{3+} + SCN^- \rightleftharpoons [Fe(H_2O)_5SCN]^{2+} + H_2O$$

Suggest, with reasoning, how the solution could be made to change
colour again without further additions to the solution.

(2 marks)

8 An analytical chemist is measuring the manganese content of a sample of steel.
The following method is used:

• A 1.50 g sample is fully dissolved in 250.0 cm³ of warm nitric acid,
in order to oxidise the manganese to manganese(II).

• A 25.0 cm³ sample is taken, and the manganese(II) is further oxidised to manganate(VII)
by addition of excess sodium bismuthate ($NaBiO_3$), which is a strong oxidising agent.
$NaBiO_3$ is reduced to bismuth oxide (Bi_2O_3), containing bismuth(III) ions, in the redox reaction.

• The manganate(VII) solution is purified of bismuth compounds, and then titrated against
0.100 mol dm⁻³ iron(II) sulfate. The end point is reached when 17.8 cm³ of iron(II) sulfate
has been added.

The reduction half-equation for manganate(VII) is: $MnO_4^- + 8H^+ + 5e^- \rightarrow Mn^{2+} + 4H_2O$
The reduction half-equation for iron(III) is: $Fe^{3+} + e^- \rightarrow Fe^{2+}$

(a) Determine the redox equation for the reaction of sodium bismuthate with manganese(II).
Show your working.

(3 marks)

(b)* Determine the percentage by mass of manganese in the original steel sample.

(6 marks)

(c) The manganate(VII) sample was purified of bismuth compounds by filtration.
Suggest how this method may affect the accuracy of the percentage mass of manganese calculated.

(1 mark)

(d) Given that manganate(VII) ions form a purple solution, outline a method other than titration
for determining the concentration of manganate(VII) in the solution after it was filtered.

(3 marks)

9 Propenal is the simplest unsaturated aldehyde. Its structure is shown in **Figure 5**.

Figure 5

(a) Describe how propenal, propanal and propanone can be distinguished
from one another by simple chemical tests.

(3 marks)

(b) Potassium cyanide can react with propenal in a nucleophilic addition reaction.
Draw the mechanism for the reaction between propenal and acidified potassium cyanide.

(4 marks)

* The quality of your extended response will be assessed for this question.

Synoptic Practice

(c) Acidified potassium cyanide will only react with one of the double bonds in propenal. Explain why it reacts with one double bond but not the other.

(2 marks)

(d) Propenal can form an addition polymer. Draw the repeat unit of this polymer.

(1 mark)

10 A research chemist has synthesised and purified an organic substance, X. She analyses a sample with different techniques to verify the structure of the compound.

(a) A 1.25 g sample of X was found to contain:

C: 0.563 g   H: 0.082 g   Cl: 0.417 g   O: 0.188 g

A mass spectrum of compound X showed a M^+ peak at 213.0.
Deduce the molecular formula of compound X. Show all of your workings.

(3 marks)

(b) Infrared (**Figure 6**) and ^1H NMR (**Figure 7**) analyses were carried out on compound X. **Table 4** shows the infrared frequencies absorbed by a range of bonds in organic molecules.

Figure 6

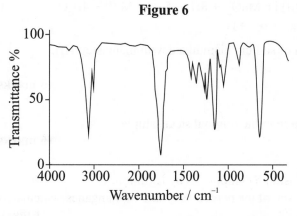

Figure 7

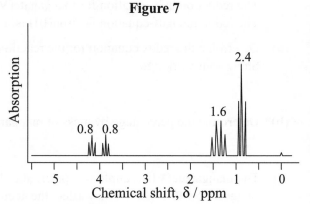

Table 4

Bond	Wavenumber / cm⁻¹
C–C	750 - 1100
C–O	1000 - 1300
C=C	1620 - 1680
C=O	1630 - 1820
O–H (acids)	2500 - 3300
C–H	2850 - 3100

Use the diagram showing ^1H NMR chemical shifts on page 102 and the data in **Table 4** to deduce the structure of X.

(8 marks)

(c) The chemist analyses a sample of compound X using gas chromatography. Suggest what result the chemist would see in the chromatogram if the sample was pure.

(1 mark)

Answers

Module 5: Section 1 — Rates, Equilibrium & pH

Page 5 — Rates of Reaction
1   e.g. monitoring pH / monitoring conductivity *[1 mark]*.

Page 7 — Reaction Orders
1 a) 1st order *[1 mark]*
   b)

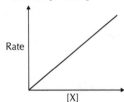

   [1 mark for correctly labelled axes, 1 mark for correct line]
   c) You could measure the volume of hydrogen gas produced in a unit of time *[1 mark]*.
2   C *[1 mark]*

Page 9 — The Rate Constant
1 a) Rate = $k[NO_{(g)}]^2 [H_{2(g)}]$ *[1 mark]*
   b) $0.00267 = k \times (0.00400)^2 \times 0.00200$
       $k = 8.34 \times 10^4 \, dm^6 \, mol^{-2} \, s^{-1}$
       [1 mark for answer, 1 mark for units].
       Units: $k = mol \, dm^{-3} \, s^{-1} \div [(mol \, dm^{-3})^2 \times (mol \, dm^{-3})]$
       $= mol^{-2} \, dm^6 \, s^{-1}$.
2 a)

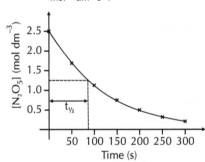

   [1 mark for correct axes, 1 mark for correctly plotted points, 1 mark for best-fit curve]
   b) From graph, half-life = 85 s *[1 mark, allow 85 ± 2]*
       $k = \dfrac{\ln 2}{t_{1/2}} = \dfrac{\ln 2}{85\,s} = 8.2 \times 10^{-3} \, s^{-1}$ *[1 mark, allow 8.2 ± 0.2 × 10⁻³]*
3   The reaction is first order with respect to CH_3COOCH_3, so rate = $k[CH_3COOH]$, and the gradient of the graph = k *[1 mark]*.

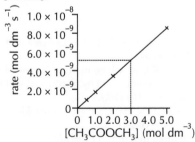

   $k = \dfrac{5.0 \times 10^{-9} \, mol \, dm^{-3} \, s^{-1}}{3.0 \, mol \, dm^{-3}} = \mathbf{1.7 \times 10^{-9} \, s^{-1}}$ *[1 mark]*

Page 11 — The Rate-Determining Step
1 a) rate = $k[H_2][ICl]$ *[1 mark]*
   b) i)   If the molecule is in the rate equation, it must be in the rate-determining step *[1 mark]*. The reaction is first order with respect to both H_2 and ICl. So there will be one molecule of H_2 and one molecule of ICl in the rate determining step *[1 mark]*.
       ii) Incorrect *[1 mark]*. H_2 and ICl are both in the rate equation, so they must both be in the rate-determining step / the order of the reaction with respect to ICl is 1, so there must be only one molecule of ICl in the rate-determining step *[1 mark]*.
2 a) The rate equation is first order with respect to HBr and O_2 so only 1 molecule of HBr (and O_2) is involved in the rate-determining step *[1 mark]*. There must be more steps as 4 molecules of HBr are in the equation *[1 mark]*.
   b) $HBr + O_2 \rightarrow HBrO_2$ (rate-determining step) *[1 mark]*
       $HBr + HBrO_2 \rightarrow 2HBrO$ *[1 mark]*
       $HBr + HBrO \rightarrow H_2O + Br_2$ *[1 mark]*
       $HBr + HBrO \rightarrow H_2O + Br_2$ *[1 mark]*
       Part b) is pretty tricky — you need to do a fair bit of detective work and some trial and error. Make sure you use all of the clues in the question...

Page 13 — The Arrhenius Equation
1 a)

T (K)	k	1/T (K⁻¹)	ln k
305	0.181	0.00328	−1.71
313	0.468	**0.00319**	**−0.759**
323	1.34	**0.00310**	**0.293**
333	3.29	0.00300	1.19
344	10.1	**0.00291**	**2.31**
353	22.7	0.00283	3.12

   [1 mark for all 3 1/T values, 1 mark for all 3 ln k values]
   b)

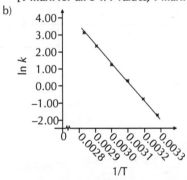

   [1 mark for correct axes, 1 mark for correctly plotted points, 1 mark for line of best fit]
   c) Gradient = −10 750 ± 250 *[1 mark]*
       $\dfrac{-E_a}{R} = -10\,750$
       $E_a = 10\,750 \times 8.31 = \mathbf{89\,300 \, J \, mol^{-1}}$ OR **89.3 kJ mol⁻¹** *[1 mark]*
   d) By substituting values into the expression $\ln k = \dfrac{-E_a}{RT} + \ln A$
       $-0.76 = -10\,750 \times 0.00319 + \ln A$
       $\ln A = 33.5 \pm 0.1$
       $A = e^{33.5} = \mathbf{3.54 \times 10^{14}}$ *[1 mark]*
       You can't use the graph to find the value of ln A (by extrapolation to find the y-intercept) because the x axis has a broken scale — it isn't all shown.

Answers

Page 15 — The Equilibrium Constant

PQs 1 $K_c = \dfrac{[NO_2]^2}{[N_2][O_2]}$

2 units $= \dfrac{(mol\,dm^{-3})^2}{mol\,dm^{-3} \times mol\,dm^{-3}} = $ no units

1 moles of N_2O_4 = mass ÷ M_r = 23.0 ÷ 92.0 = 0.250 mol
concentration N_2O_4 = moles ÷ volume = 0.250 ÷ 6.00
= 0.0417 mol dm^{-3} *[1 mark]*.
moles NO_2 = mass ÷ M_r = 0.389 ÷ 46 = 8.46 × 10^{-3} mol
concentration NO_2 = moles ÷ volume = 8.46 × 10^{-3} ÷ 6.00
= 1.41 × 10^{-3} mol dm^{-3} *[1 mark]*.
$K_c = \dfrac{[NO_2]^2}{[N_2O_4]} = \dfrac{(1.41 \times 10^{-3})^2}{0.0417} = $ **4.77 × 10^{-5}** *[1 mark]*

units $= \dfrac{(mol\,dm^{-3})^2}{(mol\,dm^{-3})} = $ **mol dm^{-3}** *[1 mark]*

2 a) $K_c = \dfrac{[[Co(NH_3)_6]^{2+}]}{[[Co(H_2O)_6]^{2+}][NH_3]^6}$ *[1 mark]*

b) $K_c = \dfrac{(2.19)}{(0.541) \times (0.234)^6} = $ **2.47 × 10^4** *[1 mark]*

units $= \dfrac{(mol\,dm^{-3})}{(mol\,dm^{-3}) \times (mol\,dm^{-3})^6} = $ **mol^{-6} dm^{18}** *[1 mark]*

Page 17 — Equilibrium Concentrations

PQs 1 $K_c = \dfrac{[C]}{[A][B]}$ so [C] = K_c[A][B]

2 [C] = 7.35 × 0.152 × 0.586 = **0.655 mol^{-1} dm^3**

1 a) moles = mass ÷ M_r = 42.5 ÷ 46 = **0.924 mol** *[1 mark]*
b) Initial concentration NO_2 = moles ÷ volume = 0.924 ÷ 22.8
= 0.0405 mol dm^{-3}
So the component concentrations are as follows:

Equilibrium component	$NO_{2(g)}$	$NO_{(g)}$	$O_{2(g)}$
Initial concentration (mol dm^{-3})	0.0405	0	0
Equilibrium concentration (mol dm^{-3})	0.0405 − 2x	2x	x

[1 mark]

$K_c = \dfrac{[NO]^2[O_2]}{[NO_2]^2} = \dfrac{(2x)^2(x)}{(0.0405-2x)^2}$ *[1 mark]*

c) moles of O_2 = mass ÷ M_r = 14.1 ÷ 32 = 0.441 mol *[1 mark]*
concentration O_2 = moles ÷ volume = 0.441 ÷ 22.8
= 0.0193 mol dm^{-3}.
So x = 0.0193 mol dm^{-3} *[1 mark]*

$K_c = \dfrac{(2x)^2(x)}{(0.0405-2x)^2} = \dfrac{(2 \times 0.0193)^2 \times (0.0193)}{(0.0405-(2 \times 0.0193))^2} = $ **7.97 mol dm^{-3}**
[1 mark]
(Units = (mol dm^{-3})^2 × (mol dm^{-3}) ÷ (mol dm^{-3})^2 = mol dm^{-3})

2 a) $K_c = \dfrac{[CrO_4^{2-}]^2[H^+]^2}{[CrO_7^{2-}][H_2O]}$ *[1 mark]*

b) i) Since there's 0.0300 moles of $Cr_2O_7^{2-}$ at equilibrium, from the
equation there must also be 0.0300 moles of H_2O.
[H_2O] = 0.0300 ÷ 0.100 = **0.300 mol dm^{-3}** *[1 mark]*
ii) 0.0700 moles of $Cr_2O_7^{2-}$ must have reacted, which will give
0.140 moles of CrO_4^{2-}.
[CrO_4^{2-}] = 0.140 ÷ 0.100 = **1.40 mol dm^{-3}** *[1 mark]*
iii) [CrO_4^{2-}] = [H^+] = 0.140 ÷ 0.100 = **1.40 mol dm^{-3}** *[1 mark]*
*You can see from molar ratios in the equation that $Cr_2O_7^{2-}$ reacts to
produce double the amount of CrO_4^{2-} and H^+.*
c) Concentration of $Cr_2O_7^{2-}$ = 0.0300 ÷ 0.100 = 0.300 mol dm^{-3}
$K_c = \dfrac{1.4^2 \times 1.4^2}{0.3 \times 0.3} = $ **42.7 mol^2 dm^{-6}**
[1 mark for correct numerical value, 1 mark for correct units]

Page 19 — Gas Equilibria

1 a) $K_P = \dfrac{p(SO_2)p(Cl_2)}{p(SO_2Cl_2)}$ *[1 mark]*

b) Cl_2 and SO_2 are produced in equal amounts so
$p(Cl_2) = p(SO_2)$ = 60.2 kPa *[1 mark]*
Total pressure = $p(SO_2Cl_2) + p(Cl_2) + p(SO_2)$ so
$p(SO_2Cl_2)$ = 141 − 60.2 − 60.2 = **20.6 kPa** *[1 mark]*
c) $K_P = \dfrac{60.2\,kPa \times 60.2\,kPa}{20.6\,kPa} = 176$ *[1 mark]* kPa *[1 mark]*
(Units = (kPa × kPa)/ kPa = kPa)
2 a) $p(O_2)$ = ½ × 36 = 18 kPa *[1 mark]*
b) $p(NO_2)$ = total pressure − $p(NO)$ − $p(O_2)$
= 99 − 36 − 18 = **45 kPa** *[1 mark]*
c) $K_P = \dfrac{p(NO_2)^2}{p(NO)^2 p(O_2)}$ *[1 mark]*

$= \dfrac{(45\,kPa)^2}{(36\,kPa)^2 \times (18\,kPa)} = $ **0.087 kPa^{-1}** *[1 mark]*

(Units = kPa^2/(kPa^2 × kPa) = kPa^{-1})

Page 21 — More on Equilibrium Constants

1 a) T_2 is lower than T_1 *[1 mark]*.
A decrease in temperature shifts the position of equilibrium in the
exothermic direction, producing more product *[1 mark]*.
More product means K_c increases *[1 mark]*.
*A negative ΔH means the forward reaction is exothermic —
it gives out heat.*
b) The yield of SO_3 increases *[1 mark]*. (A decrease in volume
means an increase in pressure.) This shifts the equilibrium
position to the right where there are fewer moles of gas. K_c is
unchanged *[1 mark]*.

2 a) $K_P = \dfrac{p(CO)p(H_2)^3}{p(CH_4)p(H_2O)}$ *[1 mark]*

b) A *[1 mark]*

Page 23 — Acids and Bases

1 a) H^+ or H_3O^+ and SO_4^{2-} *[1 mark]*
b) $2H^+_{(aq)} + Mg_{(s)} \rightarrow Mg^{2+}_{(aq)} + H_{2(g)}$ *[1 mark]*
c) HSO_4^- *[1 mark]*
2 a) $HCN_{(aq)} + H_2O_{(l)} \rightleftharpoons H_3O^+_{(aq)} + CN^-_{(aq)}$ *[1 mark]*
b) The pairs are HCN and CN^- *[1 mark]*
AND H_2O and H_3O^+ *[1 mark]*.
c) H^+ *[1 mark]*
3 a) $NH_3 + H_2O \rightleftharpoons NH_4^+ + OH^-$ *[1 mark]*
b) An acid as it donates a proton *[1 mark]*
c) OH^- *[1 mark]*

Page 25 — pH

1 a) It's a strong monobasic acid, so [H^+] = [HBr] = 0.32 mol dm^{-3}.
pH = $-\log_{10} 0.32$ = **0.49** *[1 mark]*
b) HBr is a stronger acid than HCl, so will be more dissociated in
solution. This means the concentration of hydrogen ions will be
higher, so the pH will be lower. *[1 mark]*.
2 a) Moles of NaOH = 2.50 ÷ 40.0 = 0.0625 moles *[1 mark]*
1 mole of NaOH gives 1 mole of OH^-.
So [OH^-] = [NaOH] = **0.0625 mol dm^{-3}** *[1 mark]*.
b) K_w = [H^+][OH^-]
[H^+] = 1 × 10^{-14} ÷ 0.0625 = 1.60 × 10^{-13} *[1 mark]*
pH = $-\log_{10}(1.60 \times 10^{-13})$ = **12.80** *[1 mark]*
3 K_w = [H^+][OH^-]
[OH^-] = [NaOH] = 0.0370
[H^+] = K_w ÷ [OH^-] = (1 × 10^{-14}) ÷ 0.0370 = 2.70 × 10^{-13} *[1 mark]*
pH = $-\log_{10}[H^+]$ = $-\log_{10}(2.70 \times 10^{-13})$ = **12.57** *[1 mark]*

Answers

Page 27 — The Acid Dissociation Constant

1 a) $K_a = \dfrac{[H^+][A^-]}{[HA]}$ *[1 mark]*

b) $K_a = \dfrac{[H^+]^2}{[HA]}$

[HA] is 0.280 because only a small amount of HA will dissociate

$[H^+] = \sqrt{(5.60\times10^{-4})\times(0.280)} = 0.0125$ mol dm^{-3} *[1 mark]*

pH $= -\log_{10}[H^+] = -\log_{10}(0.0125) = $ **1.90** *[1 mark]*

2 a) $[H^+] = 10^{-2.65} = $ **2.24×10^{-3} mol dm^{-3}** *[1 mark]*

$K_a = \dfrac{[H^+]^2}{[HX]} = \dfrac{(2.24\times10^{-3})^2}{0.150}$

$= $ **3.35×10^{-5} mol dm^{-3}** *[1 mark]*

b) $pK_a = -\log_{10}K_a = -\log_{10}(3.35 \times 10^{-5}) = $ **4.47** *[1 mark]*

3 $K_a = 10^{-pK_a} = 10^{-4.2} = 6.3 \times 10^{-5}$ *[1 mark]*

$K_a = \dfrac{[H^+]^2}{[HA]}$ so $[H^+] = \sqrt{K_a\times[HA]}$

$\sqrt{(6.3\times10^{-5})\times(1.6\times10^{-4})} = \sqrt{1.0\times10^{-8}}$

$= 1.0 \times 10^{-4}$ mol dm^{-3} *[1 mark]*

pH $= -\log_{10}[H^+] = -\log_{10}(1.0 \times 10^{-4}) = $ **4.00** *[1 mark]*

Page 29 — Buffers

1 a) $K_a = \dfrac{[C_6H_5COO^-][H^+]}{[C_6H_5COOH]}$

$[H^+] = 6.4\times10^{-5}\times\dfrac{0.40}{0.20} = 1.28\times10^{-4}$ mol dm^{-3} *[1 mark]*

pH $= -\log_{10}(1.28 \times 10^{-4}) = $ **3.89** *[1 mark]*

b) $C_6H_5COOH \rightleftharpoons H^+ + C_6H_5COO^-$

Adding H_2SO_4 increases the concentration of H^+.
The equilibrium shifts left to reduce the concentration of H^+, so the pH will only change very slightly *[1 mark]*.

2 a) $CH_3(CH_2)_2COOH \rightleftharpoons H^+ + CH_3(CH_2)_2COO^-$ *[1 mark]*

b) $[CH_3(CH_2)_2COOH] = [CH_3(CH_2)_2COO^-]$,
so $[CH_3(CH_2)_2COOH] \div [CH_3(CH_2)_2COO^-] = 1$ *[1 mark]*
and $K_a = [H^+]$.
pH $= -\log_{10}(1.5 \times 10^{-5}) = $ **4.82** *[1 mark]*
If the concentrations of the weak acid and the salt are equal, they cancel from the K_a expression and the buffer pH $= pK_a$.

Page 31 — pH Curves and Titrations

1 Nitric acid:

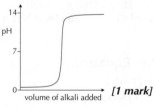

[1 mark]

Ethanoic acid:

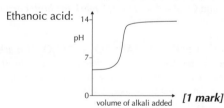

[1 mark]

2 Thymol blue *[1 mark]*. It's a weak acid/strong base titration so the equivalence point is above pH 8 *[1 mark]*.

Module 5: Section 2 — Energy

Page 33 — Lattice Enthalpy and Born-Haber Cycles

1 a)

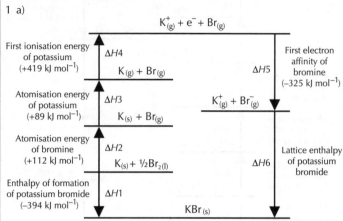

[1 mark for correct enthalpy changes. 1 mark for formulas/state symbols. 1 mark for correct directions of arrows.]

b) Lattice enthalpy, $\Delta H6 = -\Delta H5 - \Delta H4 - \Delta H3 - \Delta H2 + \Delta H1$
$= -(-325) - (+419) - (+89) - (+112) + (-394)$ *[1 mark]*
$= $ **-689 kJ mol^{-1}** *[1 mark]*

2 a)

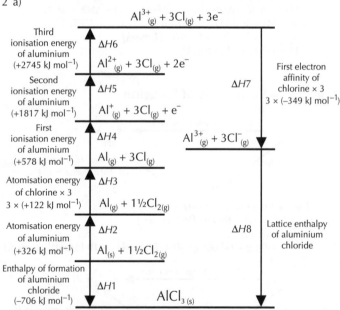

[1 mark for correct enthalpy changes and correctly multiplying all the enthalpies. 1 mark for formulas/state symbols. 1 mark for correct directions of arrows.]

b) Lattice enthalpy, $\Delta H8$
$= -\Delta H7 - \Delta H6 - \Delta H5 - \Delta H4 - \Delta H3 - \Delta H2 + \Delta H1$
$= -3(-349) - (+2745) - (+1817) - (+578) - 3(+122) - (+326) + (-706)$ *[1 mark]*
$= $ **-5491 kJ mol^{-1}** *[1 mark]*

Answers

3 a)

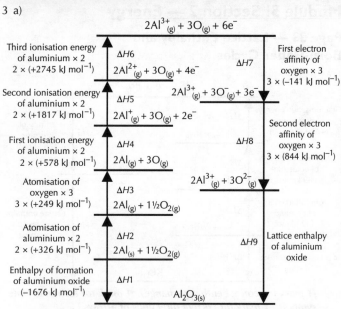

[1 mark for correct enthalpy changes and correctly multiplying all the enthalpies. 1 mark for formulas/state symbols. 1 mark for correct directions of arrows.]

b) Lattice enthalpy, $\Delta H9$
$= -\Delta H8 - \Delta H7 - \Delta H6 - \Delta H5 - \Delta H4 - \Delta H3 - \Delta H2 + \Delta H1$
$= -3(+844) - 3(-141) - 2(+2745) - 2(+1817) - 2(+578)$
$\quad - 3(+249) - 2(+326) + (-1676)$ [1 mark]
$= -15\ 464\ \text{kJ mol}^{-1}$ [1 mark]

Page 35 — Enthalpies of Solution

1 a)

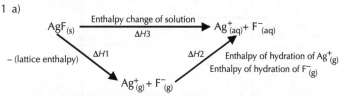

[1 mark for a complete correct cycle, 1 mark for correctly labelled arrows.]

b) $\Delta H3 = \Delta H1 + \Delta H2$
$= -(-960) + (-506) + (-464)$ [1 mark] $= -10\ \text{kJ mol}^{-1}$ [1 mark]

2 a)

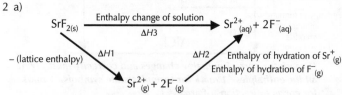

[1 mark for a complete correct cycle, 1 mark correctly labelled arrows.]

b) $-(-2492) + (-1480) + (2 \times -506)$ [1 mark] $= 0\ \text{kJ mol}^{-1}$ [1 mark]
Don't forget — you have to double the enthalpy of hydration for F^- because there are two F^- ions in SrF_2.

3 By Hess's law:
Enthalpy change of solution ($MgCl_{2(s)}$)
$= -$lattice enthalpy ($MgCl_{2(s)}$) + enthalpy of hydration ($Mg^{2+}_{(g)}$)
$\quad + (2 \times$ enthalpy of hydration ($Cl^-_{(g)}$)) [1 mark]
So enthalpy of hydration ($Cl^-_{(g)}$)
$= $ [enthalpy change of solution ($MgCl_{2(s)}$) +
$\quad$ lattice enthalpy ($MgCl_{2(s)}$) $-$ enthalpy of hydration ($Mg^{2+}_{(g)}$)] $\div 2$
$= $ [$(-122) + (-2526) - (-1920)$] $\div 2$ [1 mark]
$= -728 \div 2 = -364\ \text{kJ mol}^{-1}$ [1 mark]

4 Ca^{2+} will have a greater enthalpy of hydration [1 mark] because it is smaller and has a higher charge / has a higher charge density than K^+ [1 mark]. This means there is a stronger attraction between Ca^{2+} and the water molecules, so more energy is released when bonds are formed between them [1 mark].

Page 37 — Entropy

1 a) The reaction is not likely be feasible [1 mark] because there are fewer moles of product than moles of reactants and therefore a decrease in entropy [1 mark].
Remember — more particles means more entropy.
There's 1½ moles of reactants and only 1 mole of product.

b) $\Delta S = 26.9 - (32.7 + (½ \times 205))$ [1 mark]
$= -108\ \text{J K}^{-1}\text{mol}^{-1}$ [1 mark]

c) The reaction is not likely to be feasible because ΔS is negative/there is a decrease in entropy [1 mark].

2 a) $\Delta S = 48 - 70$ [1 mark]
$= -22\ \text{J K}^{-1}\text{mol}^{-1}$ [1 mark]

b) Despite the negative entropy change, the reaction might still be feasible because other factors such as enthalpy, temperature and kinetics also play a part in whether or not a reaction occurs [1 mark].

Page 39 — Free Energy

1 a) $\Delta S = [214 + (2 \times 69.9)] - [186 + (2 \times 205)]$
$= -242.2\ \text{J K}^{-1}\text{mol}^{-1}$ [1 mark]
$\Delta G = -730\ 000 - (298 \times -242.2)$
$\approx -658\ 000\ \text{J mol}^{-1}$ (3 s.f.) $(= -658\ \text{kJ mol}^{-1})$ [1 mark]

b) The reaction is feasible at 298 K because ΔG is negative [1 mark].

c) $T = \dfrac{\Delta H}{\Delta S} = -730\ 000 \div -242.2$ [1 mark] $= 3010\ \text{K}$ [1 mark]

2 First find ΔH:
$q = mc\Delta T = 100 \times 4.18 \times 3.5 = 1463\ \text{J}$ [1 mark]
$M_r(C_3H_7OH) = (3 \times 12.0) + (8 \times 1.0) + 16.0 = 60.0$
So, number of moles of $C_3H_7OH = 48.5 \div 60.0 = 0.808$ [1 mark]
$\Delta H = -1463 \div 0.808 = -1810\ \text{J mol}^{-1}$ [1 mark]
ΔH is negative because the combustion reaction is exothermic.
Now find ΔS:
$\Delta S = [(3 \times 214) + (4 \times 69.9)] - [193 + (4½ \times 205)]$
$= -193.9\ \text{J K}^{-1}\text{mol}^{-1}$ [1 mark]
Finally, find ΔG:
$\Delta G = \Delta H - T\Delta S = -1810 - (298 \times -193.9)$
$\approx 56\ 000\ \text{J mol}^{-1}$ (3 s.f.) $(= 56\ \text{kJ mol}^{-1})$ [1 mark]

Page 41 — Redox Equations

1 $Cl_2 + 2e^- \rightarrow 2Cl^-$ [1 mark]
$Fe^{2+} \rightarrow Fe^{3+} + e^-$ [1 mark]

2 a) $Al \rightarrow Al^{3+} + 3e^-$ and $O_2 + 4e^- \rightarrow 2O^{2-}$ [1 mark for both correct]

b) $4Al \rightarrow 4Al^{3+} + 12e^-$
$3O_2 + 12e^- \rightarrow 6O^{2-}$
$4Al + 3O_2 \rightarrow 4Al^{3+} + 6O^{2-}$ OR $4Al + 3O_2 \rightarrow 2Al_2O_3$ [1 mark]
You have to balance the number of electrons before you can combine the half-equations. And always double-check that your equation definitely balances. It's easy to slip up and throw away marks.

3 $2MnO_4^- + 16H^+ + 10e^- \rightarrow 2Mn^{2+} + 8H_2O$
$10I^- \rightarrow 5I_2 + 10e^-$
$2MnO_4^- + 16H^+ + 10I^- \rightarrow 2Mn^{2+} + 8H_2O + 5I_2$ [1 mark]

4 a) $Cr_2O_7^{2-} \rightarrow 2Cr^{3+}$
  $Cr_2O_7^{2-} \rightarrow 2Cr^{3+} + 7H_2O$
  $Cr_2O_7^{2-} + 14H^+ \rightarrow 2Cr^{3+} + 7H_2O$ *[1 mark]*
  $Cr_2O_7^{2-} + 14H^+ + 6e^- \rightarrow 2Cr^{3+} + 7H_2O$ *[1 mark]*
  $Cr_2O_7^{2-} + 14H^+ \rightarrow 2Cr^{3+} + 7H_2O$
    (−2)   (+14)   (+6)   O
  The total charge is +12 on the left hand side and +6 on the right hand side, so you need to add 6 electrons to the left hand side to balance the charges.
b) $Cr_2O_7^{2-} + 14H^+ + 3Zn \rightarrow 2Cr^{3+} + 7H_2O + 3Zn^{2+}$ *[1 mark]*
  Six electrons are needed to reduce each dichromate ion. Each zinc atom loses two electrons, so you need to multiply the zinc half-equation by three: $3Zn \rightarrow 3Zn^{2+} + 6e^-$. When the two half-equations are combined, the electrons cancel each other out.

Page 43 — Redox Titrations

1 a) Number of moles = (concentration × volume) ÷ 1000
  = (20 × 0.10) ÷ 1000 = **0.0020 mol** *[1 mark]*
b) 2 moles of MnO_4^- react with 5 moles of Sn^{2+}.
  (0.0020 ÷ 2) × 5 = **0.0050 mol** *[1 mark]*
c) Concentration = (number of moles ÷ volume) × 1000
  = (0.0050 ÷ 10) × 1000 = **0.50 mol dm^{-3}** *[1 mark]*
2 a) $MnO_4^- + 8H^+ + 5Fe^{2+} \rightarrow Mn^{2+} + 4H_2O + 5Fe^{3+}$ *[1 mark]*
b) Number of moles = (concentration × volume) ÷ 1000
  = (0.400 × 11.5) ÷ 1000 = 0.00460 *[1 mark]*
  Moles of Fe^{2+} = moles of $MnO_4^- × 5$ = 0.0230 *[1 mark]*
  Concentration = (number of moles ÷ volume) × 1000
  = (0.0230 ÷ 50.0) × 1000 = **0.460 mol dm^{-3}** *[1 mark]*
c) Mass of substance = moles × relative atomic mass
  Mass of iron in solution = (0.0230) × 55.8 = 1.2834 g *[1 mark]*
  % iron in steel wool = (1.2834 ÷ 1.30) × 100 = **98.7 %** *[1 mark]*

Page 45 — Iodine Thiosulfate Titrations

1 a) $IO_3^- + 5I^- + 6H^+ \rightarrow 3I_2 + 3H_2O$ *[1 mark]*
b) Number of moles = (concentration × volume) ÷ 1000
  Number of moles of thiosulfate = (0.150 × 24.0) ÷ 1000
  = **3.60 × 10^{-3}** *[1 mark]*
c) 2 moles of thiosulfate react with 1 mole of iodine, so there were
  (3.60 × 10^{-3}) ÷ 2 = **1.80 × 10^{-3}** moles of iodine *[1 mark]*.
d) 1/3 mole *[1 mark]*
e) There must be 1.80 × 10^{-3} ÷ 3 = 6.00 × 10^{-4} moles of iodate(V) in the solution *[1 mark]*.
  So concentration of potassium iodate(V) =
  (6.00 × 10^{-4}) ÷ (10.0 ÷ 1000) = **0.0600 mol dm^{-3}** *[1 mark]*.
2 Number of moles = (concentration × volume) ÷ 1000
  Number of moles of thiosulfate = (0.300 × 12.5) ÷ 1000
  = 3.75 × 10^{-3} *[1 mark]*
  2 moles of thiosulfate react with 1 mole of iodine.
  So there must have been (3.75 × 10^{-3}) ÷ 2 = 1.875 × 10^{-3} moles of iodine produced *[1 mark]*.
  2 moles of manganate(VII) ions produce 5 moles of iodine molecules
  So there must have been (1.875 × 10^{-3}) × (2 ÷ 5)
  = 7.50 × 10^{-4} moles of manganate(VII) in the solution *[1 mark]*.
  Concentration of potassium manganate(VII)
  = (7.50 × 10^{-4} moles) ÷ (18.0 ÷ 1000) = **0.0417 mol dm^{-3}** *[1 mark]*

Page 47 — Electrochemical Cells

1 a) Iron *[1 mark]* as it has a more negative electrode potential/ it loses electrons more easily than lead *[1 mark]*.
b) Standard cell potential = −0.13 − (−0.44) = **+0.31 V** *[1 mark]*
2 a) +0.80 V − (−0.76 V) = **+1.56 V** *[1 mark]*
b) The concentration of Zn^{2+} ions or Ag^+ ions was not 1.00 mol dm^{-3} or equimolar *[1 mark]*. The pressure wasn't 100 kPa *[1 mark]*.

Page 49 — The Electrochemical Series

1 a) $Zn_{(s)} + Ni^{2+}_{(aq)} \rightleftharpoons Zn^{2+}_{(aq)} + Ni_{(s)}$ *[1 mark]*
  $E^{\ominus} = (−0.25) − (−0.76) = $ **+0.51 V** *[1 mark]*
b) $2MnO_4^-_{(aq)} + 16H^+_{(aq)} + 5Sn^{2+}_{(aq)} \rightleftharpoons$
    $2Mn^{2+}_{(aq)} + 8H_2O_{(l)} + 5Sn^{4+}_{(aq)}$ *[1 mark]*
  $E^{\ominus} = (+1.51) − (+0.14) = $ **+1.37 V** *[1 mark]*
c) No reaction *[1 mark]*. Both reactants are in their oxidised form *[1 mark]*.
2 $KMnO_4$ *[1 mark]* because it has a more positive/less negative electrode potential *[1 mark]*.
3 a) $Cu^{2+}_{(aq)} + 2e^- \rightleftharpoons Cu_{(s)}$ *[1 mark]*
  $Ni^{2+}_{(aq)} + 2e^- \rightleftharpoons Ni_{(s)}$ *[1 mark]*
b) 0.34 − (−0.25) = **+0.59 V** *[1 mark]*
c) $Cu^{2+}_{(aq)} + Ni_{(s)} \rightleftharpoons Cu_{(s)} + Ni^{2+}_{(aq)}$ *[1 mark]*
d) If the copper solution was more dilute, the $E^{\ominus}$ of the copper half-cell would be lower (the equilibrium will shift to the left/ the copper will lose electrons more easily), so the overall cell potential would be lower *[1 mark]*.

Page 51 — Storage and Fuel Cells

1 a)

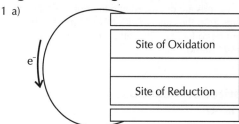

  [1 mark for each correct label — total of 2 marks for part i) and 1 mark for part ii).]
b) Anode: $H_2 \rightarrow 2H^+ + 2e^-$ *[1 mark]*
  Cathode: $\frac{1}{2}O_2 + 2H^+ + 2e^- \rightarrow H_2O$ *[1 mark]*
c) It only allows the H^+ across *[1 mark]* and forces the e^- to travel around the circuit to get to the cathode. This creates an electrical current *[1 mark]*.
2 a) +0.52 − (−0.88) = **1.4 V** *[1 mark]*
b) $Cd_{(s)} + 2NiO(OH)_{(s)} + 2H_2O_{(l)} \rightarrow Cd(OH)_{2(s)} + 2Ni(OH)_{2(s)}$
  [1 mark]

Module 5: Section 3 — Transition Elements

Page 53 — The d-block

1 C *[1 mark]*
2 a) $1s^2\, 2s^2\, 2p^6\, 3s^2\, 3p^6\, 3d^8\, 4s^2$ *[1 mark]*
b) $1s^2\, 2s^2\, 2p^6\, 3s^2\, 3p^6\, 3d^6$ *[1 mark]*
c) $1s^2\, 2s^2\, 2p^6\, 3s^2\, 3p^6\, 3d^9$ *[1 mark]*
d) $1s^2\, 2s^2\, 2p^6\, 3s^2\, 3p^6\, 3d^1$ *[1 mark]*
3 a) 3 *[1 mark]*
b) 6 *[1 mark]*
c) 3 *[1 mark]*
d) 0 *[1 mark]*
4 The student is right that both scandium and titanium are period 4 elements, but only titanium is a transition element *[1 mark]*. Scandium isn't a transition element because it doesn't form an ion with an incomplete d sub-shell *[1 mark]*.

Page 55 — Properties of Transition Elements

1 a) iron *[1 mark]*
b) chromium *[1 mark]*
c) manganese *[1 mark]*

Answers

Page 57 — Ligands and Complex Ions

1 a)

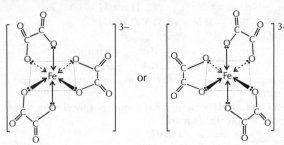

[1 mark]

b) Optical isomerism is a type of stereoisomerism that happens when a molecule can exist in two non-superimposable mirror images *[1 mark]*.

2 a)

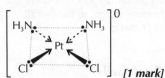

[1 mark]

b) The two chloride ligands are displaced and their places taken by two nitrogen atoms from the cancer cell's DNA *[1 mark]*. This stops the cell from reproducing. The cell is unable to repair the damage, and dies *[1 mark]*.

Page 59 — Substitution Reactions

1 a) $[Cu(H_2O)_6]^{2+}$ *[1 mark]*

b) i) $[Cu(H_2O)_6]^{2+}_{(aq)} + 4NH_{3(aq)} \rightleftharpoons$
$[Cu(NH_3)_4(H_2O)_2]^{2+}_{(aq)} + 4H_2O_{(l)}$
[1 mark for correct formula of new complex formed, 1 mark for the rest of the equation being correctly balanced.]

ii) Deep blue *[1 mark]*

iii) Octahedral *[1 mark]*

2 a) i) The water ligand is replaced with an oxygen ligand *[1 mark]*.

ii) It is the basis of the oxygen transportation mechanism in the bloodstream *[1 mark]*.

b) Carbon monoxide will bind to the haemoglobin complex and will not exchange with an oxygen (or water) ligand *[1 mark]*. The haemoglobin can't transport oxygen any more, so cells of the body will get less oxygen *[1 mark]*.

Page 61 — Reactions of Ions

1 $2MnO_4^- + 6H^+ + 5H_2O_2 \rightarrow 2Mn^{2+} + 8H_2O + 5O_2$ *[1 mark]*
The electrons have to be cancelled out by multiplying the manganate half-equation by 2 and the H_2O_2 half-equation by 5.

2 E.g. CuI_2 *[1 mark]*

Extra Exam Practice for Module 5

Pages 62-63

2 a) $Br^- \rightarrow \frac{1}{2}Br_2 + e^-$ *[1 mark]*
$BrO_3^- + 6H^+ + 5e^- \rightarrow \frac{1}{2}Br_2 + 3H_2O$ *[1 mark]*
You'll also get full marks if your equations have different multiples, as long as they're still correctly balanced.

b) E.g. using this balance will produce a high percentage error, so it won't give an accurate reading *[1 mark]*.
The uncertainty of the balance is ±0.005. This gives a percentage error of (0.005 ÷ 0.05) × 100 = 10%

c) E.g. repeat the experiment at several different temperatures, keeping the concentrations of the reactants constant *[1 mark]*. Use a water bath to vary the temperature *[1 mark]*. Calculate the rate of the reaction at each temperature (T), hence the rate constant (k) at each temperature *[1 mark]*. Plot a graph of ln k against $\frac{1}{T}$ and determine the gradient, which is $\frac{-E_a}{R}$ *[1 mark]*.
Rearrange the equation for the gradient to find E_a:
$E_a = -(gradient \times R)$ *[1 mark]*

d) $E_a = (\ln A - \ln k) \times RT$
$= (\ln 3.07 \times 10^{12} - \ln 353) \times (8.314 \times (25 + 273))$
$= 56702.284... $ J mol^{-1} = **56.7 kJ mol^{-1} (3 s.f.)**
[2 marks for correct answer, otherwise 1 mark for the rearrangement of the equation to find E_a]

3 a) $\Delta S = S_{products} - S_{reactants}$
$= (197.9 + 188.7) - (130.6 + 213.7)$
$= 42.3$ J K^{-1} mol^{-1}
$\Delta G = \Delta H - T\Delta S = 41\ 200 - (298 \times 42.3) = 28\ 594.6$ J mol^{-1}
$= $ **28.6 kJ mol^{-1} (3 s.f.)**
[4 marks for correct answer, otherwise 1 mark for calculating the entropy change, 1 mark for the correct ΔS value, and 1 mark for substituting the correct values into the free energy change equation.]

b) From the reaction equation, the equilibrium mixture contains 0.6 mol of H_2O, 1.6 − 0.6 = 1.0 mol H_2 and 1.6 − 0.6 =1.0 mol CO_2.
So there are a total of 1.0 + 1.0 + 0.6 + 0.6 = 3.2 moles of gas in the equilibrium mixture.
Mole fraction of gas = moles of gas ÷ total moles of gas in mixture
Partial pressure = mole fraction of gas × total pressure of mixture
Partial pressure (H_2) = (1.0 ÷ 3.2) × 101 = 31.5625 kPa
Partial pressure (CO_2) = (1.0 ÷ 3.2) × 101 = 31.5625 kPa
Partial pressure (CO) = (0.6 ÷ 3.2) × 101 = 18.9375 kPa
Partial pressure (H_2O) = (0.6 ÷ 3.2) × 101 = 18.9375 kPa
$K_p = \frac{p(CO)p(H_2O)}{p(H_2)p(CO_2)} = \frac{18.9375 \times 18.9375}{31.5625 \times 31.5625} = $ **0.36**
$K_p = \frac{kPa \times kPa}{kPa \times kPa} = 1$ (hence no units are required for K_p)
[5 marks — 1 mark for correct moles of H_2, CO_2 and H_2O at equilibrium, 1 mark for correct partial pressures, 1 mark for equilibrium constant equation, 1 mark for correct K_p and 1 mark for showing units aren't needed.]

c) E.g. the complex involved is haemoglobin, which contains a central Fe^{2+} ion that forms 6 coordinate bonds / bonds with haem, globin and oxygen/water *[1 mark]*. Carbon monoxide replaces the oxygen/water ligand in the complex ion *[1 mark]* in a ligand substitution reaction *[1 mark]*.

d) E.g. nickel makes a good catalyst as it can easily change oxidation states (between 0 and 2+) by losing or gaining electrons from its 4s orbital *[1 mark]* / it is good at adsorbing substances onto its surface to lower the activation energy of reactions *[1 mark]*.

Answers

Module 6: Section 1 — Aromatic Compounds & Carbonyls

Page 65 — Benzene and Aromatic Compounds

1 a) The model suggests that there should be two different bond lengths in the molecule, corresponding to C=C and C–C *[1 mark]*.
   b) X-ray diffraction shows that all the carbon–carbon bond lengths in benzene are actually the same, which doesn't fit the Kekulé model *[1 mark]*.
   c) E.g. If the Kekulé model were true, and benzene contained three double bonds, you'd expect the enthalpy of hydrogenation to be three times that of cyclohexene *[1 mark]*. The enthalpy of hydrogenation is in fact less exothermic than expected, implying that benzene is actually more stable than the Kekulé model predicts. This is thought to be due to the delocalised ring of electrons *[1 mark]*.

Page 67 — Electrophilic Substitution

1 a) Cyclohexene would decolorise bromine water, benzene would not *[1 mark]*. This is because orange bromine reacts in an electrophilic addition reaction with cyclohexene, due to the localised electrons in the double bond, *[1 mark]* to form a colourless dibromocycloalkane, leaving a clear solution. Benzene has a delocalised π system which spreads out the negative charge and makes it very stable, so it doesn't react with bromine water and the solution stays orange *[1 mark]*.
   b) i) It acts as a halogen carrier *[1 mark]*.
      ii)

      [3 marks available — 1 mark for each stage above.]

Page 69 — Substituted Benzene Rings

1 a)

      [1 mark]
   b)

      2-methyl-4-nitrophenol   2-methyl-6-nitrophenol
      [2 marks — 1 mark for each correct structure and name.]
2 a) With benzene, there will be no reaction but with phenol a reaction will occur which decolorises the bromine water and forms a precipitate *[1 mark]*. The product from the reaction with phenol is 2,4,6-tribromophenol *[1 mark]*.
   b) Electrons from one of oxygen's p-orbitals overlap with the benzene ring's delocalised system, increasing its electron density *[1 mark]*. This makes the ring more likely to be attacked by electrophiles. *[1 mark]*
   c) Electrophilic substitution *[1 mark]*

Page 71 — Aldehydes and Ketones

1 a) Both compounds react with 2,4-dinitrophenylhydrazine to form an orange precipitate, so they must both be carbonyl compounds *[1 mark]*. The only carbonyl compounds with the molecular formula C_3H_6O are propanone (CH_3COCH_3) and propanal (CH_3CH_2CHO). Compound Y reacts with Tollens' reagent to form a silver mirror, so must be the aldehyde propanal *[1 mark]*. Compound X has no reaction with Tollens' reagent so it is the ketone propanone *[1 mark]*.
   b)

      [2 marks — 1 mark for correct mechanism, 1 mark for correct product]
   c) Compound Y (propanal) *[1 mark]*

Page 73 — Carboxylic Acids and Acyl Chlorides

1 a) Sodium 3-methylbutanoate *[1 mark]*.
   b) cold water *[1 mark]*.
   c)

[1 mark].
   d) Ammonia *[1 mark]*.

Page 75 — Esters

1 a) Propan-1-ol *[1 mark]*
   b) Any two from:
      Ethanoic acid: Ethanoyl chloride: Ethanoic anhydride:

      [2 marks — 1 mark for each correct structure and name.]
2 a) A and D *[1 mark]*.
   b) 2-methylpropanol and sodium pentanoate *[1 mark]*.

Module 6: Section 2 — Nitrogen Compounds, Polymers & Synthesis

Page 77 — Amines and Amides

1 a) Any two from: propylamine / dipropylamine / tripropylamine / tetrapropylamine ion *[2 marks — 1 mark for each correct name]*.
   b) fractional distillation *[1 mark]*
   c) React nitrobenzene with tin and concentrated hydrochloric acid under reflux *[1 mark]*, then react the product with sodium hydroxide *[1 mark]*.
2   C *[1 mark]*

Answers

Page 79 — Chirality

1 a)

[1 mark]

b)

[4 marks — 1 mark for each correct isomer]

Page 81 — Polymers

1 a) It's a polyamide *[1 mark]* and it's made by condensation polymerisation *[1 mark]*.

b) A dicarboxylic acid and a diamine *[1 mark]*.

c) Hydrolysis with an acid / base *[1 mark]*.

Page 83 — More on Polymers

1 a)

b) condensation polymerisation *[1 mark]*

2 a)

b)

Page 87 — Carbon-Carbon Bond Synthesis

1 a) KCN or NaCN *[1 mark]*, ethanol, reflux *[1 mark]*.

b)

[1 mark]

c) Reflux benzene with AlCl₃ (or any other appropriate halogen carrier, e.g. FeCl₃) *[1 mark]* and 1-bromo-4-chloro-2-methylbutane *[1 mark]*.

This is the structure of 1-bromo-4-chloro-2-methylbutane:

2

[1 mark]

Page 89 — Organic Synthesis — Practical Techniques

1 a) The purer sample will have the higher melting point, so the sample that melts at 69 °C is purer *[1 mark]*.

b) To purify the sample you could dissolve it in hot propanone to make a saturated solution *[1 mark]* and cool the solution slowly so that the product recrystallises *[1 mark]*. You'd then filter the crystals under reduced pressure, wash them with very cold propanone *[1 mark]* and dry them.

c) E.g. the purity could be checked by measuring the melting point and comparing it against the known melting point of stearic acid *[1 mark]*.

2 B *[1 mark]*

Page 91 — Functional Groups

1 a) A — alcohol / hydroxyl *[1 mark]*
   B — alcohol / hydroxyl and alkene / alkenyl *[1 mark]*
   C — alcohol / hydroxyl and aromatic ring / phenyl *[1 mark]*

b) C *[1 mark]*

c) A *[1 mark]*

d) B *[1 mark]*

Page 93 — Synthetic Routes

1 E.g. Step 1: The methanol is refluxed with K₂Cr₂O₇ and acid to form methanoic acid *[1 mark]*.
Step 2: The methanoic acid is heated with ethanol using an acid catalyst to make ethyl methanoate *[1 mark]*.

2 E.g. Step 1: React propane with bromine in the presence of UV light to form bromopropane *[1 mark]*.
Step 2: Bromopropane is then refluxed with aqueous sodium hydroxide solution to form propanol *[1 mark]*.

Module 6: Section 3 — Analysis

Page 95 — Tests for Organic Functional Groups

1 B *[1 mark]*
Cyclohexene is an alkene so it decolourises bromine water.

2 E.g. put 2 cm³ of the solution that you want to test in a test tube and add some sodium carbonate *[1 mark]*. If the solution is a carboxylic acid, the mixture will fizz *[1 mark]*. If you collect the gas produced and bubble it through limewater, the limewater should turn cloudy *[1 mark]*.

Page 98 — Chromatography

1 a) R_f value = $\dfrac{\text{Distance travelled by spot}}{\text{Distance travelled by solvent}}$ *[1 mark]*

R_f value of spot A = 7 ÷ 8 = 0.875 *[1 mark]*
The R_f value has no units, because it's a ratio.

b) Substance A has moved further up the plate because it's less strongly adsorbed onto the surface than substance B *[1 mark]*.

2 a) The peak at 5 minutes *[1 mark]*.

b) The retention time for ethene will be shorter *[1 mark]* because it has a lower boiling point that hexene, so will spend less time condensed as a liquid and will travel faster through the tube *[1 mark]*.

Answers

3 a) The mixture is injected into a stream of carrier gas, which takes it through a tube over the oil / solid *[1 mark]*. The components of the mixture dissolve in the oil / on the solid *[1 mark]*, evaporate into the gas *[1 mark]*, and redissolve, gradually travelling along the tube to the detector *[1 mark]*.

b) The substances separate because they have different solubilities in the oil / on the solid *[1 mark]*, so they take different amounts of time to move through the tube *[1 mark]*.

c) The areas under the peaks will be proportional to the relative amount of each substance in the mixture OR the area under the benzene peak will be three times greater than the area under the ethanol peak *[1 mark]*.

4   C *[1 mark]*

Page 101 — NMR Spectroscopy

1 a) The peak at δ = 0 is produced by the reference compound, tetramethylsilane/TMS *[1 mark]*.

b) All three carbon atoms in the molecule $CH_3CH_2CH_2NH_2$ are in different environments *[1 mark]*. There are only two peaks on the carbon-13 NMR spectrum shown *[1 mark]*.
The ^{13}C NMR spectrum of $CH_3CH_2CH_2NH_2$ would have three peaks because this molecule has three carbon environments.

c) The peak at δ ≈ 25 represents carbons in C–C bonds *[1 mark]*. The peak at δ ≈ 40 represents a carbon in a C–N bond *[1 mark]*. The spectrum has two peaks, so the molecule must have two carbon environments *[1 mark]*.
So the structure of the molecule must be:

$$H-\overset{\overset{\displaystyle H}{|}}{\underset{\underset{\displaystyle H}{|}}{C}}-\overset{\overset{\displaystyle NH_2}{|}}{\underset{\underset{\displaystyle H}{|}}{C}}-\overset{\overset{\displaystyle H}{|}}{\underset{\underset{\displaystyle H}{|}}{C}}-H$$

[1 mark].
The two carbon environments are CH_3–$CH(NH_2)$–CH_3 and $CH(NH_2)$–$(CH_3)_2$.

2   C *[1 mark]*

Page 103 — Proton NMR

1 a) A CH_2 group adjacent to a halogen *[1 mark]*.
You've got to read the question carefully — it tells you it's an alkyl halide. So the group at 3.6 ppm can't have oxygen in it. It can't be halogen-CH_3 either, as this has 3 hydrogens in it.

b) A CH_3 group *[1 mark]*.

c) CH_2 added to CH_3 gives a mass of 29.0, so the halogen must be chlorine with a mass of 35.5. *[1 mark]*.
So a likely structure is CH_3CH_2Cl *[1 mark]*.

d) The quartet at 3.6 ppm is caused by 3 protons on the adjacent carbon. The n + 1 rule tells you that 3 protons give 3 + 1 = 4 peaks *[1 mark]*. Similarly the triplet at 1.3 ppm is due to 2 adjacent protons giving 2 + 1 = 3 peaks *[1 mark]*.

Page 105 — More on Spectra

1 a) Mass of molecule = 73 *[1 mark]*
You can tell this from the mass spectrum — the mass of the molecular ion is 73.

b) Structure of the molecule:

$$H-\overset{\overset{\displaystyle H}{|}}{\underset{\underset{\displaystyle H}{|}}{C}}-\overset{\overset{\displaystyle H}{|}}{\underset{\underset{\displaystyle H}{|}}{C}}-C\overset{NH_2}{\underset{O}{\diagdown}}$$

[1 mark]

Explanation: *[Award 1 mark each for the following pieces of reasoning, up to a total of 5 marks]*:
The infrared spectrum of the molecule shows a strong absorbance at about 3200 cm^{-1}, which suggests that the molecule contains an amine or amide group.
It also has a trough at about 1700 cm^{-1}, which suggests that the molecule contains a C=O group.
The ^{13}C NMR spectrum tells you that the molecule has three carbon environments.
One of the ^{13}C NMR peaks has a chemical shift of about 170, which corresponds to a carbonyl group in an amide.
The ^1H NMR spectrum has a quartet at δ ≈ 2, and a triplet at δ ≈ 1 — to give this splitting pattern the molecule must contain a CH_2CH_3 group.
The ^1H NMR spectrum has a singlet at δ ≈ 6, corresponding to H atoms in an amine or amide group.
The mass spectrum shows a peak at m/z = 15 which corresponds to a CH_3 group.
The mass spectrum shows a peak at m/z = 29 which corresponds to a CH_2CH_3 group.
The mass spectrum shows a peak at m/z = 44 which corresponds to a $CONH_2$ group.

2 a) Mass of molecule = 60 *[1 mark]*
You can tell this from the mass spectrum — the mass of the molecular ion is 60.

b) Structure of the molecule:

$$H-\overset{\overset{\displaystyle H}{|}}{\underset{\underset{\displaystyle H}{|}}{C}}-\overset{\overset{\displaystyle H}{|}}{\underset{\underset{\displaystyle H}{|}}{C}}-\overset{\overset{\displaystyle H}{|}}{\underset{\underset{\displaystyle H}{|}}{C}}-OH$$

[1 mark]

Explanation: *[Award 1 mark each for the following pieces of reasoning, up to a total of 5 marks]*:
The ^{13}C NMR spectrum tells you that the molecule has three carbon environments.
One of the ^{13}C NMR peaks has a chemical shift of 60 — which corresponds to a C–O group.
The infrared spectrum of the molecule has a trough at about 3300 cm^{-1}, which suggests that the molecule contains an alcoholic OH group.
It also has a trough at about 1200 cm^{-1}, which suggests that the molecule also contains a C–O group.
The mass spectrum shows a peak at m/z = 15 which corresponds to a CH_3 group.
The mass spectrum shows a peak at m/z = 17 which corresponds to an OH group.
The mass spectrum shows a peak at m/z = 29 which corresponds to a C_2H_5 group.
The mass spectrum shows a peak at m/z = 31 which corresponds to a CH_2OH group.
The mass spectrum shows a peak at m/z = 43 which corresponds to a C_3H_7 group.
The ^1H NMR spectrum has 4 peaks, showing that the molecule has 4 proton environments.
The ^1H NMR spectrum has a singlet at δ ≈ 2, corresponding to H atoms in an OH group.
The ^1H NMR spectrum has a sextuplet with an integration trace of 2 at δ ≈ 1.5, a quartet with an integration trace of 2 at δ ≈ 3.5, and a triplet with an integration trace of 3 at δ ≈ 1 — to give this splitting pattern the molecule must contain a $CH_3CH_2CH_2$ group.

Answers

Extra Exam Practice for Module 6

Pages 106-107

2 a) A chiral molecule has a chiral centre, which means it has two optical isomers *[1 mark]* which are mirror images of one another that cannot be superimposed over one another *[1 mark]*.

chiral centre

[1 mark]

b)

[1 mark for AlCl₃ catalyst, 1 mark for curly arrow from Cl lone pair to Al and 1 mark for the correct structure of carbocation and catalytic intermediate.]

(+ HCl + AlCl₃)

[1 mark for curly arrow from benzene ring to carbocation, 1 mark for curly arrow from Al–Cl bond to ring hydrogen and 1 mark for curly arrow from C–H bond to ring.]

You would also get the marks if you correctly used any other sensible halogen carrier catalyst in your mechanism.

c) Dissolve the impure zingerone in a minimum volume of hot solvent *[1 mark]*. Allow the filtrate to cool and the zingerone to crystallise *[1 mark]*. Filter the mixture through a Büchner funnel/under reduced pressure *[1 mark]*. Rinse the crystals with ice cold solvent *[1 mark]* and leave them to dry *[1 mark]*.

3 a)

[1 mark]

The question doesn't specify how to draw the structure here (e.g. to use displayed formula, skeletal formula etc.) — so as long as your structure's correct, you get full marks whatever format you used.

b)

[1 mark]

You **must** include the empty bonds stretching off each side here, to show that the chain continues. Since it's the repeating unit (not the formula), you don't need to include brackets or an 'n' — but if you did include them, you don't lose the mark.

c)

[1 mark]

Synoptic Practice

Pages 110-116

1 a) magnesium cell: 1.00 mol dm⁻³ Mg²⁺(aq), Mg electrode, 298 K, 100 kPa *[1 mark]*, zinc cell: 1.00 mol dm⁻³ Zn²⁺(aq), Zn electrode, 298 K, 100 kPa *[1 mark]*, saturated salt bridge *[1 mark]*
$Mg_{(s)} + Zn^{2+}_{(aq)} \rightarrow Mg^{2+}_{(aq)} + Zn_{(s)}$ *[1 mark]*
$E^{\ominus}_{cell} = E^{\ominus}_{reduced} - E^{\ominus}_{oxidised}$
You're looking for a combination of cells that produces a standard cell potential of 1.61 V. The difference between the magnesium and zinc half-cells is $-0.76 - (-2.37) = 1.61$ V.

b) Iron is a stronger reducing agent than silver / loses electrons more easily / the iron half-cell has a more negative electrode potential than the silver half-cell *[1 mark]* so iron metal will reduce silver(I) ions to silver metal *[1 mark]*.

c) i) $M_r(FeSO_4.7H_2O)$
$= 55.8 + 32.1 + (4 \times 16.0) + (14 \times 1.0) + (7 \times 16.0) = 277.9$
$M_r(Fe(NO_3)_3.9H_2O)$
$= 55.8 + (3 \times 14.0) + (9 \times 16.0) + (18 \times 1.0) + (9 \times 16.0)$
$= 403.8$
moles required for solution = concentration × volume
$= 1.00$ mol dm⁻³ × 0.250 dm³ = 0.250 mol
mass of $FeSO_4.7H_2O = 277.9 \times 0.250 = $ **69.48 g**
mass of $Fe(NO_3)_3.9H_2O = 403.8 \times 0.250 = $ **100.95 g**
[3 marks for both masses correct, otherwise 1 mark for calculating M_r of both substances and 1 mark for calculating the number of moles required.]

ii) E.g. wear goggles/gloves when handling the solutions *[1 mark]*.

iii) The $E^{\ominus}$ of the iron half-cell is more negative than the chromate half-cell, so the Fe^{2+} will be oxidised.
reduction: $Cr_2O_7^{2-}_{(aq)} + 14H^+_{(aq)} + 6e^- \rightarrow 2Cr^{3+}_{(aq)} + 7H_2O_{(l)}$
oxidation: $6Fe^{2+}_{(aq)} \rightarrow 6Fe^{3+}_{(aq)} + 6e^-$
redox reaction: $6Fe^{2+}_{(aq)} + Cr_2O_7^{2-}_{(aq)} + 14H^+_{(aq)} \rightarrow 6Fe^{3+}_{(aq)} + 2Cr^{3+}_{(aq)} + 7H_2O_{(l)}$ *[1 mark]*

2 a) $MCO_{3(s)} + 2H^+_{(aq)} \rightarrow M^{2+}_{(aq)} + H_2O_{(l)} + CO_{2(g)}$ *[1 mark]*

b) i) $MCO_3 + 2HCl \rightarrow MCl_2 + H_2O + CO_2$
moles of $MCO_3 : CO_2 \Rightarrow 1 : 1$,
so moles of $CO_2 = 3.56 \times 10^{-3}$
$PV = nRT \Rightarrow V = \dfrac{nRT}{p}$
50 °C = 323 K, 101 kPa = 101 × 10³ Pa
$V = \dfrac{(3.56 \times 10^{-3})(8.314)(323)}{101 \times 10^3} = 9.4654... \times 10^{-5}$ m³
$= $ **9.47 × 10⁻⁵ m³** (3 s.f.)
[3 marks for correct answer, otherwise 1 mark for correctly rearranging ideal gas equation and 1 mark for substituting correct values into the equation.]

Answers

ii) $M_r(MCO_3) = \dfrac{\text{mass of substance}}{\text{number of moles}}$

$= 0.300 \div (3.56 \times 10^{-3}) = 84.26...$

$M_r(M) = 84.26... - M_r(CO_3{}^{2-}) = 84.26... - 60.0 = \mathbf{24.3}$

therefore M is Mg

[3 marks —1 mark for calculating relative formula mass of metal carbonate, 1 mark for finding relative formula mass of metal and 1 mark for identifying metal as Mg.]

c) E.g. Step 4: mixture should be stirred thoroughly to ensure the sodium carbonate is fully dissolved *[1 mark]*. Step 5: glass rod/ large beaker/funnel should be washed with deionised water into the volumetric flask *[1 mark]*. Step 6: the solution should be mixed thoroughly *[1 mark]*.

d) moles of HCl added at the start = $0.200 \times 0.0500 = 0.0100$ mol

moles of HCl : MCO_3 in reaction $\Rightarrow$ 2 : 1

so moles of HCl reacting with $MCO_3 = 2 \times 3.56 \times 10^{-3}$
$= 7.12 \times 10^{-3}$

So if all MCO_3 reacted, there would be $0.0100 - 7.12 \times 10^{-3} = 2.88 \times 10^{-3}$ moles of HCl left that would be neutralised by NaOH. Reading of equivalence point = 36.0 cm^3

moles of NaOH = $0.0800 \times 0.0360 = 2.88 \times 10^{-3}$ mol

$HCl + NaOH \rightarrow NaCl + H_2O$

ratio of NaOH : HCl = 1:1

moles of HCl neutralised = $\mathbf{2.88 \times 10^{-3}}$ mol

therefore all of the MCO_3 reacted.

[8 marks — 1 mark for moles of HCl added, 1 mark for moles of HCl that should have reacted, 1 mark for moles of HCl that should be left, 1 mark for reading equivalence point, 1 mark for moles of NaOH, 1 mark for balanced equation, 1 mark for moles of HCl neutralised, 1 mark for comparing results of titration to predicted result (to work out if all MCO_3 reacted).]

3 a) E.g. the reaction equations are:

$HNO_3 + H_2SO_4 \rightarrow H_2NO_3{}^+ + HSO_4{}^-$
$H_2NO_3{}^+ \rightarrow NO_2{}^+ + H_2O$ *[1 mark]*. The oxidation state of nitrogen in HNO_3 is +5, oxidation state of nitrogen in $NO_2{}^+$ is +5, therefore no redox reaction has occurred *[1 mark]*.

b) The delocalised electron ring / π system causes benzene to be more energetically stable (than the equivalent Kekulé model) *[1 mark]*. If there was an addition to a benzene ring carbon, the delocalised system would be broken (leaving two carbon-carbon double bonds) *[1 mark]*. If a substitution reaction occurs, the delocalised system remains intact after the reaction so substitution reactions are more favourable than addition reactions *[1 mark]*.

c) 2-nitromethylbenzene will have more peaks on its carbon-13 NMR spectrum than 4-nitromethylbenzene *[1 mark]* because it has seven unique carbon environments *[1 mark]* while 4-nitromethylbenzene has five unique carbon environments *[1 marks]*.

d) $2C_7H_5(NO_2)_3 \rightarrow 7CO + 7C + 5H_2O + 3N_2$

$\Delta_rH = \Delta_fH(\text{products}) - \Delta_fH(\text{reactants})$
$= [(7 \times -110.5) + (5 \times -241.8)] - (2 \times -63.2)$
$= -1856.1 = \mathbf{-1860\ kJ\ mol^{-1}}$ **(3 s.f.)**

[4 marks for correct answer, otherwise 1 mark for the correct balanced equation, 1 mark for stating the formula, and 1 mark for substituting the correct enthalpies into the formula.]

4 a) E.g.

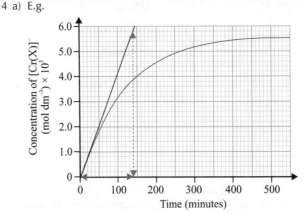

initial rate $= \dfrac{\text{change in } y}{\text{change in } x} = \dfrac{5.8 \times 10^{-3}}{140} = 4.1428... \times 10^{-5}$
$= \mathbf{4.1 \times 10^{-5}\ mol\ dm^{-3}\ min^{-1}}$ (2 s.f.)

[2 marks for value between 3.5×10^{-5} mol dm^{-3} min^{-1} and 5.0×10^{-5} mol dm^{-3} min^{-1}, otherwise 1 mark for correctly drawn tangent at 0 minutes.]

b) $1s^2\ 2s^2\ 2p^6\ 3s^2\ 3p^6\ 3d^3$ *[1 mark]*

c) The colour change is from green to purple *[1 mark]*.
$[Cr(H_2O)_6]^{3+} + 6NH_3 \rightarrow [Cr(NH_3)_6]^{3+} + 6H_2O$ *[1 mark]*

d) E.g. add a few drops of sodium hydroxide to a test tube of the solution *[1 mark]*. If chromium(III) ions are present a grey-green precipitate will form *[1 mark]*.

5 a) i)

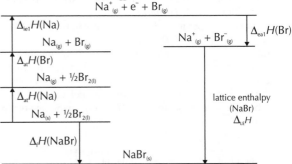

To find lattice enthalpy, $\Delta_{LE}H$:

$\Delta_{LE}H(NaBr) = - (-325) - (+496) - (+112) - (+107) + (-361)$
$= -751$ kJ mol^{-1}

Enthalpy of solution $= 751 + (-406) + (-348) = \mathbf{-3\ kJ\ mol^{-1}}$

[6 marks for correct answer, otherwise 1 mark for correct enthalpy changes to find lattice enthalpy, 1 mark for the correct species for each line, 1 mark for correct direction of arrows, 1 mark for the correct value of lattice enthalpy, 1 mark for correct enthalpy changes to find enthalpy of solution.]

ii) The first ionisation energy of lithium would be higher than sodium's, because lithium has fewer electron shells than sodium *[1 mark]* so lithium's outer electron is closer to the nucleus and less shielded from the attractive force of the nucleus *[1 mark]* meaning more energy is required to overcome the attraction *[1 mark]*.

b) $M_r(HBr) = 1.0 + 79.9 = 80.9$

number of moles of HBr $= 0.0400 \div 80.9 = 4.94... \times 10^{-4}$ mol
$[H^+] = 4.94 \times 10^{-4} \div 0.0500 = 9.88... \times 10^{-3}$ mol dm^{-3}
$pH = -\log[H^+] = -\log(9.88... \times 10^{-3}) = \mathbf{2.00}$ (3 s.f.)

[3 marks for correct answer, otherwise 1 mark for moles HBr and 1 mark for calculating $[H^+]$.]

Answers

c) Assume $[H^+] = [A^-]$ and $[HA]_{aq} = [HA]_{start}$

so $K_a = \dfrac{[H^+]^2}{[HA]}$ and $[HA] = [H^+]^2 \div K_a$ *[1 mark]*

$K_a = 10^{-pKa} = 10^{-2.90} = 1.25... \times 10^{-3}$ *[1 mark]*

$[H^+] = 10^{-pH} = 10^{-1.50} = 0.0316...$ *[1 mark]*

$[HA] = \dfrac{(0.0316...)^2}{1.25...\times10^{-3}} = 0.794... = \textbf{0.794 mol dm}^{-3}$ (3 s.f.) *[1 mark]*

d)

OH, Br (positions 2 and 6), Br (position 4) — 2,4,6-tribromophenol structure *[1 mark]*

6 a) The mechanism is a free radical substitution reaction *[1 mark]*.

Initiation: $Br_2 \xrightarrow{UV} 2Br\bullet$
[1 mark for showing free radicals being produced.]

Propagation: $Br\bullet + C_3H_8 \rightarrow HBr + \bullet C_3H_7$
[1 mark for showing free radicals being used up.]

$\bullet C_3H_7 + Br_2 \rightarrow C_3H_7Br + Br\bullet$
[1 mark for showing free radicals being reformed.]

Termination: e.g. $Br\bullet + \bullet C_3H_7 \rightarrow C_3H_7Br$
[1 mark for reaction showing two free radicals combining.]

b)

$H_3C-C=C-H \rightarrow H_3C-C-C-H \rightarrow H_3C-C-C-H$ (with Br additions)

Name of mechanism: electrophilic addition
[5 marks — 1 mark for curly arrow from C=C to Br atom, 1 mark for curly arrow from Br-Br bond to other Br atom, 1 mark for curly arrow from Br^- to C^+, 1 mark for correct structure of product and 1 mark for correctly naming the mechanism.]

c) Doubling $[C_2H_5CBr(CH_3)CH_3]$ doubles the rate (by comparing experiments 1 and 2) implying first order with respect to $C_2H_5CBr(CH_3)CH_3$ *[1 mark]*.

Comparing experiment 1 with 3, $[NaOH]$: $0.28 \div 0.14 = 2$,
$[C_2H_5CBr(CH_3)CH_3]$: $0.45 \div 0.3 = 1.5$,
rate: $(6.75 \times 10^{-5}) \div (4.5 \times 10^{-5}) = 1.5$. Doubling the concentration of NaOH doesn't affect the rate, implying zero order with respect to NaOH *[1 mark]*. This means the rate determining step involves one molecule of 2-bromo-2-methylbutane only *[1 mark]*, so the rate determining step is:

(structure) $\rightarrow$ (structure) Br^- *[1 mark]*

d) The major product would be 2-bromopropane *[1 mark]*. HBr is a polar molecule, and since the hydrogen atom has a $\delta+$ charge it bonds to the propene first *[1 mark]* forming either a primary ($CH_3CH_2C^+H_2$) or a secondary ($CH_3C^+HCH_3$) carbocation *[1 mark]*. The secondary carbocation is more stable so is more likely to form *[1 mark]*.

e)

(structures) *[1 mark for both structures correct.]*

(structures) *[1 mark for both structures correct.]*

The first step of the reaction is the formation of a bromocarbocation, which reacts with the chloride ions present forming bromochloropropane *[1 mark]*.

7 a) i) $\Delta G = \Delta H - T\Delta S \Rightarrow \Delta S = \dfrac{\Delta H - \Delta G}{T}$, 25.0 °C = 298 K

$\Delta S = \dfrac{(-102 \times 10^3) - (-49 \times 10^3)}{298} = -177.85...$
$= \textbf{-178 J K}^{-1}\textbf{ mol}^{-1}$ (3 s.f.)

[3 marks for correct answer, otherwise 1 mark for correct equation for ΔS and 1 mark for correct values in equation.]

ii) Spontaneous reactions occur when $\Delta G \leq 0$ so
$0 = \Delta H - T\Delta S \Rightarrow T = \dfrac{\Delta H}{\Delta S}$
$T = \dfrac{-102 \times 10^3}{-177.85...} = 573.509... = \textbf{574 K}$ (3 s.f.)
[2 marks for correct answer, otherwise 1 mark for correct equation for T.]

If you got an incorrect value for ΔS in part (i), or if you used the rounded value, you can still get full marks for part (ii) if all the working is correct.

b) i)

(four complex structures) *[4 marks — 1 mark for each correct structure]*

For the stereoisomers of the ammonia-nickel complex, you might not have drawn the ligands in exactly same places as above, but as long as you've drawn one isomer with the H_2O ligands next to each other and one with them opposite to each other then you'd get the marks.

ii) $[Ni(NH_3)_4(H_2O)_2]^{2+}$ can show cis-trans isomerism *[1 mark]*. The $(en)_3Ni$ complex can show optical isomerism *[1 mark]*.

c) Heating up the solution will change the colour of the solution *[1 mark]*. When heated, the position of equilibrium will shift to the left in the exothermic direction, making the solution less red / return to yellow *[1 mark]*.

8 a) Oxidation state of Bi in $NaBiO_3$ is +5, and in Bi^{3+} it's +3 so the half-equation for reduction of Bi is:
$BiO_3^- + 6H^+ + 2e^- \rightarrow Bi^{3+} + 3H_2O$
$(Mn^{2+} + 4H_2O \rightarrow MnO_4^- + 8H^+ + 5e^-) \times 2$
$\Rightarrow 2Mn^{2+} + 8H_2O \rightarrow 2MnO_4^- + 16H^+ + 10e^-$
$(BiO_3^- + 6H^+ + 2e^- \rightarrow Bi^{3+} + 3H_2O) \times 5$
$\Rightarrow 5BiO_3^- + 30H^+ + 10e^- \rightarrow 5Bi^{3+} + 15H_2O$
Redox equation:
$5BiO_3^- + 14H^+ + 2Mn^{2+} \rightarrow 5Bi^{3+} + 7H_2O + 2MnO_4^-$
[3 marks for correctly balanced redox equation, otherwise 1 mark for Bi half-equation and 1 mark for correctly balancing the half-equations.]

Answers

b) **5-6 marks:**
All stages of the working are present and fully correct.
The calculation steps are laid out in a logical order.
3-4 marks:
Not all the stages of the working are present, but those that are present are correct OR all stages are present but with mistakes made. The steps of the calculation may not follow a completely logical order.
1-2 marks:
Only one stage of the working is present and correct OR attempts have been made at parts of the calculations but with errors present and no logical method followed.
0 marks:
There is no relevant working.
Here are some points your answer may include:
Writing the balanced redox equation for
the reaction between Fe^{2+} ions and MnO_4^-
Fe^{2+} is being oxidised so direction of half-equation is:
$Fe^{2+} \rightarrow Fe^{3+} + e^-$
$(Fe^{2+} \rightarrow Fe^{3+} + e^-) \times 5 \Rightarrow 5Fe^{2+} \rightarrow 5Fe^{3+} + 5e^-$
$MnO_4^- + 8H^+ + 5e^- \rightarrow Mn^{2+} + 4H_2O$
Redox equation:
$MnO_4^- + 5Fe^{2+} + 8H^+ \rightarrow Mn^{2+} + 4H_2O + 5Fe^{3+}$
Finding the mass of manganese(II) in the 25 cm³ sample
moles = concentration × volume
moles $(Fe^{2+}) = 0.100 \times (17.8 \div 1000) = 1.78 \times 10^{-3}$ mol
From redox equation, ratio $MnO_4^- : Fe^{2+} = 1 : 5$, so
moles $(MnO_4^-) = 1.78 \times 10^{-3} \div 5 = 3.56 \times 10^{-4}$ mol
moles (Mn^{2+}) = moles (MnO_4^-)
mass = moles × molar mass
mass $(Mn^{2+}) = (3.56 \times 10^{-4}) \times 54.9 = 0.01954...$ g in 25.0 cm³
Finding the percentage of Mn in the original sample
0.01954 g $\times 10 = 0.1954$ g in 250 cm³ in the original sample.
1.50 g of steel was dissolved, so percentage by mass of Mn
$= \dfrac{0.1954...}{1.50} \times 100 = \textbf{13.0\%}$ (3 s.f.)

c) Some of the sample could be lost during the filtration, meaning the percentage mass of manganese would be less than expected *[1 mark]*.

d) E.g. make up a set of solutions of potassium manganate(VII) of known concentration *[1 mark]*. Measure the absorbance of each solution, and plot these values on a graph against the concentration (to make a calibration curve/graph) *[1 mark]*. Measure the absorbance of the manganate(VII) solution from the steel sample, and determine the concentration from the calibration graph *[1 mark]*.

9 a) Propenal will react with bromine water and with Tollens' reagent, giving a positive result for both *[1 mark]*. Propanal will only react with Tollens' reagent *[1 mark]* and propanone will react with neither *[1 mark]*.

b)

[1 mark for curly arrow from C=O bond to O, 1 mark for curly arrow from CN⁻ to C, 1 mark for correct intermediate, 1 mark for curly arrow from O⁻ to H⁺.]

c) The cyanide ion reacts with the carbonyl carbon since the C=O bond is polar and so the carbon has a partial positive charge *[1 mark]*. By contrast, the C=C bond is non-polar (as both atoms have the same electronegativity) so the cyanide ion is not attracted to either carbon *[1 mark]*.

d)

[1 mark]

10a)

Element	C	H	Cl	O
$\dfrac{\text{mass}}{A_r}$	$\dfrac{0.563}{12.0}$	$\dfrac{0.082}{1.0}$	$\dfrac{0.417}{35.5}$	$\dfrac{0.188}{16.0}$
Moles	0.0469...	0.082	0.0117...	0.01175
Whole number ratio	$\dfrac{0.0469...}{0.0117...}$ = 4	$\dfrac{0.082}{0.0117...}$ = 7	$\dfrac{0.0117...}{0.0117...}$ = 1	$\dfrac{0.01175}{0.0117...}$ = 1

[1 mark for correct moles of each element.]
Empirical formula: C_4H_7ClO *[1 mark]*
$M_r(C_4H_7ClO) = 106.5$, $\dfrac{213.0}{106.5} = 2$, therefore molecular formula is twice empirical formula $= C_8H_{14}Cl_2O_2$ *[1 mark]*

b) IR spectrum: peak at about 1700 cm⁻¹ indicating a C=O, peak at about 1200 cm⁻¹ indicating a C–O.

¹H NMR δ	Whole number ratio	Adjacent H	Possible environments
0.9	3	2	CH_3
1.4	2	3	CH_2
3.9	1	2	OCH / ClCH
4.2	1	2	ClCH / OCH

Structure is:

[8 marks — 1 mark for identifying C=O and 1 mark for identifying C–O in IR spectrum, 1 mark for identifying four hydrogen environments, 1 mark for identifying two CH environments, 1 mark for identifying an OCH environment, 1 mark for identifying a ClCH environment, 1 mark for the whole number ratio for each peak in ¹H spectrum, 1 mark for correct structure.]

There are no ¹H peaks for a carboxylic acid or single peak for an alcohol, so the peaks in the IR spectrum are likely produced by an ester. To work out the structure, start with the ester (RCOOCH) group — the OCH hydrogen environment has 2 adjacent Hs so there must be another carbon (with hydrogens) attached. This can't be the CH_3 group as there's only 2 Hs in the adjacent environment, and it can't be the CH_2 group because that has 3 adjacent Hs. So it must be ClCH. This is adjacent to 2 Hs so there must be 2 Hs in the OCH environment, so the ratio should be doubled. What's left is 2 CH_2 groups with 3 adjacent Hs and 2 CH_3 groups with 2 adjacent Hs — this suggests they are 2 separate chains of -CH_2CH_3. Add them to a carbon on the 'R' end of the RCOOCH group. There are no more adjacent H environments so this carbon likely has another Cl — you can double-check your structure against the molecular formula you found in (a) to make sure.

c) E.g. if it was pure, there would be only one peak / there would not be any extra peaks (compared to a standard solution of the substance) *[1 mark]*.

Specification Map

This specification map tells you where each part of the OCR specification that you'll need for your exams is covered in this book.

Module 5: Physical chemistry and transition elements

Module 6: Organic chemistry and analysis

Index

Index

Index

The Periodic Table

Key:

Relative Atomic Mass	1.0
	H
Atomic number	Hydrogen
	1

(1)	(2)												(3)	(4)	(5)	(6)	(7)	(0)
																		4.0 **He** Helium 2
6.9 **Li** Lithium 3	9.0 **Be** Beryllium 4												10.8 **B** Boron 5	12.0 **C** Carbon 6	14.0 **N** Nitrogen 7	16.0 **O** Oxygen 8	19.0 **F** Fluorine 9	20.2 **Ne** Neon 10
23.0 **Na** Sodium 11	24.3 **Mg** Magnesium 12												27.0 **Al** Aluminium 13	28.1 **Si** Silicon 14	31.0 **P** Phosphorus 15	32.1 **S** Sulfur 16	35.5 **Cl** Chlorine 17	39.9 **Ar** Argon 18
39.1 **K** Potassium 19	40.1 **Ca** Calcium 20	45.0 **Sc** Scandium 21	47.9 **Ti** Titanium 22	50.9 **V** Vanadium 23	52.0 **Cr** Chromium 24	54.9 **Mn** Manganese 25	55.8 **Fe** Iron 26	58.9 **Co** Cobalt 27	58.7 **Ni** Nickel 28	63.5 **Cu** Copper 29	65.4 **Zn** Zinc 30	69.7 **Ga** Gallium 31	72.6 **Ge** Germanium 32	74.9 **As** Arsenic 33	79.0 **Se** Selenium 34	79.9 **Br** Bromine 35	83.8 **Kr** Krypton 36
85.5 **Rb** Rubidium 37	87.6 **Sr** Strontium 38	88.9 **Y** Yttrium 39	91.2 **Zr** Zirconium 40	92.9 **Nb** Niobium 41	95.9 **Mo** Molybdenum 42	**Tc** Technetium 43	101.1 **Ru** Ruthenium 44	102.9 **Rh** Rhodium 45	106.4 **Pd** Palladium 46	107.9 **Ag** Silver 47	112.4 **Cd** Cadmium 48	114.8 **In** Indium 49	118.7 **Sn** Tin 50	121.8 **Sb** Antimony 51	127.6 **Te** Tellurium 52	126.9 **I** Iodine 53	131.3 **Xe** Xenon 54
132.9 **Cs** Caesium 55	137.3 **Ba** Barium 56	138.9 **La** Lanthanum 57	178.5 **Hf** Hafnium 72	180.9 **Ta** Tantalum 73	183.8 **W** Tungsten 74	186.2 **Re** Rhenium 75	190.2 **Os** Osmium 76	192.2 **Ir** Iridium 77	195.1 **Pt** Platinum 78	197.0 **Au** Gold 79	200.6 **Hg** Mercury 80	204.4 **Tl** Thallium 81	207.2 **Pb** Lead 82	209.0 **Bi** Bismuth 83	**Po** Polonium 84	**At** Astatine 85	**Rn** Radon 86
132.9 **Fr** Francium 87	**Ra** Radium 88	**Ac** Actinium 89	**Rf** Rutherfordium 104	**Db** Dubnium 105	**Sg** Seaborgium 106	**Bh** Bohrium 107	**Hs** Hassium 108	**Mt** Meitnerium 109	**Ds** Darmstadtium 110	**Rg** Roentgenium 111	**Cn** Copernicium 112	**Fl** Flerovium 114	**Lv** Livermorium 116				

The Lanthanides

140.1 **Ce** Cerium 58	140.9 **Pr** Praseodymium 59	144.2 **Nd** Neodymium 60	144.9 **Pm** Promethium 61	150.4 **Sm** Samarium 62	152.0 **Eu** Europium 63	157.2 **Gd** Gadolinium 64	158.9 **Tb** Terbium 65	162.5 **Dy** Dysprosium 66	164.9 **Ho** Holmium 67	167.3 **Er** Erbium 68	168.9 **Tm** Thulium 69	173.0 **Yb** Ytterbium 70	175.0 **Lu** Lutetium 71

The Actinides

232.0 **Th** Thorium 90	**Pa** Protactinium 91	238.1 **U** Uranium 92	**Np** Neptunium 93	**Pu** Plutonium 94	**Am** Americium 95	**Cm** Curium 96	**Bk** Berkelium 97	**Cf** Californium 98	**Es** Einsteinium 99	**Fm** Fermium 100	**Md** Mendelevium 101	**No** Nobelium 102	**Lr** Lawrencium 103